I0022706

Anonymous

The Atlantic & gulf ship canal across the peninsula of Florida

connecting the Atlantic ocean with the Gulf of Mexico and Caribbean Sea

Anonymous

The Atlantic & gulf ship canal across the peninsula of Florida
connecting the Atlantic ocean with the Gulf of Mexico and Caribbean Sea

ISBN/EAN: 9783337146733

Printed in Europe, USA, Canada, Australia, Japan

Cover: Foto ©Andreas Hilbeck / pixelio.de

More available books at **www.hansebooks.com**

Privately Printed. }
Only 20 Copies. }

THE

ATLANTIC & GULF SHIP CANAL

ACROSS

THE PENINSULA OF FLORIDA,

CONNECTING

THE ATLANTIC OCEAN

WITH

THE GULF OF MEXICO AND CARIBBEAN SEA.

ALSO,

THE GREAT TIDE-WATER CANAL ROUTE,

FROM

THE PORT OF FERNANDINA, THROUGH THE PENINSULA

TO

THE PORT OF KEY WEST, AND CUBA,

THEIR

COMMERCIAL AND FINANCIAL CHARACTER, AND PROPERTIES.

LONDON.

1877.

THE ATLANTIC AND GULF SHIP-CANAL

ACROSS

THE PENINSULA OF FLORIDA,

CONNECTING

THE ATLANTIC OCEAN

WITH

THE GULF OF MEXICO AND CARIBBEAN SEA.

PART FIRST.

THE present large commerce of the Atlantic Ocean with the Pacific Ocean, and both these oceans with the nations and countries contiguous to the Gulf of Mexico and the Caribbean Sea—especially including the vast amount and value of the productions, exports, and imports of the Great Mississippi Valley, and the Gulf States of the United States of America, interchanged through these Central Seas, and transported over other tributary channels and routes ; also, the great importance, necessity, and incalculable benefits of this grand Maritime Ship Canal to facilitate the interchange of this gigantic amount of international and national commerce and trade—are fully shown from the official reports of the Governments of

> THE UNITED STATES,
> GREAT BRITAIN, and
> RUSSIA—

From Official Reports of States—Reports of the proceedings in Convention of Twenty-seven States—Reports of Boards of Commerce and Trade in Cities in the United States and Canada—and from other high Authorities, Official Surveys, Maps, and Reports therewith connected.

From these high authorities the Promoter and Attorney of this Ship-Canal enterprise has compiled and published an elaborate and complete Report, fully exhibiting the commercial and financial character of this Canal, with a description of it and accompanying maps, cost of construction, earnings ; also, the valuable properties, charters, franchises, rights, and privileges belonging thereto ; also, various other matters of interest bearing upon the same, which Report is herewith submitted.

In order to form a correct judgment of the merits of the whole enterprise, this Report must be studied.

THE

ATLANTIC AND GULF SHIP CANAL

OF

FLORIDA,

AND

GREAT TIDE WATER CANAL ROUTE

THROUGH

THE PENINSULA.

SYLLABUS.

CHAPTER I.

THE COMMERCIAL CONSIDERATIONS OF THE ENTERPRISE.

Great importance, necessity, and incalculable benefits of this Ship Canal to International and National Commerce and Trade, as shown from Official Reports of the Governments of

The United States,
Great Britain and
Russia;

from the States of Florida and Alabama; Reports of the Convention of twenty-seven States; of Boards of Commerce and Trade of Cities in the United States and Canada, and from other high authorities, Official Surveys, Maps, &c., &c., &c.

The international character of this Ship Canal is shown from the large number of nations and countries directly engaged in the commerce and trade with the Gulf of Mexico and Caribbean Sea nations (p. 7.)

The "Straits of Florida," through "Gulf Stream," is the Chief Ocean Route for the passage of this commerce (p. 7.)

The United States' Government estimated "the amount of commerce compelled to use this passage twenty-five years ago at $420,000,000." The amount now annually obliged to pass through this channel, and over costly railway transit, is computed at 10,000,000 tons net, valued at $1,000,000,000 (p. 7), (and on the opening of the mouth of the Mississippi River, this amount will be more than doubled from the Mississippi Valley.)

The "Straits of Florida" are notoriously known to be the most dangerous ship route to navigate on the earth. The wrecks and losses of ships and cargoes are enormous (pp. 8, 9.)

The annual loss in ships, cargoes, extra insurance, extra high freights, &c., &c., consequent upon this commerce being shipped through this dangerous channel and over costly railway transit, is computed at over $40,000,000, or £8,000,000 (pp. 9, 10). Half of this annual loss will construct the Ship Canal.

This commerce will and must pass through the Ship Canal, for self-evident reasons:—1. It will shorten the sailing distance from London, Liverpool, New York, Philadelphia, &c., to New Orleans, Mobile, Pensacola, Galveston, St. Louis, Cincinnati, and Ports of Mexico, about 1,100 miles, or 2,200 miles for the out and return voyage. It will save, in *sailing time*, eight days for steam ships, and twenty-two days for sailing vessels; also a large *pro rata* saving of distance and time to and from other Gulf and the Caribbean sea-ports. It will avoid the dangerous and costly navigation of the "Straits of Florida; will save the extra high insurance and high freights; it will save the extra wages and supplies now required on the present long voyages; will save the interest on capital on this commerce and ships, wear and tear of ships; and ships will be earning new freights, and merchants making profits on their merchandise, during this extra time, for the long voyages now required. In short, this commerce can pay $10,000,000 Canal tolls annually, and then save over $30,000,000 by its shipment through the Canal (pp. 9, 10.)

The Gulf of Mexico commercially considered. Its rapid increase, and the ultimate amount of commerce of this *central sea of the world*, are fully shown by Commodore Maury and Dr. Fontaine, which will repay a careful reading (pp. 11, 12.)

Near causes, which will increase this trade—1st. From the increase of population of the contiguous foreign nations (p. 12.) 2nd. From the Trans-Continental Railways now being constructed (p. 13.) 3rd.

A

From the Darien Ship Canal, with its minimum commerce, estimated at $450,000,000 per annum, making a saving thereon of $49,000,000. Three-fourths of this commerce must pass through the Florida Ship Canal (pp. 13, 14.)

The immediate, vast-increasing commerce of the Gulf now comes, and always must come, from the Mississippi Valley, and the Gulf States which form a portion of that Valley.

The gigantic commerce which this Valley is now annually producing for export, and is increasing with unparalleled rapidity, will furnish the Florida Ship Canal all the freight, for time to come, to make this Canal the grandest financial success of the world.

The Report, from pages 14 to 31, fully exhibits the area, productions, commerce, and capabilities of this Royal Valley.

The head-notes, page 14, indicate the topics treated off. (Please read them first).

Area of this valley, nearly 3,000,000 square miles (p. 14). Its present population is over 27,500,000; many of its states and cities more than double *their* population and wealth every ten years (p. 15). It possesses the most magnificent river system of the world, affording nearly 50,000 miles in length of river and canal navigation, upon which upwards of 10,000 steamers, besides large fleets of auxiliary vessels are engaged in the commerce of these waters (p. 15).

The grand railway system of this valley amounts to 44,000 miles of completed roads in active operation (p. 15).

THE ANNUAL PRODUCTIONS AND COMMERCE OF THIS VALLEY ARE SIMPLY COLOSSAL.

40,000,000 tons net, of agricultural, mineral, and other productions are annually transported on those rivers and canals (p. 17). The Lake commerce of 1872, mostly from this valley, amounted to the value of $1,000,000,000, an average of one vessel every nine minutes, day and night, during one whole season, passed Fort Gratiot Lighthouse, near Port Huron (p. 17). "The value of commodities moved by the railroads in 1872 is estimated at over $10,000,000,000, and their gross freight receipts reached the enormous sum of $473,241,055." (Three-fourths of this amount are exports and imports of this valley.) "The commerce of the Ohio River alone (one of the tributaries of the Mississippi) has been carefully estimated at over $1,623,000,000 per annum" (p. 17).

An immense amount of its products are shipped to the Southern States, also to foreign countries—*via* the Mississippi River. The coastwise shipping trade of the United States amounts to 61,000,000 tons net annually (pp. 17 and 18). A large portion of this is from the Mississippi Valley, and yet, after supplying all its home consumption, and exporting a vast amount, there is left on the hands of the producers 15,000,000 tons of Grain and Meat alone of surplus annual productions for Export from the Mississippi Valley needed in Foreign Markets, but which the Northern Lakes, Canals, and Railways, taxed to their fullest carrying capacity, cannot transport to the Atlantic Seaboard—The annual surplus productions of the Mississippi Valley and Gulf States needed in the markets of the Atlantic Seaboard, in Europe, in South America, the West Indies, Central America, and in Mexico (pp. 18, 19, 22, 26, 28.)

Statistics.—It will be observed that these 15,000,000 tons represent only "grain and meat." To this must be added the long list of other productions, as cotton, tobacco, sugar, rice, hay, butter, cheese, potatoes, fruit, and other crops, coal, iron, lead, copper, timber, lumber, wool, and numerous other articles, aggregating many times the tonnage of the "Cereals," of which more than 20,000,000 tons could be exported every year to foreign and Atlantic seaboard markets, if there were transportation facilities to do so. (See pp. 16 and 17, and especially read the "Commercial Reports of Great Britain," p. 26.) But none of this surplus of grain, nor much of these other products, can get to the seaboard now. The Northern Lakes, Canals, and Railways carry all they can, and still leave this vast surplus annually in this valley.

Hence Mr. Kingsford, of Canada, declares: "In many localities the produce is even without value, for it is without a market." "Out of 500,000,000 bushels of Indian corn or maize, not 5 per cent. of this amount finds its way to the seaboard." "That out of 60 cents paid in New England for a bushel of corn, *only 9 cents* go to the producer, the remainder being expended in freights and commissions" (p. 20). Commodore Maury says: "These figures of the Agricultural Bureau in Washington bring out the *startling fact* that the Western farmer sending his corn to the sea by the present routes, is required to give for freights, canal tolls, insurance commissions, and profits, 82 *bushels out of every 100 that go forward*" (p. 21). The Report of the National Board of Trade says: "Even in the State of Illinois, corn—the staff of life—needed at the East to feed hungry mouths, has been burned as fuel" (p. 19). The fact is notorious that in sundry of the States and territories west of the Mississippi, corn is burned for fuel, cattle slaughtered for their hides and tallow, and so, too, with sheep to a great extent.

The British Reports on Commerce (p. 26) declare: "*As a matter of fact, the country (the Mississippi Valley) presents the anomalous condition of being the richest in the world in products useful to man, and yet one of the poorest in proper facilities of distribution of those products.*" "*That inquiry from season to season only elicits the reply that (the 660,000,900 bushels of surplus grain left in the producers' hands), when not burned, it lies over deteriorating, and is applied to some inferior purpose, or used for manure. Besides these cereal products, there are also 481,531,389 lbs. of meat in excess, and, whether these be in the living or slaughtered state, equally a waste.*" "*These products, at the cash prices given in the official returns of the export values, amount to the sum of $517,935,405.*" *This is a practical loss to the farmer per annum.*

The Chamber of Commerce of the State of New York declares, that if only 5,000,000 tons of this surplus grain could be conveyed to the Eastern markets, it would net to the farmers $200,000,000 a year, to the carriers $200,000,000, and increase the sales at the East, say, chiefly at New York, by $400,000,000" (p. 19. See also the Report itself.)

Look at the possibilities of the amount of wheat production. This valley possesses 3,000,000 square miles area, or 1,920,000,000 acres. Allowing for all waste lands and poor crops, this will yield, at least, 10 bushels per acre, or 19,200,000,000 bushels of wheat. Allowing each man, woman, and child to eat 10 bushels a year, this would feed a population of 1,920,000,000 souls. If cultivated in Indian corn and barley, it would more than double these figures. Hence *all the* Reports herein on this subject declare this valley has capabilities of almost an infinite amount of production. The British Report says: "*The agricultural resources* of these States" (not including the territories equal to all the States) "are all but unlimited. With capital and labour, the present yield of cotton and cereals might be doubled in a few years" (p. 26.)

THE QUESTION SOLVED.—The Mississippi River and Gulf route declared by the Congress of the United States, and many other deliberative bodies, the cheapest and most feasible route for the shipment of this surplus to the Atlantic Seaboard and to Europe—Late law of Congress making $7,000,000 appropriations in money, and directing the Mississippi River and its mouth to be improved, to make this the great commercial artery for the outlet of the productions of the Mississippi Valley (pp. 22, 23.)

In General Sherman's St. Louis address he declared: —"If as industrious as their fathers, the surplus of food for shipment abroad from this valley will be simply infinite, plenty to give occupation to the Northern lakes and canals, and every railroad leading Eastward, as well as the vaster amount that must flow down the Mississippi to go to the Ocean markets" (p. 24.)

The Times article of September 21, 1875, reviewing the address of the Hon. Jefferson Davis, concludes as follows:—"He then spoke at considerable length upon the vast agricultural resources of the country, and the future development of the commerce of the Mississippi Valley, and its advantages and importance to the nation, and predicted that the time would soon come when fleets of iron barges would float down the mighty Mississippi bearing a commerce greater than that of the whole world" (p. 24.)

The British Report on Commerce (pp. 26, 27) shows that a cargo of 336,000 bushels of coal were shipped by a cheap steamboat and her barges down the Ohio and Mississippi Rivers to New Orleans, 2,000 miles, for $13,440, considered a remunerative trip. To have shipped the same by railway would have cost $268,000, making a saving of freight on this single cargo of $254,560 by water over railway transport—being a difference in favour of this grand and cheap water-way of over 2,000 per cent., or twenty times cheaper.

THE RUSSIAN GOVERNMENT understands this subject quite well. The Report (p. 27) is short, and should be read in full.

Russia concedes that the United States will supply and control the corn markets of Western Europe. "Hitherto all the North American corn destined for Europe went by rail from Chicago to New York, and the costs of freights to England were so high as to amount to three times the value of the grain at Chicago" (besides twice the value of corn in the farmers' hands west of the Mississippi to get it to Chicago).— On the completion of the improvements at the mouth of the Mississippi River "there will be cheap water carriage the whole way from Chicago to Europe." The Report further concedes that the United States can ship grain in quantity, and so cheap as to "render her absolutely the controller of the prices of the London market; that Russia will be utterly unable to compete with her."

And the Report concludes:—

"The following will be the result: 'The corn trade of Odessa and of Russia generally will share the fate of our wool trade. As Australia, South Africa, and South America have driven our wool from the markets of Western Europe, so will the United States drive from them our corn trade.' Other competitors are comparatively unimportant."

The Atlantic and Gulf Ship Canal across the Peninsula of Florida, the "short-cut" to the Atlantic Ocean from the Gulf of Mexico for this commerce. The Mississippi River, Gulf, and Florida Ship Canal, the cheapest and shortest possible water route from the centre of the Mississippi Valley to Liverpool and other European ports on the Atlantic—Steam Ships can sail from Europe and New York direct to the City of St. Louis, in the heart of the Great Mississippi Valley—Navigation on the routes by the Northern Lakes and Canals through the United States and Canada is stopped and closed by ICE an average of six months each year—This Ship Canal and the Mississippi River route open to Navigation all the year, and never obstructed or closed by ice—This route will go far towards promoting direct trade between England and the Mississippi Valley—The Mississippi Valley and Gulf States, through this cheap transportation route, can supply Western Europe with bread, meat, cotton, &c., of first-class quality, cheaper than any other country on the globe."

Summary of Conclusions on the Mississippi Valley Commerce, and the Advantages of the Mississippi River, Gulf, and Florida Ship Canal Route, over the Northern Lakes, Canals, and Railway Routes, all combined. These conclusions contain all the material facts in the premises (pp. 28, 29.)

The amount of merchandise ready to pass through this Canal, on its completion, will be safe to estimate at 25,000,000 tons net. Compare this with the results of the Suez Canal (pp. 30 and 53.)

Reasons assigned why a large number of foreign ships now running to New York, Boston, Philadelphia, Baltimore, and Canada, should be put on this New Orleans Route (p. 30.)

New Orleans, before the war, was the largest exporting port of the United States, excepting New York. It must become so again; and will, no doubt, in course of time, far exceed New York.

Three-fourths of the tonnage and value of the entire annual exports from the United States to foreign markets is the production of the Mississippi Valley and the Gulf States (p. 18.)

CHAPTER II.

ATLANTIC AND GULF SHIP CANAL, AND THE GREAT TIDE WATER CANAL ROUTE.

Maps designated, showing the Peninsula, location of Canals, surrounding Waters, and Countries, also a description of the Canals.

The East portion of the Ship Canal, running through the St. John's River, and inside Tide Waters, with their connecting Canal, and thence through the Harbour and Channel of Fernandina into the Atlantic Ocean, together with the great Tide Water Canal Route, is designated the "EAST DIVISION." That portion of the Ship Canal running West from the St. John's into the Gulf of

Mexico, the "WEST DIVISION."—No engineering difficulties to encounter in construction.—Capacity of Ship Canal sufficient for all classes of Ocean Steam Ships and Sailing Vessels to pass through.—The only possible outlet for a Ship Canal into the Atlantic Ocean. —Costs of entire construction estimated at £4,000,000 (Cost of Suez Canal, £19,000,000).—Balance to complete "EAST DIVISION."—Amount of Work done on "EAST DIVISION."—Large traffic and earnings of "EAST DIVISION" before construction of "WEST DIVISION."— Legislative acts, charters, and rights secured to the Company.—They are liberal and complete.—No competing Ship Canal across the Peninsula possible, and in this respect it possesses as absolute a monopoly as the Suez Canal.

Interesting chain of Navigable Rivers, Lakes, Sounds, Lagoons, Bays and Harbours, aggregating 1,500 miles, connected and utilized by these Canals, and made tributary to the Company's Canal earnings. (See full chapter, pp. 31—36).

The commercial importance of the Tide Water Canal Route is fully detailed in the Report, (p. 35.)

CHAPTER III.

COMPANY'S PROPERTY AND SECURITIES.

Amount of Share Capital and Bonds proposed to be issued shall be sufficient to cover construction costs, equipment, purchase of real estate, erection of wharves, docks, and warehouses, improvement of real estate, construction of steamers, barges, tow boats, &c., &c. Proposed share capital, £8,000,000 ; Bonded Mortgage Debt, £5,000,000 (p. 36).

The canals and earnings will constitute a solid property and guarantee to make the Share Capital and Bonded Debt safe and desirable investment securities (p. 36).

But the real estate and timber resources thereon, without the canals and their earnings, will repay every share of stock and the Bonded Debt, and will make these the most valuable and desirable Land Grant Bonds known in the markets (p. 36).

The value of Land Grants in aid of canal and railway construction practically shown. The average price of all the land grant lands sold to 1872 was $7 per acre. The Illinois Central Railroad had about 2,500,000 acres, and realized $30,000,000 from the sale of its lands (p. 36).

The Company owns, by grants and perfect fee simple titles, 2,300,000 acres, and is in position to acquire by grants and purchase a further amount of 6,000,000 acres which, at the above minimum sale price, should realize $58,100,000 to the Company (p. 37).

Accurate official surveys of these lands, with maps, also Topographical Reports, describing the soil, forests, timber, and other resources thereon, have been made by the United States' Government and published annually. These Reports contain reliable information, by which alone the Government disposes of her lands. The United States' Official Agricultural Reports and Florida Land Office Reports furnish cumulative evidence. The Company possesses all these Reports, and they contain conclusive evidence of the great value of the Company's lands (p. 37).

FORESTS.—Florida is the best timbered State in the Union (p. 40.) The Land Office Report of the United States for the year 1870 contains an interesting description of the lands, soils, forests, and other resources of the State of Florida. On page 45 it says : "Four-fifths of the entire State is covered with heavy forests, consisting of yellow and pitch pine, live and water oak, cypress, hickory, ash, birch, cedar, magnolia, mahogany, and other timber. The yellow and pitch pine attain great size, and furnish the finest quality of pine timber." This timber is fully described (pp. 40—41). It commands a premium in the New York market of 10 per cent., an account of its superior quality (p. 41). The large quantity per acre, and especially its superior quality for naval construction and building materials caused the United States' Government to select and set aside nearly all her forest lands from the State of Florida required by the Government. The present timber production from Florida amounts to $25,000,000 per annum (p. 40). In 1869 the timber product was $10,000,000 (p. 40).

Official (Government) estimates are made of the quantity of timber, lumber, ship spars, &c., per acre. Please read Mr. Judah's Report, adopted by the United States' and State Governments as correct (p. 41—42). Gross value of timber and lumber on the Company's 8,300,000 acres is computed at $228,000,000 ; net value on the $114,000,000 ; net value on the Company's 2,300,000 acres, $16,000,000 (p. 42.)

Location of the Company's 2,300,000 acres in the St. John's and Indian River Valleys is on the Great Tide Water Canal Route and on the Atlantic Coast, the most advantageous location for the shipment of its timber, agricultural, and horticultural productions of any lands in the United States—practically, all right on the seaboard.

The agricultural and horticultural capabilities and productions of the Florida lands, including those of the Company, are fully described herein from the Government Official and other Reports, and forms a most interesting topic for close perusal to all interested in such industries (pp. 38, 39, 40, 44, 46, 47, 48, 49, 50, and 56 to 61).

From those reports, quoted and named, the facts are established—that the long, or Sea Island Cotton, the most valuable fabric the soil can grow, and ranking next to silk in value—grows all over the State of Florida, and can be made to supply the markets of the world in this article (p. 39, and U.S. Land Office Reports) ; that her sugar lands grow double the quantity of sugar per acre that can be grown on the rich sugar lands of Louisiana and Texas, and, consequently, double the profits per acre (see U.S. Land Office Reports 1868, 1869, and 1870 ; also Florida Land Office Reports) ; that the costly Cuban tobacco is grown there successfully, and at larger profits per acre than in Cuba (see same authorities last quoted) ; that all the vegetable productions of the torrid and temperate zones successfully grow, winter and summer, in Florida, and can be supplied in the markets of the Northern States and Cities during the five winter months, when no other State in the Federal Union can do this (pp. 39, 44, 60, &c.) ; that all the fruits of both the torrid and temperate zones are cultivated and produced there with great success and in great perfection, and at immense profits on capital and labour (see all the Reports quoted above on Florida productions) ; and that in the culture of these fruits, and the growth of the garden vegetable during the winter months, Florida enjoys an absolute monopoly of the markets, and can supply much of the fruits and vegetables consumed in the Northern cities alone, computed at $200,000,000 per annum (p. 40, 47, 48, 51).

The immense profits per acre in this fruit culture has no parallel in any other portion of North America. "Oranges, lemons, pine-apples, bananas, and various other tropical fruits raised in Florida, will yield an average profit of about $1,000 per acre yearly" (p. 40). The *Times* of June 23, 1876, in one of its leaders, in speaking of the profits of orange culture in Florida, in the St. John's River Valley, in the very centre of the Company's grants, of 2,300,000 acres, says: "*Florida, as a fruit-producing country, has not a rival in the world.*" "*The Orange groves of Florida are in themselves sources of wealth as rich as the most famous lodes of Nevada*" (meaning the silver mines of Nevada, which are producing their tens of millions of dollars annually), "*and yield in full bearing from 1,000 to 2,500 per cent. per acre to the owner at present prices, and with but trifling labour.*" *A large tract was purchased on the St. John's River (in Orange County) eight years ago at about one dollar per acre, and has lately been re-sold for Orange planting at prices varying from 50 dollars to 120 dollars, while other estates, bought some four or five years ago at $25 per acre, and planted with Orange trees, brought a couple of years since not less than 1,000 dollars an acre*" (p. 47).

The British Official Report on Commerce and Trade, No. 6, for 1876, through the British Legation Office, of Washington, says of the St. John's Valley: "*Florida would, like Texas, appear especially to have been favoured in rapid development of its resources and increase of wealth.*" "*The almost fabulous returns (from horticulture) are attracting crowds, who are thrown out of employment by the crisis of the North.*" "*Amongst other things that might be cited as instances of the latent wealth of this favoured region may be especially mentioned Oranges—which are cultivated as easily, and produce as quickly as the apple, and yield in full bearing from 1,000 to 2,500 per cent. per acre to the owner on the ground at present prices, and with but trifling labour.*" Then, in speaking of the Sanford Grant in Orange County, of twenty-five miles square, which was purchased in 1868 at about one dollar per acre, "*Lands for Orange culture upon it have been sold in the past year at an average of 50 dollars and up to 150 dollars per acre.*" "*Lands there purchased four years ago at 25 dollars an acre, and planted in Orange trees, have been sold three years later at 1,000 dollars per acre, and its neighbourhood in Orange County abounds in similar instances*" (pp. 47, 48).

THE VALUE OF THE COMPANY'S LANDS PER ACRE.

The heavy immigration into Florida is chiefly into the St. John's and Indian River Valleys. The agricultural and horticultural developments, rapid improvements, and great rise in the price of lands are going on in those localities, and immediately about the Company's grants (pp. 45, 47-51.) In these valleys along on the Company's Tide Water Canal Route, the visiting population spend their winter months. At the numerous water-places on this route, life and gaiety rules the hour (pp. 44, 47-51, 58.)

The Indian River Valley—in history, demonstrated by late experience, is the most celebrated region for tropical fruit culture—far superior to the St. John's Valley. The richest sugar and cotton lands of the State lie in the Indian River Valley. Frost never touches the most delicate fruits, plants, or sugar-cane in this Royal Valley, and the fruits grown here command a premium in the markets over the St. John's fruits, on account of their superior quality (pp. 44, 48—51).

About 1,000,000 acres of the Company's lands are situated in the Indian River Valley. The residue and much the largest portion in the Valleys of the St. John's and Halifax Rivers. The Halifax is in all respects like the Indian River Valley. (Land Office Reports of Florida).

The Governor of Florida and his cabinet officers scheduled and valued the Company's lands in the Trust Deed at $10 average per acre (p. 46). The United States' land surveyors who had surveyed and selected these lands, valued them in 1870 at from $8 to $25 per acre, &c. (pp. 44, 45).

A highly respectable firm of London Solicitors compiled the official evidence from the United States' Land Office and Agricultural Reports, also from the Florida Land Office Reports, and exhibit at a glance the value per acre of the Company's lands in the different counties. This evidence is official and entitled to the highest consideration. This firm came to the conclusion, after long and careful search, that the Company's lands are worth, and will sell in the markets now, at from $5 to $100 per acre. Please read this report fully (pp. 43—46).

Upon the completion of the short canal connecting Lake Washington with Indian River, the Company will possess about 450,000 acres of the richest sugar and cotton lands on the American continent, every acre thoroughly drained off, and in excellent condition for agriculture, and for fruit and garden vegetable productions. These lands will then rent readily at $10 per acre. Good sugar and cotton lands do so now in other States. The time will soon come, by holding on to these lands, when the Company will realize an annual ground rent therefrom of over $4,000,000 (p. 43).

Then, too, town and village sites will be located at every five to ten miles along the Company's canal routes on the Company's Lands. Wharves will be constructed at these points, and population will settle rapidly at these locations, and will purchase and improve town lots. Railway and canal companies have done so in other instances, and have from this source realized large incomes (p. 43).

A clear summary of conclusions upon the Company's real estate, its great value, with estimates of annual incomes therefrom, is found on page 51.

It is reasonable to estimate the value of their lands now at $30,000,000, and that the incomes from the sales of agricultural lands, town lots, ground and other rents, sale of timber, &c., when the Company's improvements shall be in full operation, will be safe to estimate at from $3,000,000 to $5,000,000 per annum.

An interesting communication from Haarlem is published in the *Daily News*, London, October 30th, 1876, on the construction of THE NORTH SEA CANAL in Holland.

On "Next Wednesday, the 1st of November, it will be opened by the King of Holland, in person," and an interesting fact is disclosed which will be worthy of mention here.

" That the land on each side of the canal has been re-claimed, and has fetched enormously high prices, amounting in some cases to £120 an acre. There are nearly 12,000 acres of reclaimed land, and by the concession they become the property of the Company."

The construction costs do not fall *" far short of two-and-a-half million sterling."*

Hence this little body of *reclaimed swamp-land*, at this rate, paid nearly *three-fifths of the entire construction costs.* Another circumstance worthy of note is the important fact—so often illustrated in the United States, that lands through which canals and railways are constructed, always rise rapidly in price, and at central points to enormous values.

Apply this rule to the Company's 2,300,000 acres now in hand, lying along the great Ship Canal and Tide Water Canal Routes, and who can compute their value? They have already doubled in price several times since the Company owns them; and they will do so again on the completion of their canal improvements.

CHAPTER IV.

Canal Properties Considered Financially.

Their net earnings are more certain and greater in proportion to construction costs than Railway or other internal improvements, and they afford the cheapest freights of all artificial improvements (p. 52).

The Erie Canal of New York is a horse canal of 363 miles long, open to navigation about six months each year. Its total earnings in twenty-five years amounted to $81,952,010 ; costs for operating $22,075,570, and its net incomes were $59,876,440, or 73 per cent. of the gross incomes during that period. The net annual profits realised amounted to $2,302,940 (p. 52).

The Suez Universal Canal is a grand Ship Canal success.

The amount of its Share Capital is ... £8,000,000
Total costs of construction... ... £19,000,000

Amount of net tonnage through in 1875, 2,009,984 tons. It earned a dividend on its share capital in 1875-6, over all costs for operating and preferential charges, of about 6½ per cent. Its future commercial and financial results are unquestionable. The *Economist* compares its future exhibits and the larger returns to the stock in the New River Company of North London (pp. 52 and 53).

The Dutch Canals of Holland amount to 400 miles in length, and earn net profits of £625 per mile per annum. This challenges the Railway system of any States, while canal freights are from 300 to 500 per cent. cheaper than Railway freights (pp. 53 and 54).

CHAPTER V.

Recapitulation.

Estimates of the Gross and Net Earnings of the Ship Canal and the Tide Water Canal.

Ship Canal net ...	...	$21,250,000
Tide Water Canal ,, ...	...	3,400,000
Total net ...	...	24,650,000
Forest Products, net ...	...	1,000,000
Land Sales, Rents, Issues, and Profits, net ...	...	2,550,000
Total net Incomes	...	$28,200,000

The above estimate of freights is based at less than one half the rate of the Suez Canal. At one-fourth the rate of the Suez Canal, the construction costs would be repaid within two years.

These stupendous results can only be appreciated and reconciled from the fact that the commerce *which must pass* through this Canal exists now, ready to go through it from its opening. The Government Reports on Commerce and Trade, quoted, leave no room for doubt.

The only point to determine is how high or low the tariff shall be.

APPENDIX.

Note " A."—Capt. Townsend, of 2nd Life Guards, of London, gives an interesting history of the settlement and changes in Florida (p. 56.)

Finest climate in the world (pp. 56, 57.)

As respects *health* the climate of Florida stands pre-eminent, and exhibits the best health-bill of any country in the world (p. 57.)

50,000 people visit the State annually, and spend their winters in Florida for health and pleasure, and to avoid the rigours of the Northern winters (p. 58.)

Interesting notes on Agriculture and Horticulture of Florida, and large profits in tropical Fruit Culture (pp. 58—61.)

Note "B."—Mr. Little's statement to London timber importers on the consumption and exhaustion of timber supplies of North America. Interesting details (pp. 61, 63).

Report of United States' Congress on Forestry—evidence quoted, showing the consumption of timber products in the United States amounts annally to about $1,000,000,000, and also showing the increasing demand for timber. Here is a home market for all the Company's timber products (pp. 63, 64).

CHAPTER I.

These North Atlantic nations and countries are the

>United States,
>Canada,
>Great Britain,
>France,
>Prussia,
>Holland,
>Belgium,
>Spain, and other nations.

The countries on the Gulf of Mexico and Caribbean Sea embrace the

>United States on the Gulf, and the great Mississippi Valley,
>Mexico,
>The West Indies,
>Central America, and portions of South America and
>Pacific Regions.

Amount of Commerce, Foreign and Coastwise, between the Atlantic and Southern Countries above-named, annually Transported through the "Florida Pass."

The Federal Government estimated "the amount of Commerce compelled to use this passage twenty-five years ago at $420,000,000 per annum."

From the Official Statistics on Commerce and Navigation for the year 1871, issued by the United States, Great Britain, and other Countries interested in this trade, it appears that the Foreign and United States Coastwise Trade amounted to 9,180,287 tons, valued at $100 per ton (part gold) $918,028,700.

Add to this the Gulf trade, passing over the railway from Cedar Keys to Fernandina, which

is all Ocean Commerce, and we have an annual aggregate of commerce and trade of about 10,000,000 tons, valued at $1,000,000,000, now passing around and through the Peninsula of Florida.

The increased commerce of the Gulf of Mexico will exceed 20,000,000 tons, as hereinafter detailed from authorities and statistics published by the United States' and British Governments, &c.

THE PENINSULA OF FLORIDA,

As shown upon any correct geographical map of the Western Continent, extends south nearly to Cuba; and, with its surrounding "keys," "coral reefs," shoals, rocks, and insidious currents, runs through more than 8½ degrees of north latitude, and possesses an average breadth of over 120 miles.

The official Land Office Report of the United States' Government for the year 1870 says:—

"The Islands of Cuba and San Domingo may be regarded as a *prolongation* of the Florida Peninsula, from which they are separated only by *narrow and comparatively shallow channels.*

"The Peninsula separates the waters of the Atlantic Ocean from the Gulf of Mexico, and lies directly across the line of a short ship route from the North Atlantic Ocean into the Gulf of Mexico and Caribbean Sea.

"The *Gulf Stream* passes around the Peninsula of Florida, and runs northerly between the Bahama Islands and banks, and the Atlantic coast of Florida. This passage constitutes the Straits of Florida."

Dangerous Navigation through the Straits of Florida. Immense Annual Loss to the Commercial World consequent upon this Navigation, which the Florida Ship Canal will save.

The accumulated evidence from history, commercial and official sources, would fill volumes, detailing the dangers, casualties, and heavy losses of ships and commerce consequent upon the navigation of the Straits of Florida and passage around this Peninsula.

The United States' Land Office Report for 1869 says :—

"South of Cape Canaveral, and extending from Cape Florida on the Peninsula, a series of sandbanks, islands, and reefs, or keys, attached and belonging to the State of Florida, extend east and south-westward a distance of 220 miles, in a curve terminating in a cluster of sandbanks and rocks, inside the entrance of the Gulf. These keys are separated from the mainland by Florida Bay, Bay Biscayne, Carp's Sound and Barn's Sound. South of this series of keys lie the Florida reefs, being narrow coral reefs, here constituting the left bank of Gulf Stream."

The United States' Senate Report of 1874, in answer to a Special Message from the President of the United States on Transportation Routes to the seaboard, report the evidence, that—

" The immense extent of the actual risks incurred and heavy commercial losses sustained will be better appreciated by a knowledge of the number of vessels partially wrecked in the Florida Straits and Channel (south of Cape Canaveral) from 1848 to 1859 inclusive, with the values of the vessels and cargoes, adjudicated in the courts at Key West, upon which salvage was allowed, and aggregate as follows:—

" Number of vessels, 618 ; salvage and expenses allowed, $4,261,489 ; value of cargoes, $23,043,327 ; and the total wrecks and losses south of Cape Canaveral unadjudicated," during the same period " foot up an equal amount in number and losses," or about 600 vessels and cargoes, valued at $23,000,000, wholly .lost ; aggregating total number of vessels wrecked, 1,218, with cargoes valued at $46,043,327.

Estimated annual loss in ships and cargoes over $2,500,000.

This is an annual loss of 120 ships for a series of years.

The Report further says :—

" In a national point of view the importance of the Florida Ship Canal cannot be overrated. The passage around the southerly point of Florida, which vessels engaged in the North Atlantic trade, entering and leaving the Gulf, are compelled to make for about 500 miles, is narrow, subject to tornadoes, and is beset with concealed reefs, upon which a rapid current has a tendency to carry vessels. The consequent dangers are such that it costs on *an average* one and three-eighths per cent. more to insure for a Gulf than for an Atlantic port."

" Twenty-five years ago the Acting-Secretary of the United States' Treasury estimated the amount of commerce then compelled to use this passage at $420,000,000 per annum, on which the sum of $2,376,000, as the increased amount

of insurance, was paid annually on account of the dangers of the Straits of Florida."

The memorial and resolution from the Legislature and Governor Hart, of Florida, addressed to the Congress of the United States in 1873, asking "Land Grant," or "a loan of the National Credit," in aid of the construction of the Florida Ship Canal, declares " the losses by shipwreck upon the Florida Coast within the last year alone are credibly estimated at $5,000,000."

The Official Guide of Florida for the year 1873 says :—

" Key West is the principal rendezvous of the wreckers along the Florida reefs (east from Key West), and the fact that during the past year (1873) 700 cases have been heard and decided in the Salvage Court, presided over by Judge Locke, shows the extensive character of the business.

The Official Statistical Register of Alabama for 1871, p. 49, says :—

" The rates of insurance from New York to Fernandina are five-eighths per cent., and to New Orleans or Mobile, around the Florida Peninsula, one and five-eighths per cent.

The extra insurance now amounts annually, from the most reliable estimates, to $3,000,000.

" Rather than risk the dangers of the Florida Pass, shippers in Mobile now prefer 160 miles of rail, from Cedar Keys to Fernandina, in Florida, with a delay of several days, and all the expenses, loss, and inconvenience involved in two transhipments, one from ship to rail, the other from rail to ship."

A leader in the *Daily Telegraph* says—

" It has long been notorious that the navigation of the Straits of Florida is fraught with no ordinary peril. The Florida reefs and keys enjoy the reputation of having wrecked more vessels than any other coast upon earth."

In a book just published in London by Captain Townsend, of the 2nd Life Guards, he says :—

" Wrecking is one of the regular industries of the inhabitants in Southern Florida ; and so numerous are the vessels annually cast away on the reefs and keys, owing to the dangerous character of the navigation of those seas, and the terrific hurricanes to which they are liable, that a profitable business is done by the wreckers."

Commodore Mathew F. Maury, LL.D., quoted by the United States' and British Governments as good authority on commerce and navigation. He is author of " Physical Geography of the Seas," a book for " Sailing Directions," and author of a series of Civil Geographies used in Schools and Colleges, all held in high estimation ; has written fully on the dangers and commercial losses in navigating the Florida

Straits. The extracts are made from his works. His "Manual of Geography," p. 51, says of the dangers of the Straits of Florida :—

"The Gulf Stream sweeps around this State and separates it from the Great Bahama banks and islands, which are also of coral, making navigation dangerous ; Key West is a famous wrecking station, where the property secured from shipwreck is brought to be disposed of."

In his Special Report on the "Florida Pass," he says :—

"And rather than incur the risks of that dangerous navigation, four times the equivalent of railway transportation, with the delays and expenses of two transhipments, are preferred *across the Peninsula.*"

Again, "How much commerce has been paying on account of the dangers of the Florida Keys and Bahama Banks, which would have been *saved* by a practical Ship Canal across the Peninsula, is difficult to ascertain. But the losses entailed by wrecks and disasters, and the sums paid for extra insurance, on account of the dangers of that Pass, foot up many hundreds of millions of dollars. Notwithstanding the perfection of charts, the erection of light-houses, the knowledge acquired concerning the winds and currents of the sea, &c., *insurances* on voyages using the Pass still range as high as 2¼ per cent. upon the value of ship and cargo."

"As an evidence of the dangers of this Pass, it may be mentioned that wrecking is the chief business of Key West. There it is a regular occupation, and there the United States have established a Court of Admiralty especially for the adjudication of Salvage."

"The Dangers of the Florida Pass are what in Navigation are called *hidden dangers.* They lurk there in the shape of insidious currents, sunken rocks, reefs, and shoals. There is nothing in the surface to mark their existence. The water looks open and the way all clear, but an error in the reckoning of a minute, or even less, is often fatal to the ship and cargo, if not the crew."

"*To sailing vessels* the calms that prevail there at certain seasons increase the dangers, for in them vessels are often silently *swept by the currents and stranded* with total loss."

"Added to these are the storms and hurricanes."

"They, alternating with the most vexatious calms, rage from the middle of July till the middle of March. During these eight months the dangers increase, and the rates of insurance go up, for the dangers to a vessel are greatly aggravated when she is overtaken by storms in this crooked and narrow passage-way. Scenes the most awfully grand and sublime that are known at sea, sometimes take place in the hurricanes and tornadoes that prevail here, in them the waters are piled up ; the Gulf Stream is turned back, or forced over reefs with a violence that no skill can countervail—no ship withstand."

"Maury's Physical Geography of the Sea," and "Maury's Sailing Directions" (Large Volume) cite extraordinary cases of these wrecks.

"To avoid such dangers, cotton is now shipped from Mountgomery, 382 miles by rail to Savannah, and thence by sea to New York, at $7.50 per bale of 500lbs., or $30 per ton of 2,000lbs. Mobile shippers avoid these rates and shun this Pass by fetching their cotton to Mountgomery by river, transhipping it and forwarding it thence to Cedar Keys by sea. Here it is transhipped again, and sent 160 miles by rail to Fernandina, to undergo another shipment, and be forwarded thence to New York by steamer, all for $6 per bale."

"But it costs one per cent., or $2 a bale additional, to insure by this route, making a total charge of $28 per ton by weight on this light and bulky article."

"Notwithstanding all these transhipments, forwarders find it cheaper and better to send by this route than to encounter the dangers of the Florida Pass and the high risks that way."

The British Report on Commerce and Trade of Her Majesty's Vice-Consul at Key West, for the year 1874, published by the Government, pages 294 and 295, fully corroborates the foregoing statements, and concludes by saying :—" The wrecking vessels of Key West are not allowed to pursue their calling on the Bahama Banks, neither are the Bahama wreckers on the American Coast. A District Admiralty Court of the United States was established at Key West in 1847. At the present time *seventy two vessels are licensed by the Judge of the Court as wreckers.*"

Another authority says :—" On the Bahama side a larger number of vessels are licensed for the same purpose, which alone shows the very extensive number of ships wrecked, and the consequent large loss of cargoes."

TOTAL LOSS ACCOUNT.

In consequence of the great southerly projection of the Florida Peninsula, the coast line of Florida, commencing at Fernandina, and which runs south on the Atlantic side, around the southerly point, and up the Gulf coast to Pensacola, is estimated (see United States' Land Office Reports) at over 1,200 miles long ; hence ships sailing from the North Atlantic to the Gulf and Caribbean Sea ports, through the "Florida Pass," and keeping well in the

B

channel from the keys, reefs, rocks, and sand-banks on the Atlantic side, are *obliged to sail* an immense irregular circle of extra distance in doubling the Peninsula, and require from 6 to 32 days extra time to sail these extra distances. Hence the annual losses, consequent upon the navigation of this dangerous "Florida Pass," in ships and cargoes—in extra insurance on account of extra risks—in extra time required to sail the long circuitous route around the Peninsula, requiring additional coal, and other supplies, wages, interest on capital employed *for the extra time*, also use of ships, and wear and tear of machinery, and, above all, increased rates of freight on account of these losses, dangers, and extra time, &c., all aggregate a total annual loss of over $40,000,000, or £8,000,000, to the commercial world.

This large amount, less canal tolls, will be practically saved annually upon the completion of this "Short-cut" Ship Canal, and internal steam line, connecting the Atlantic Ocean with the Gulf of Mexico, thereby making the shortest possible and only practicable ship route (being almost a straight line) from Liverpool and New York City into the Gulf, and thence continuing on the straight route through the Channel of Yucatan, into the Caribbean Sea. See full report.

ATLANTIC AND GULF SHIP CANAL—THE ONLY DIRECT ROUTE—AVOIDS ALL DANGERS OF THE STRAITS OF FLORIDA—IMMENSE SAVING OF DISTANCE, TIME, AND MONEY.—THIS COMMERCE MUST PASS THROUGH THE CANAL.

The official survey and map of the Peninsula, and the Florida Ship Canal route, made by the United States' Government in 1856, and re-affirmed by the Government in 1873, shows this is the shortest possible ship route across the narrowest part of the Peninsula.

The United States' Senate Report, on "Transportation Routes to the Seaboard," contains a portion of these Survey Reports, and also other Survey Reports, as well as very voluminous evidence, all showing the international and national importance of this Ship Canal, from which the following extracts are made :—

"The object of a Ship Canal across the Peninsula of Florida is too obvious to need more than a passing notice."

Attention has been turned to this subject since 1824, and examinations of different routes made. The interest which such an improvement possesses to the whole commercial world increases from year to year, as the vast commerce passing through the Straits of Florida increases, and accidents attending that navigation become more frequent and more generally known.

"It involves the interest of the whole Gulf, and the greater portion of the commerce of the Caribbean Sea with the North Atlantic Ocean.

"It will shorten the sailing distance for all the North Atlantic commerce now obliged to go through the Florida Pass to and from the United States' Gulf Ports, and the Gulf commerce from the Mississippi Valley and Mexico, 1,100 miles each voyage, or 2,200 miles for the outward and return voyage, and for all the commerce of the Caribbean Sea, passing both ways, through the Channel of Yucatan and the Florida Pass, it will prove another saving of 500 miles on each voyage, 1,000 miles for the round voyage.

"Then there is the consequent corresponding saving of time from 6 to 10 days for steamships, and from 8 to 22 days for sailing vessels, in making these voyages.

"It will avoid the dangerous and expensive navigation around the Florida Capes, and avoid the great loss of ships and cargoes.

"It will greatly reduce the costs of freights and the millions of extra insurance of cargoes and ships—items of vast importance.

"It will save the extra wages, extra supplies, and other costs, in the difference of time, between these long and short-time voyages.

"It will save the interest on the capital employed, and the wear and tear of ships for this extra time, and ships will be earning new freights, and merchants making profits in this commerce during this extra time."

But the question may be asked, What assurance is there that this commerce will pass through the Florida Ship Canal?

The answer is self-evident from the facts already stated.

Suppose 25 per cent. of the present loss (or $10,000,000) be deducted annually from the total loss account for canal tolls, this sum, in connection with the local earnings of the Canal, and the great through route to Cuba, together with the incomes from the Company's vast amount of real estate and timber thereon, will make this Ship Canal Company enterprise a great financial success. This would leave an annual saving of $30,000,000 in money, which is now lost as above detailed.

Now, then, will this commerce still continue to go through the most dangerous ship passage on the globe? still navigate this extra distance of 1,100 to 2,200 miles, still lose from 6 to 22 days extra time to run this extra distance, and still lose annually $30,000,000 cash, which will *all* be *saved* by its passing through the Florida Ship Canal? But the amount of commerce already stated, awaiting the completion of this Ship Canal, is a small fraction only of that vast and rapidly increasing commerce from and to the Gulf and Caribbean Sea, which is now increasing with astonishing rapidity.

THE GULF OF MEXICO THE CENTRE OF A VAST
EXPANDING COMMERCE, THE GREATER PART
OF WHICH MUST PASS THROUGH THE FLORIDA
SHIP CANAL.

Commodore M. F. Maury, L.L.D., on "The
Future Importance and Commerce of the Gulf
of Mexico" (see 'Alabama Official Register')
thus :—

"A sea is important for commerce in proportion to the length of the rivers that empty
into it, and to the extent and fertility of the
river basins that are drained by it. The
quantity and value of the staples that are
brought down to market depend upon these.
The Red Sea is in a riverless district. Few
are the people and small are the towns along
its coast. Its shores are without valleys, not
a river emptying into it, for there is no basin
for it to drain. Commercially speaking, what
are its staples, in comparison to those of the
Mediterranean, which gives outlet to rivers
that drain and fertilize basins containing not
less than three million and a quarter square
miles of fruitful lands? Commercial cities
have never existed on the shores of the Red
Sea. Commerce loves the sea, but it depends
for life and health upon the land. It derives
its sustenance from the rivers and the basins
which they drain, and increases the opulence
of nations in proportion to the facility of
intercourse which these nations have with the
outlets of such basins.

"The river basins drained into the Gulf and
Caribbean Sea greatly exceed in extent of area
and capacity of production the river basins of
the Mediterranean. The countries in Africa,
Asia, and Europe, which comprise the river
basins of the Mediterranean are, in superficial
extent, but little more than one-fourth the size
of those which are drained by this sea in our
midst. It is the Mediterranean of the New
World, and Nature has laid it out on a scale
for commerce far more grand than its type in
the Old—that is, about forty-five degrees of
longitude in length, by an average of seven
degrees of latitude in breadth. Ours is broader,
but not so long; it is therefore more compact.
Ships can sail to and fro across it in much less
time, and gather its articles of commerce at
much less cost.

"Had it been left to man to plan the form
of a basin for commerce on a large scale—a
basin for the waters of our rivers and the products of our lands—he could not have drawn
the figure of one better adapted for it than that
of the Gulf, nor placed it in a position half so
admirable. The Mississippi and the Amazon
are the two great commercial arteries of the
continent. They are fed by tributaries with
navigable length of channel more than enough
to encircle the globe.

"The products of the basin of the Mississippi,
when they arrive at Balize, may in a few days
be landed on the banks of the Orinoco and
Amazon. Thus, in our favoured position here
in the New World, we have, at a distance of
only a few days' sail, an extent of fruitful
basins for commercial intercourse which they
of the Old World have to compass seas and land,
and to sail the world around, to reach.

"*On this Continent Nature has been prodigal
of her bounties. Here, upon this central sea,
she has, with a lavish hand, grouped and
arranged in juxtaposition all those physical
circumstances which make nations truly great.
Here she has laid the foundation for a commerce the most magnificent the world ever
saw. Here she has brought within the distance
of a few days the mouths of her two greatest
rivers. Here she has placed in close proximity
the natural outlets of her grandest river basins.
With unheard-of powers of production, these
valleys range through all the producing latitudes of the earth. They embrace every
agricultural climate under the sun; they are
capable of all varieties of productions which the
whole world besides can afford. On their green
bosom rests the throne of the vegetable kingdom. Here commerce, too, in time to come, will
hold its Court.*

"The three great outlets of commerce—the
Delta of the Mississippi, the mouths of the
Hudson and Amazon, are all within two
thousand miles (6 days' sail) of Darien. It is
a barrier that separates us from the markets of
six hundred millions of people, three-fourths of
the population of the earth. Break it down by
the construction of the Central American Ship
Canal, therefore, and this country is placed
midway between Europe and Asia; this sea
becomes the centre of the world and the focus
of the world's commerce. This is a highway
that will give vent to commerce, scope to
energy, and range to enterprise; which, in a
few years hence, will make gay with steam and
canvas parts of the ocean that are now un-
frequented and almost unknown. Old channels
of trade will be broken up and new ones opened.
We desire to see our own country the standard-
bearer in this great work."

Professor Edward Fontaine, in an address
before the Chicago Chamber of Commerce, said :

"Look to the South ! There are the Indies,
whose imperial treasures enriched old Spain;
and there is the source from which England
still obtains her wealth. That nation, or city,
whatever it may be, will be the wealthiest and
most prosperous whose manufacturers and
merchants supply most extensively the demands
of this El Dorado of the New World."

"The gateways of the West, the most
practicable ports of the Gulf, look out upon
the India of Columbus. New Orleans, Mobile,

and Pensacola invite the tropical productions of the Caribbean Sea to exchange with the cereals of the West. The Central American States and Mexico, Venezuela, Brazil, and the West Indies possess all the articles of commerce which the Western States need, and which they cannot produce; while they cannot make flour or bacon, and are destitute of iron, lead, and hardware, cutlery, arms, ammunition, agricultural implements, and the hundreds of various kinds *of Western produce and manufactures which they require.* The Amazon empties directly with one great mouth into the equatorial current which flows against the whole eastern coast of the Western Hemisphere in its northern course, and touches the shores of Brazil, the Guianas, Venezuela, New Granada, Costa Rica, Guatemala, Honduras, Mexico, Texas, and Louisiana; *and bears so strongly against the mouth of the Mississippi that it erodes the bottom of the ocean to the depth of more than 7,000 feet at that point.* A vessel can start from the mouth of the Amazon, and without unfurling a sail, can steer along this strong current which forms the Gulf Stream, 'with bare pole,' directly to the mouth of South-west Pass. Bottles thrown out at the mouth of the Amazon are always stranded by this current on Galveston Island, Terrebone parish, or some other parts of the coast of Texas or Louisiana. It receives the mouths of the Amazon, Orinoco, Magdalena, Rio Grande, Brazos, and Mississippi, indicating the natural course of the tropical trade, and proving that the great Creator intended that the valleys of these rivers should interchange their products by their mouths, which he has singularly linked together."

"In the winter of 1868-9 cargoes of coffee from Rio Janeiro were received at Mobile, shipped over the long line of the Mobile and Ohio Railroad, to St. Louis, and sold there for less than they could have been laid down at the same point by way of Baltimore, and the lines connecting Baltimore with the West. The same result would hold true of all other South American and West Indian products."

"Not only do the ports of Gulf States look out upon the India of Columbus, but they also look out upon the India which Columbus sought."

"They look across the Isthmus of Darien toward the commerce of the Pacific. The Western Continent is a repetition of the Eastern. To the one the Gulf of Mexico is what the Mediterranean is to the other. The Isthmus of Darien bears the same relation to the New World which the Isthmus of Suez bears to the Old. Across both lies the road to the Indies. When the caravans which followed the route marked out by the Crusaders, greeted the products of Europe with the riches of the Orient upon the shores of the Mediterranean, the cities of that genial inland sea rose into beauty and magnificence. They gave arts and sciences to mankind, and broke with a rising sun through the gloom of the mediæval ages."

"The discovery of the Cape of Good Hope gave a cheap water route to India, and destroyed the commerce of the Mediterranean cities."

"Now, the Isthmus of Suez is cut by a ship canal, and the wealth of India will again flow through the Italian cities, if they will only stretch out their hands to grasp it. Now, also, the mission of Mr. Cushing to the Columbian Government determines the cutting of the Isthmus of Darien, and the opening of India to the commerce of the Gulf."

CAUSES AND IMPROVEMENTS WHICH ARE BOUND TO INCREASE THE COMMERCE OF THE GULF OF MEXICO TO AN IMMENSE EXTENT, THE GREATER PORTION OF WHICH MUST PASS THROUGH THE FLORIDA SHIP CANAL.

FIRST.—*From the rapid increase of Population, and subsequent enlarged Commerce of the Countries bounded upon and contributory to the Gulf and Caribbean Sea. United States' Senate's Transportation Report* (p. 195, VOL. I.,) says :—

"Some idea of the possible development of Trade with the following-named countries and islands may be formed by referring to the statistics of their population—our commerce with them, and their total commerce with all foreign countries :—

POPULATION.

Mexico ...	...	...	9,175,000
Central America		...	2,665,000
South America...		...	26,259,000
West Indies	...	...	4,000,000
Total		...	42,099,000 "

"Statement showing the value of commerce of Great Britain with Mexico, Central America, West Indies, and South America, during the year 1872 :—

Total Value of Imports into Great Britain	... ...	$189,612,344
Total Value of Exports from Great Britain	... ...	163,774,597
Total Imports and Exports		$353,386,941

"The total value of the commerce of these southern countries and colonies, and the value of their commerce with Great Britain and the United States, may be stated as follows:—

Commerce with Great Britain	$397,560,308
Commerce with the United States	272,279,162
Commerce with all other countries	66,660,530
	$736,500,000."

SECOND.—FROM THE TEXAS PACIFIC RAILWAY (running from San Diego to Shreveport, and thence to New Orleans, by the Trunk Line of the New Orleans, Baton Rouge, and Shreveport Road).

Also the HONDURAS and TEHUANTEPEC RAILWAYS projected.

The Texas Pacific Road is now being rapidly constructed, and its completion can be calculated upon as certain.

The earnings of the Union Pacific Railway for 1874 were:—

Gross earnings	...	$24,137,192
Net earnings ...	...	13,504,838

The freights which must pass over the Texas Pacific will greatly exceed that of the Union Pacific.

A large portion of the *through traffic* of these three trans-continental railways will be ocean commerce, and must pass through the Gulf of Mexico and the Florida Ship Canal as the quickest, cheapest, and most practicable route.

THIRD.—FROM THE ATLANTIC AND PACIFIC SHIP CANAL THROUGH THE ISTHMUS OF CENTRAL AMERICA.

The construction of this great international ship-passage connecting the two great oceans may now be reckoned upon as a foregone conclusion. Its construction has long since been contemplated, and the Old and New Worlds are now taking steps for its consummation. The saving in time and money to the commercial world demand its immediate construction. Look at a few facts.

IMMENSE SAVING OF TIME AND DISTANCE.

The time and distance saved to England, France, and Germany, Holland, Belgium, and other European countries to and from the Pacific Coast of the United States and Territories, the British Possessions, Mexico, Central America, South America, and also to the Sandwich Islands, Australia, New Zealand, and other Pacific countries is very great.

As, for instance, the saving of distance, from Liverpool and New York to San Francisco by way of this canal is 14,000 miles, and from all to all the other countries named in proportion. But this not *all* the distance saved.

Nearly all the commerce which will pass through the Darien Ship Canal must also pass through the Florida Ship Canal, and thereby save 500 miles more, and twice this distance, or 1,000 miles, for the out and return voyage. An examination of any correct map of ocean routes and distances proves this fact.

Upon the completion of these canals, then, the distances saved from Liverpool to Sydney will be 2,820 miles, and from New York and England to San Francisco 14,500 miles, and to the other countries proportionately as great.

The saving of time is from 18 to 129 days, each voyage.

ESTIMATED VALUE OF COMMERCE WHICH WILL ULTIMATELY PASS THROUGH THE DARIEN SHIP CANAL, TO WIT:—

United States	...	$238,682,220
England	...	300,000,000
France	...	90,600,000
Other countries	...	100,000,000
Total	...	$728,682,220

The data are from Mr. Stone's commercial statements.

The Committee of the United States' Senate in 1874, took evidence relating to the importance of this Isthmus Ship Canal, and its bearings on the commerce of the Gulf (see " Transportation Routes to the Seaboard"), and says:—

" The Inter-oceanic Canal across the Isthmus of Darien will have a minimum trade whose annual value is about $450,000,000, and it is claimed, and no doubt correctly, that it will save annually some $49,000,000."

Compare these facts, and add this to the commerce which now passes through the Straits of Florida, exceeding $900,000,000, sustaining an annual loss (which will be saved by its passage through the Florida Ship Canal) amounting to about $40,000,000, and the commercial necessity for the immediate construction of these two great international highways seem self-evident to any business mind.

The United States' Senate Report on Cheap Transportation Routes, VOL. I., page 92, says:—

" The tonnage that passed through the Suez Canal in both directions in 1871 was 761,367 tons."

The commerce which must pass through the Florida Ship Canal will always be several times greater than the *joint amount of both the Darien and Suez Canals together.* The statistical facts already stated prove this point. The geographical location of the Florida Ship Canal produces this result :—

1st. The commerce between Europe and the Atlantic side of the Western Continent will always be greater than the commerce of the Pacific can ever become. A large portion of this will pass through the Florida Canal, and not through either of the others.

2nd. The coastwise trade between the United States, Atlantic, and Gulf ports, must all pass through the Florida Canal, and will exceed the amount that will pass through the other canals. Nearly all that immense amount of the surplus productions of the Great Mississippi Valley, as we shall presently see, will pass through the Florida Ship Canal.

3rd. While it is also quite true that fully three-fourths or more of the commerce which will pass through the Darien Ship Canal, will also pass through the Florida Ship Canal, and thence go to the North American Atlantic Seaboard, and to the markets of Europe.

These facts cannot be successfully controverted.

The Darien Canal is the gateway for the interchange of commerce between the two great Oceans. The United States' Government has just completed the survey for this Canal, and has found a practicable ship-route.

We now come to the great Mississippi Valley and the Gulf States, which properly form a part of this Valley.

The gigantic commerce which this Valley is now annually producing for export, and is increasing with unparalleled rapidity, will furnish the Florida Ship Canal all the freight, for time to come, to make this Canal the grandest financial success of the world.

The full Report, from page 12 to 28, gives a practical insight of the wealth and unlimited capabilities of this great region of the earth, and is treated of under the following heads :—

4th. *The Great Mississippi Valley—An Empire in area—Her remarkable Rivers and Railroad Systems—Large Population and increasing rapidly—The greatest agricultural, horticultural, and stock-raising country on the globe—Cheap bread and cheap meat for the millions in foreign countries—Immense annual surplus productions of the "cereals," meat, cotton, &c., &c.—The lakes, canals, and railways taxed to their fullest capacity are incapable* *to transport half of this surplus to the Atlantic Seaboard—General demand for cheaper transportation and sufficient facilities to move this surplus and increasing production—The President of the United States and Congress, 27 States in Convention, the Boards of Commerce and Trade of the Atlantic and Western Cities, and the merchants, farmers, and planters all taking action to promote this object—The Mississippi River, Gulf of Mexico, and Florida Ship Canal declared the cheapest and best route to the Atlantic Seaboard and to Europe—United States' Senate Report in favour of the Mississippi River Route as the cheapest and best possible—The Congress of the United States have just passed "an Act," with $7,000,000 appropriations to remove obstructions in the Mississippi River, and improve the Bar at its mouth, to permit all classes of ocean vessels to enter the port of New Orleans—Then this great untaxed highway will "let out" to the Gulf and Atlantic direct the vast surplus products of the Mississippi Valley and Gulf States—This will tend to establish "direct trade" between the Mississippi Valley and England—This Route will save 1,500 miles costly railway transport from the Mississippi Valley to New York—The routes by the northern lakes and canals to New York and through Canada, closed by ice over five months each year—The Mississippi route open all the year round—The surplus products west of the Mississippi River, and for some distance east of it, and all south of the mouth of the Ohio River, can be delivered over 200 per cent. cheaper at the port of New Orleans than at Chicago—From Chicago and New Orleans to Liverpool, New Orleans has full 200 per cent. the advantage. The following exhibit shows the different routes to the Atlantic Seaboard, establishes the foregoing facts, and that the leading commerce of the Gulf of Mexico is from the Mississippi Valley, and will so continue.*

The area of this agricultural Empire is nearly 3,000,000 square miles, or larger than all Europe, excepting less than one half of Russia in Europe from the calculation. (P. 12.)

The unsurpassed fertility and productiveness of this Valley and the Gulf States, and enormous yields of agricultural and horticultural crops, are elaborately treated of in history, geography, agricultural reports published by the United States' Government, census statistics, &c.

It is sufficient to say that this Valley can support a population of 200,000,000 people, and then export bread-stuffs and meat sufficient to supply the deficiency of the markets of the world besides; while her cotton and other staple productions, and her coal and iron minerals are practically without limit in amount, and of the finest quality.

But a few years ago this vast region was a

wilderness; now it has a population of over 27,500,000. Many of its States, cities, and towns have doubled their population and wealth each decade. History furnishes no parallel of such rapid growth in population and wealth. (P. 12).

Gen. Palmer, who is good authority, says: "The growth of the West is measured by the increase in population of its cities and towns."

An English Report, on The Resources of Missouri says :—

"St. Louis, the capital of Missouri, has become, to use the words of Horace Greely, 'the seat of an immense industry, and the home of a far-reaching, ever-expanding commerce.' 'She advances surely and steadily to her predestined station of first inland city of the globe.' In the year 1800 there were less than a thousand inhabitants of St. Louis; in 1830 her citizens reached 5,852; in 1840, 16,469; in 1850, 74,439; in 1860, 160,000; in 1870 (despite the Civil War) no less than 312,980 (and in 1875, 550,000!) This marvellous increase no doubt arises mainly from the position of St. Louis. The city is, and must be, the very centre of the commerce of America. The Mississippi, on which St. Louis is placed (about 20 miles below the junction with the river Missouri), has an unbroken navigation, *from New Orleans to Canada*, of no less than 2,131 miles. In connection with its tributaries, it affords 20,000 miles of inland navigation, more than three-fourths of which bear directly on the interests of St. Louis. Upwards of 10,000 steamers are actively engaged in the commerce of these waters, besides large fleets of auxiliary vessels.

"Whilst St. Louis is thus the centre of the whole river-commerce of America, she is also the very central point of the railway communications between the Atlantic and Pacific Oceans. The railroad system of the United States comprehends, at the present time, about 72,000 miles of road. Of these railways no less than 18 distinct trunk railroads centre at St. Louis, besides five more in construction, and four projected. By means of this grand system, St. Louis is, at the present time, only distant four days from San Francisco, and less than two days from New York or New Orleans."

INCREASE OF POPULATION OF MISSISSIPPI VALLEY.

Cities.	1830.	1840.	1850.	1860.	1870.	1874.
Chicago ...	70	4,853	28,047	120,000	298,977	500,000
Cincinnati ...	52,000	80,145	156,844	216,000	268,000	325,000
Pittsburg ...	60,000	81,235	138,290	178,931	262,200	310,000
Cleaveland ...	10,000	26,500	48,099	78,033	132,010	165,000
Detroit	6,000	24,173	42,760	75,547	119,098	140,000
Indianopolis..	7,100	16,080	24,103	39,855	71,939	89,000
Omaha... ...	None.	None.	None.	4,328	19,982	40,000
Kansas City...	2,000	7,600	14,000	23,000	55,041	71,200

GRAND RIVER SYSTEM OF THE MISSISSIPPI VALLEY AND GULF STATES.

	Miles.
The Mississippi River and its immense tributaries and sub-tributaries afford steam navigation for an aggregate distance of ...	20,000
And the rivers of the Gulf States over	5,000
Total ...	25,000

The National Board of Trade Report says :—

"The branches of these great Rivers with slack-water and canal improvements will swell the grand total of this inland navigation to at least 50,000 miles.

This vast system of magnificent rivers permeates all portions of the Mississippi Valley and Gulf States like a net-work, affording the most complete water facilities for internal commerce, and for the transportation of the surplus productions to the Gulf of Mexico, from the Gulf States, and from this largest and most productive valley in the world, at the cheapest rates of freight possible; thence, by far the larger portion, to be transhipped to the markets of foreign countries, and to the Atlantic seaports, through the Florida Ship Canal.

RAILWAY SYSTEM OF THE MISSISSIPPI VALLEY AND GULF STATES.

Number of miles completed and in operation in the Western States in the year 1873 is ...	33,906
Number of miles in the Gulf States	9,706
Total	43,612
Miles of Railways in the Southern States (1873)	15,316

The system of railways in the South generally runs north and south, connecting the cities of the Gulf—viz., New Orleans, Galveston, Mobile, Pensacola, Jacksonville, and Fernandina, with the immense railway system of the whole Mississippi Valley, and, therefore, constitute so many additional transportation feeders to the commerce of the Gulf and Florida Ship Canal.

While this unparalleled system of rivers and railways furnishes the cheapest and quickest outlet of the exports of the Mississippi Valley and the Gulf States, it also furnishes the quickest, best, and cheapest transportation for the imports into the Gulf States and the Mississippi Valley. (P. 14)

STATISTICS.

The Annual Report of the Chamber of Commerce of the City and State of New York for 1874 shows :—

"THAT THE TOTAL PRODUCTS OF 'CEREALS' (consisting of wheat, Indian corn, oats, rye, buckwheat, and barley) in all the States and territories of the United States, amounted, in the year

1840	... ...	615,535,077 bushels
1850	... ...	867,454,032 „
1860	... ...	1,238,138,947 „
1870	... ...	1,357,230,096 „

"The aggregate cereal product of all the nations of Europe, in 1868, with a total population of 296,128,293, was reported to the International Statistical Congress at the Hague, in 1869, to be 4,754,516,604 bushels, being 16 bushels to the head. The product in the United States, in 1870, of 1,357,230,096 bushels, with a population of 38,558,371, was 35 bushels to the head.

"That the cereal products of the interior States north of the Ohio River, embracing the present States of Ohio, Indiana, Michigan, Illinois, Wisconsin, Minnesota, Iowa, Missouri, Kansas, and Nebraska were, in the year

1840	... ...	166,204,201 bushels.
1850	... ...	311,581,066 „
1860	... ...	577,255,715 „
1870	... ...	812,055,564 „

The Board of Commerce and Trade of St. Louis report the grain raised in the Mississippi, in 1871, was 1,035,094,584 bushels.

OFFICIAL STATISTICS FROM THE NATIONAL BUREAU OF AGRICULTURE, SHOWING TOTAL CEREAL PRODUCTIONS FOR THE YEAR 1872, viz. :—

	Bushels.
United States and Territories ...	1,656,198,100
Mississippi Valley and Gulf States named	1,304,129,500
The ten North-Western States ...	1,038,987,300

Mr. Ruggles, who is considered high authority by the New York Chamber of Commerce, in a speech before that body, declared " that the ten interior States north of the Ohio River and on the upper Lakes and upper Mississippi and Missouri, produced in the year 1870, amounting in round numbers to 21,000,000 tons of cereals avoirdupois surplus for export.

"There is not anything like adequate transportation at present for these surplus products, to say nothing of the enormous amount of freightage required for cattle, hogs, cotton, merchandise, and other things. At the monthly meeting of the directors of the New York Cheap Transportation Association, on Tuesday, the question was considered in its different aspects.

"The National Board of Trade, in session at Baltimore, and the National Cheap Transportation Convention, now assembled at Washington, are giving serious attention to the matter of cheap transportation."

Mr. Ruggles further said :—

"That these ten States will probably produce annually 40,000,000, or, perhaps, 50,000,000 tons surplus. It has now become a matter of vital interest, not only to the American Union, but to the common civilisation and welfare of the world, to improve to the utmost all the water ways, natural or artificial, affording cheap transportation from the immense interior of North America to the ocean. The steady progress of agriculture in over-spreading the American Union, from the Atlantic to the Pacific, as shown by the tables, with the steps already taken for improving the channels by land and water needed for transporting its products to the oceans, furnish a moral and historical element most important and instructive in tracing the evolutions of an empire on a North American continent, as yet unequalled in the history of the human race."

By comparison it will be seen that the cereal product of the Mississippi Valley and Gulf States produced in 1872 nearly as much as the whole United States and territories did in 1870. Allowing two-fifths for home consumption, then there was left surplus tonnage for export :—

1870, from ten North-Western States	...	11,000,000 tons.
1871, from Mississippi Valley	... ...	15,526,500 tons.
1872, from Mississippi Valley	... ...	20,000,000 tons.

But this was not all the surplus for export.

The United States' Census for 1870 show the number of horses, mules, asses, cattle, sheep, and swine of this Valley amounted to 85,703,913 head, exclusive of Texas, the greatest cattle-growing State of the world. Add Texas, and the increase in 1874, and we have a total of 105,703,913 head. The census further shows this Valley produced, in 1870 :—

Animals slaughtered (cash) ...	...	$300,369,531
Raised hogs...	...	23,000,003 head
Produced wool	...	64,000,000 lbs.
„ Tobacco	...	228,000,000 „
„ Butter	...	177,932,803 „
„ Cheese	...	53,000,000 „

Add to this the potato and other root crops, hay and grass seeds, flax, hemp, orchard and garden products, small fruits and berries, sugar, molasses, rice, cotton, and flax seeds, oil cake, winter vegetables, and semi-tropical fruits. Also 4,000,000 bales of cotton (of which the Valley Gulf States produce 3,500,000 bales), with a large list of additional agricultural and horticultural productions not enumerated. Also an immense amount of live stock, fish, poultry, and eggs. Also the gigantic amounts of timber, lumber, coal, iron, copper, lead, alcohol, oil, and other products, together with the amount of manufactured productions for the home markets and for export, all aggregating an annual tonnage many times the annual tonnage of grain product of this Valley already stated.

And when it is remembered that of these nineteen States and eight Territories, not one acre in every 500 has ever seen a plough, and that for extent of agricultural area, remarkable fertility and productiveness of soils, and variety and salubrity of climates, together with practically unlimited quantities of iron and coal minerals of the best quality abounding there, it must seem self-evident that the Mississippi Valley and Gulf States can have no equal or rival in the two hemispheres, and that this internal and export commerce must ultimately control the markets of the world. (See Census Statistics, Agricultural and Land Office Reports of the United States' Government, and British Reports of her Majesty's Secretaries of Embassy and Legation at Washington on the iron and coal industries and wealth of this valley.

Look at the commerce of this Valley now ?

The Report of the United States Senate on Transportation Routes, says :—

" We have no means of measuring accurately the magnitude of internal transportation ; but its colossal proportions may be inferred from two or three known facts. The value of commodities moved by the railroads in 1872 is estimated at over $10,000,000,000, and their gross freight receipts reached the enormous sum of $473,241,055. (The commerce of the cities of the Ohio River alone has been carefully estimated at over $1,623,000,000 per annum.) Some conception of the immense trade carried on upon the northern lakes may be formed from the fact that during the entire season of navigation, in 1872, an average of one vessel every nine minutes, day and night, passed Fort Gratiot Lighthouse, near Port Huron. The value of our internal commerce is many times greater than our trade with all foreign nations, and the amount annually paid for transportation is more than double the entire revenues of the Government."

From an English authority—

" The Lake Commerce in			
1841 was...	...	...	$65,000,000
" The Lake Commerce in			
1851 was...	...	...	300,000,000
" The Lake Commerce in			
1870 was...	...	...	700,000,000"

The New York Chamber of Commerce Report for 1874 says :—

" It is difficult to ascertain the actual tonnage of freight which has been carried upon the lakes. The tonnage of the vessels has increased one-half since 1862, and the trade is now valued at $1,000,000,000 (one billion dollars)."

Add to all this the commerce of the rivers and canals, amounting to 40,000,000 tons, and the very large commerce of the Gulf from this Valley hereinbefore stated. This indicates the enormous annual tonnage and value of the internal commerce of the States.

THE COASTWISE TRADE OF THE UNITED STATES OF AMERICA—GIGANTIC IN AMOUNT.

The *Iron Age* of April 22nd, 1875, published the following article :—

" In another department the United States compare more favourably with England than is generally supposed. That is in navigation. Most of the ships and steamers of England are engaged in foreign commerce. Her coastwise commerce is confined within narrow limits by the size of the British Isles ; her voyages become foreign as soon as the vessels cross the narrow seas and touch France, Spain, or Germany ; while with us the coastwise trade extends from Maine to Texas and California. In that trade, which is exclusively our own, the business is conducted with such energy and despatch that, while we are behind Europe in our foreign trade, the entries and clearances of tonnage in our ports exceed those in the ports of Great Britain. This is shown by the following extracts from a paper recently submitted to the Congress of Statisticians at St. Petersburg :—

" ' At this time more than three-fourths of the shipping of the United States is engaged in the coastwise trade, which is nearly three times as great as the foreign trade, and is wholly under the flag of the United States. It is gigantic in its proportions, comprising, as it does, the commerce between all the ports of the United States, from the Bay of Fundy to the Rio Grande, including also voyages of 18,000 miles in length around Cape Horn, between the seaports of our Atlantic coast and those of California, Oregon, and Alaska. The entries and clearances in the ports of the United States for the year ending with January, 1872, exceed the entries and clearances for the same period in the ports of Great Britain. They have been as follows :—

Entries and clearances in United States coastwise trade in ports of the United States for the year ending January 31, 1872 ... ...   Tons. 61,050,287

In foreign trade of United States in the same year   21,402,015

Total   82,452,302

Entries and clearances in the ports of Great Britain for 1871 ... } Foreign trade   35,496,234 / Coastwise ...   36,726,300

Total ...   72,222,534

"'Our tonnage in the coastwise trade, which is sedulously guarded by the nation, is nearly three times as great as that in the foreign trade in which the foreign flag has predominated. The movement in the coastwise trade is remarkable, but there is conclusive evidence to show that the movement by our canals and railways is four times as large as that in the coastwise trade. Here we find a vast commerce independent of the sea, and inaccessible to any foe, reaching from gulf to gulf, and ocean to ocean, and radiating from the great centres of production to the centres of consumption. This commerce comprises not merely the products of agriculture, but the produce of the mechanical arts, which the different sections of the Republic interchange with each other.'"

From *Harper*—

"THE MERCHANT FLEETS OF THE WORLD.—With all our talk about the decline of American shipping, our merchant marine stands first in the world in the number of ships, as we learn from the following, clipped from an English paper : 'In appendix to a memorandum by the German Government upon its navy is the following estimate of the numbers of the merchant ships of the principal Powers in 1869 : United States of America, 26,393 ; Great Britain, 26,367 ; Italy, 18,822 ; France, 15,778 ; Norway, 6,883 ; Greece, 5,512 ; Germany, 5,510 ; Sweden, 3,257 ; Austro-Hungary, 3,114 ; Denmark, 2,853 ; Russia, 2,646 ; Turkey, 2,200 ; Spain, 1,414.' The figures since 1869 have, if anything, increased in our favour."

Three-fourths of the tonnage and value of the entire annual exports from the United States to Foreign markets is the production of the Mississippi Valley and Gulf States. (Commodore Maury.)

We now come to the important consideration of this statement.

A serious drawback and embargo on the surplus productions of this great basin for export to the Atlantic seaboard and to foreign markets exist.

Not one-half of these surplus productions can now reach the Atlantic seaboard.

All the Middle States and the Alleghany, Blue Ridge, and Cumberland Mountains intervene between this Valley and the Atlantic, and from the centre of this basin to the seaboard ports it is 1,500 miles.

THE ONLY TRANSPORTATION ROUTES FROM THIS VALLEY TO THE ATLANTIC AND GULF ARE—

1st. The Mississippi River.

2nd. The Northern Lakes and Canals through New York and Canada.

3rd. The Seven Trunk Railways.

The Bar in the mouth of the Mississippi, during the late war and since, has formed accretions, so as to measurably suspend export commerce through this untaxed and cheapest transportation route known. The United States' Government is now removing this Bar.

The Northern lakes and canals are closed by ice, and navigation is entirely suspended on them for more than five months in each year, and frequently for six or seven months. Hence the only facilities for transporting all the year are over the Trunk Railways. Look at the astounding results :—

The Official Statistical Register of Alabama of 1871 says :

"The great North-west has outgrown the Northern routes to the Atlantic. The tonnage of Western products in 1860 was 33,000,000. Of this amount 20,000,000 could have been spared for market, as it is estimated that in a fertile country three-fifths of the productions are surplus. Instead of 20,000,000 tons being exported to market in that year, the amount was but 5,500,000. The facilities were not adequate in capacity, nor were the charges of transit sufficiently low to permit so vast an eastward movement of tonnage. In a comparative sense, the actual movement of tonnage as late as 1862, while the stimulus of war prices was active in bringing it forward, was very meagre."

"In 1862," says the Report of the Board of Trade and Commerce of Buffalo, 1865, "the surplus products of the West sent eastward (*through* trade) to the tide-water markets, including products of wool, agriculture, animals, manufactures, and miscellaneous commodities, was 5,176,499 tons. This includes the eastward movement of through freight over the four great roads of the United States, and the Grand Trunk and Northern Railways, and the total exports from Buffalo and Oswego by canal. If the way freights received at the Western terminal points of all these railways, and delivered in the interior, be added to the *through* freight, it is estimated that the total number of tons moved out of the West during that year exceeded 5,500,000. Of the eastward movement in 1862, 2,080,656 were sent from Buffalo, and 638,419 tons from Oswego, making nearly 50 per cent. of the total movement by the New York canals, and the remaining portion by the five through lines of railroad."

The annual Report of the Chamber of Commerce of the State of New York for 1874 says:—

"We have seen that of the surplus grain productions of the ten North-Western States in 1870, but 7,000,000 tons were transported eastward over all the channels of transport, and hence the 'skeleton in the corn-crib,' the burning of·corn as a cheap fuel; the costly conversion and necessary condensation of the cereals into animals, their products and liquors. This surplus, which the present channels of transport cannot convey to the Eastern market, would net to the farmers $200,000,000 a year, to the carriers $200,000,000, and increase the sales at the East, say, chiefly at New York, by $400,000,000.

"The simple annual increase of the products of the West exceeds the present capacity of the Trunk Railways. You cannot build railways fast enough to meet this increase.

"Only one well acquainted with the Western country, and particularly with the extremities of the drainages of trade, 'the frontiers of cereal cultivation,' can appreciate how much of the produce must be withheld from your markets for the want of transportation.

"You must go into those extremities of cultivation to realise the annual loss—nay, even the destruction of what would enhance the whole business of New York more than 10 per cent.

"The population of the ten Western States has increased at the rate of 4 per cent. per annum for each of the last ten years, and of several of them from 5 to 8 per cent. per year, and their agricultural products requiring transport to the Atlantic increase more rapidly than the population, and ten years hence will be twice as great as now—viz., more than 20,000,000 of tons; and if cheap, rapid, and certain transportation is afforded, this tonnage will exceed twenty-five millions."

The following extract from a Report made in 1869 by a committee of the National Board of Trade, composed of members from all the principal cities and shipping centres of the country, on the subject of increased facilities for transportation between the West and the Eastern markets, conveys in forcible language some of the aspects of this problem:—

TRANSPORTATION TO MARKET THE GREAT NEED OF THE WEST.

"The problem now most seriously engrossing the attention of commercial men at the North, at the East, and throughout the West, is that of cheaper inter-communication between the great interior region of our continent and the seaboard. The necessity for its solution is becoming more and more urgent every day. The railroads are overburdened with freight, and are inadequate to its transportation, at rates which draw it forth from remote parts of the interior.

"The question of cheaper transportation is only another form of the question of adequate means of transportation—for the moment that freight prices are so reduced as to permit produce to go to market, from where it is grown in the fertile West at a profit to the producer, immediately such a volume of it is mobilised as to over-tax the capacity of the avenues of transportation. The problem of cheap carriage is, therefore, no other than that of adequate means of transportation.

"The productions of the interior are magnifying every year. They grow in aggregate more rapidly than the means of transmitting them to market can be multiplied. Western production is constantly pressing unduly upon the means of transportation.

"The stimulus imparted to production by the railway and navigation systems which have been mentioned, seconded by the unexampled growth of population there going on, is producing an immense development of export products. In 1860 there were eighteen millions of tons of produce to spare from the West, not one-half of which went off! It failed to go off either from the non-existence of sufficient means of transportation, or by reason of the prohibitory cost of freightage over great distances. What the amount of produce now is which could be spared for outside markets from the interior, cannot be stated with authentic accuracy, and the statistics of the forthcoming census must be awaited. But it would be an under-statement to say that it has reached 25,000,000,000 tons. On the other hand, it would be an exaggeration to estimate that twelve and a half millions of these tons now go out to market over all the existing avenues of transit.

"And the present tonnage which could be spared by the West, and which could be forwarded to the seaboard markets, if its products were mobilised by cheap carriage, and by ample avenues of transportation, would be 25,000,000 tons annually." (See article Hunt's Magazine for August, 1868.)

"Already very many of the products of the West, wanted at the East, will not bear transportation. Even in the State of Illinois, corn, the staff of life—needed at the East to fill hungry mouths—has been burnt as fuel on the score of economy, and in Dubuque, on the western bank of the Mississippi, within the last five years, corn in the cob has been burnt for domestic purposes as cheaper than other fuel. Insufficiency in the means of outlet produces high freight charges, and the remarks of all eminent writers on political economy is true, that impassable mountain chains interpose no greater barriers to trade than high prices of freights."

Mr. W. Kingsford, C.E., the engineer for the Canals of the Dominion of Canada, depicts in vivid colours the value and importance of the Western trade. A few extracts from his *Canadian Canals* are here introduced :—

"The commerce of the North-west," he truly says, "is not any fanciful speculation, nor is its magnitude in any way questionable. It is a reality, as inquiry will establish. It has outgrown the Canals and Railways, and the complaint of the West is that the quantity carried is so immense that carriers can command their own terms. The condition of the producers of the West has been described without exaggeration as that of a man shut out from the markets of the world, oppressed by the excessive production of their own toil, which remains wasting and worthless upon their hands, depriving labour of half its reward, and paralyzing enterprise. . . . .

"In many localities the produce is even without value, for it is without a market. It is estimated that five hundred million bushels of Indian corn or maize are raised in the North-west, but not five per cent. of this amount finds its way to the seaboard, owing to the expense of getting it there; and that out of the 60 cents paid in New England for a bushel of corn, only 9 cents go to the producer, the remainder being expended in freights and commission. It is the sense of inferiority of position which has hitherto led to great discontent in the West. . . . .

"Thus surplusage of grain accounts for the extended pork trade. The hog is, indeed, regarded as corn in a concentrated (but expensive) form.

"We can, therefore, readily understand why, in the North-west, public attention has been turned to the Mississippi route.

"What the State of Illinois asks, is a direct trade between the North-western States and Liverpool, on the plea 'that the increasing volume of business cannot be maintained without recourse to the natural outlet of the lakes.' If this opportunity be vouchsafed, and the requisite facilities be given, the surplus produce will be increased with a rapidity even beyond that of the past century. It is estimated that from the State of Illinois alone there has been shipped annually for the last ten years a surplus of food sufficient to feed ten millions of people; and, at the same time, there has been a positive waste, from the inability to bring the crops profitably to market."

Commodore Maury's Report says :—

"The Canadian Government, perceiving how inadequate are the New York routes by rail, lakes, and canals from the North-western Mississippi Valley States to the Sea, have at great labour and expense constructed ship canals around Niagara Falls and other difficult passes between the Falls and the Atlantic, with a view of diverting the Western traffic from New York, and bring it out to the sea through the St. Lawrence River and Gulf. These canals admit a draft of 9 to 10 feet, and engineers are now at work making estimates, &c., for extending and enlarging them so as to pass ships drawing 15 feet.

"'To deepen these canals and gain this trade,' say the Canadian Government, 'is the policy for us to pursue. If we fail to follow it, we neglect every advantage—geographical and commercial—which we possess.'

"As for trade with Liverpool, were there a strait between the Falls of Niagara and the Gulf of St. Lawrence, as wide, as deep, and as free as the Straits of Gibraltar, the six months' ice and frosts of winter, the icebergs, and the fogs of summer, would make this route altogether impracticable. It would be available at best for only a little more than one-half of the year. For the Trans-Mississippi States, and for the greater part of the other Valley States, it cannot be used at all.

"The North Atlantic Ocean is the most tempestuous sea in the world. Cape Horn is nothing to it. The approaches to the mouth of the St. Lawrence lie through the most stormy part of this *tempestuous* ocean. When not vexed by gales in the winter, this part of it especially is in summer beset by calms, fogs, and ice—flow and drift—and by icebergs.

"This route is, therefore, obstructed by the physical geography of the sea as well as of the land, and in this fact lies the secret of the failure of the Canadian Canals to get the trade of the West. *The Western States want, and must have, a route to the Sea that is never closed a single month by the weather, much less one that is tight frozen regularly for six months every year, and rendered almost impossible at other times by the dangers of the sea.*

"*These six months' suspensions of inland navigation in winter, with the storms, fogs, and drifting ice, present insuperable difficulties to this route for all time to come, and which engineering skill and capital can never overcome.*

"*The effect upon Lake Transportation of equinoctial gales and winter storms.*

"At certain seasons of the year, obstacles interposed by the weather to cheap transportation there, which cannot be removed after the middle of September, and annually about the time of the equinoctial storms, the navigation of the Lakes becomes more boisterous, and so remains until after November, when the frost-king sets his seal upon them, and closes them up, generally till April, and sometimes till May.

"The Statistics of the Lake Board of Trade show that, with the commencement of boisterous navigation, there is a rise in freight, both by lake and rail, on all produce going forward from Chicago to Buffalo, New York, and Boston; that this equinoctial rise is from 50 to 90 per cent. upon all grain, breadstuffs, and provisions seeking transportation at that season; and that those high rates last from the autumnal equinox until the opening of navigation in the spring.

According to the tariff of railroad freights published by the Chicago Board of Trade, the freight to New York, on flour, in—

	1866.	1867.
April and May	$1.10 at $1.40 per bbl	$1.00 at $1.10
October and February	1.60 at 2.10	1.70
Fourth-class articles, ⎱ April and May ⎰	.55 at .70	.50 at .55
October and February	.10 at 1.05	.85

PARTLY BY LAKE AND PARTLY BY RAIL—*Flour.*

	1866.	1867.
May	.75 at .80 per bbl	.65 at .70
Middle of September ⎱ to November ⎰	$1.10 at $1.90	$1.30 at $1.35

Provisions per 100 pounds.

	1866	1867
May	.40 at .45	.32¼ at .38
Middle of September ⎱ to November ⎰	.75 at .95	.62¼ at .67½

"Thus it appears that in fall, winter, and early spring—the very time the crops are coming forward, and when the farmers stand most in need of cheap transportation—then, that is the time when the lake route is of the least value. At this season—whether they use lake or rail, or whether the lakes be blocked with ice or vexed by storms, they have to pay from 50 cents to $1 more on every barrel of flour, and from $3 to $3.50 more on every 1,000 pounds of provisions that they send to the seaboard, than they do in midsummer, when their water-line is clear.

"During the two and a-half months of autumnal storms on the lakes, those farmers have also to pay more, by 50 per cent., exclusive of insurance, than they do when the lakes are unvexed. This annual period of high freight commences in September and ends in April.

"*In autumn, the bulk of the crop is gathered; then, in mid-winter, is the time for sending it to market. But this is the time of all others when wind and weather conspire to make transportation from the West, by lake and rail, most expensive.*

"From the Report of the United States' Agricultural Department for 1866, it appears that the average price of corn in the six great corn-growing States of the West—viz: Kentucky, Ohio, Illinois, Indiana, Iowa, and Missouri, was 48 cents the bushel, and the average price in the State of New York and the six new England States, was $1.30. These figures of the Agricultural Bureau in Washington bring out the startling fact, that

the Western farmer in sending corn to the sea by the present routes, is required to give for freights, canal tolls, insurance, commissions and profits, 82 *bushels out of every* 100 *that go forward.*"

Of course this is financial death to the producer and consumer.

"We have seen that the farmers of Iowa and other trans-Mississippi States have to pay 68 cents the bushel to get their wheat to the Atlantic seaboard. *This is* 10 *cents the bushel more than the farmers in California would pay for sending theirs around Cape Horn to New York.*"

"Forty cents per bushel for freight and transhipment *alone*, is as much as Western grain, except at famine prices, can afford to pay for a sea market, this is at $13.20 per ton, but the Trans-Mississippi States must pay 68 cents, which is $22.44 the ton including all charges."

"The Lake trade was carried on in 1866, with 3,000 boats, but common arithmetic shows that 1,700 boats could do all this freighting, if this route were open all the year round."

Then during the six months of the ice blockade of the lakes and canals, all this vast commerce is thrown upon the railways.

In speaking of the railway capacity, the *New Orleans Picayune*, February 22, 1872, says:—

"The blockade of all the railroads of the country is again repeated this year. Each winter offers more convincing proof that ten times the number of railroads in existence, with their average rolling stock multiplied a score, could not conduct the business of the country.

"The glut of freight on all the roads running to New York and Philadelphia has never been equalled. It has been impossible to get freight room, either east or west, at any rates. The roads running south have been so completely blocked for some time past that the officers of them have not been able to keep the run of the freight, and many tons are scattered along at the different stations.

"Notwithstanding the enormous number of miles of railroad already in existence, and the apparently abnormal increase every year, it is evident that the commerce of the country would be in a state of hopeless confusion were it not for the great water-routes that afford avenues for the outlet of so many millions of tons of agricultural and mineral products. *The country never will be wealthy enough to build a sufficient number of railroads to transport all the freight to be moved, and were this done it would be impossible to handle a sufficient amount of rolling stock to move the crops to market.*

"The progress of our railroad system in the West has been pronounced by some of the ablest men of the day as too rapid to be long sustained. The capital cannot be found for a continuance of such enormous investments as have characterised the past ten years. Yet the resources of the interior have been so rapidly developed that the pressure for transportation is greater each winter. The farmer is still ahead of the track-layer, and the plough and reaper are faster than the locomotive. Industry accumulates faster than railways can move ; the cry for more railroads and more rolling stock is louder than it was five years ago."

See memorial of the merchants to Congress, full report, pp. 17 and 18, corroborating the above statement. The rates of freights are raised extortionately high, while most of the produce offered is refused transportation, "damaging the agricultural, manufacturing, and business interests of the entire country." And the evidence abounds that the produce of the trans-Mississippi States will not bear transportation to the seaboard by the railways, and lakes, and canals mentioned, and the United States' Senate Report, vol. 1st, p. 242, shows that "additional railway lines, under the control of private corporations, will afford no substantial relief, *because self-interest will invariably lead them into combination with existing lines.*"

But all these Northern routes, taxed to their fullest capacity, can only transport 7,000,000 *tons produce to sea. Hence about* 15,000,000 *tons of grain and meat have no means of reaching the market of the Atlantic, and the whole country is alive to the question and importance of increasing the transportation facilities.*

An English gentleman, resident of Liverpool, who is thoroughly acquainted with the commerce of the Mississippi Valley and the present wants of additional transport facilities, has written an able book on " Narrow-gauge Railways," in which he says :—

"The deep importance of the question of cheap transportation may be inferred by a consideration of the proposals which have been published and gravely advocated for solving it. Two only need be mentioned here. The first is the maintenance of the navigation of the Erie Canal during the five months it is closed in winter by ice, by means of hot-water pipes extending throughout its entire length of 325 miles. The second is by a double-track freight railroad of 1,300 miles, from New York to Council Bluffs, Iowa, with branches to Chicago and Saint Louis, at an estimated cost of $225,000,000 or £45,000,000 sterling. Both may be dismissed from consideration ; the first, from its impracticability ; the second, from its enormous cost."

THE QUESTION SOLVED. THE MISSISSIPPI RIVER ROUTE DECLARED THE BEST AND CHEAPEST.

The President of the United States in his Message of December, 1872, made the following recommendation to Congress :—

"The attention of Congress will be called during its present session to various enterprises for the more certain and cheaper transportation of the constantly increasing surplus of Western and Southern products to the Atlantic seaboard. The subject is one that will force itself upon the legislative branch of the Government sooner or later, and I suggest, therefore, that immediate steps be taken to gain all available information to ensure equable and just legislation."

"*That production increases more rapidly than the means of transportation, in our country, has been demonstrated by past experience. That the unprecedented growth in population and products of the whole country will require additional facilities, and cheaper ones, for the more bulky articles of commerce to reach the tide water, and a market will be demanded in the near future, is equally demonstrable.*"

"I would, therefore, suggest either a committee or commission to be authorised to consider this whole question, and to report to Congress at some future day for its better guidance in legislating on this important subject.

"Looking to the great future growth of the country and the increasing demands of commerce, it might be well, while on the subject, not only to have examined and reported upon the various practicable routes for connecting the Mississippi with tide water on the Atlantic, but the feasibility of an almost continuous land-locked navigation from Maine to the Gulf of Mexico."

43 Congress—1 Session.

UNITED STATES' SENATE REPORT OF THE SELECT COMMITTEE ON TRANSPORTATION ROUTES TO THE SEABOARD, WITH EVIDENCE AND MAPS, APRIL 24, 1874, IN ANSWER TO THE PRESIDENT'S MESSAGE. (Contains 1,499 printed pages, with Evidence, and Maps of Florida Ship Canal.)

This is one of the ablest and most exhaustive Reports which has ever emanated from a deliberative body. It shows the commerce of the Mississippi Valley, the present channels of transport, the extortionate rates of freight charged, the incapacity of the present routes to move the large annual surplus of cereals and other productions ; declares water routes afford the cheapest and best known means of transport, and that the Mississippi River is the first and most important route to let out this commerce to the seaboard by way of the Gulf of Mexico.

So important is this Report, that the British Legation at Lisbon, March 22, 1876, added a postscript to the Commercial Reports of the British Government, from the Embassy and Legation Office at Washington, United States, for the year 1875, as follows :—

" P.S.—I omitted to mention that the entire subject of ' Transportation Routes to the Sea-board ' is fully discussed in an exhaustive Report (1874) of the United States' Senate Committee on that subject, as also in various reports by engineer officers charged with the examination of different routes. These latter are, of course, technical, but all are replete with statistics, and with information on the subject."

The following conclusions and evidence copied from this Report speak for themselves, viz. :—

" THE UNITED STATES' SENATE COMMITTEE'S CHIEF SUMMARY OF CONCLUSIONS AND RECOMMENDATIONS.

" Eleventh. The uniform testimony deduced from practical results in this country, and through the commercial world, is, that water routes, when properly located, not only afford the cheapest and best known means of transport for all heavy, bulky, and cheap commodities, but they are also the natural competitors, and most effective regulators, of railway transportation.

Twelfth. The above facts and conclusions, together with the remarkable physical adaptation of our country for cheap and ample water communications, point unerringly to the improvement of our great natural water-ways, and their connection by canals, or by short freight railway portages under control of the Government, as the obvious and certain solution of the problem of cheap transportation. [Canals or railway portages not required for the Mississippi River, but extensively for the Lake and other routes.]

Thirteenth. After a most careful consideration of the merits of various proposed improvements, taking into account the cost, practicability, and probable advantages of each, the Committee have come to the unanimous conclusion that the following are the most feasible and advantageous channels of commerce to be created or improved by the national Government in case Congress shall act upon this subject, viz. :—

" 1st. The Mississippi River.

The evidence taken by this Senate Committee (see full Report, pp. 22—24), with other reliable evidence, shows the fact that wheat can be shipped on this Mississippi River route, by the barge system of transportation, to New Orleans, from the cities of St. Louis, Cincinnati, Louisville, and all the numerous smaller cities and towns down the river from these points, at 5 cents the bushel ; and from all points above these cities to the heads of navigation of the numerous tributaries of the Mississippi for 10 cents the bushel, and even less, at a fair profit to the transportation companies. These rates are as cheap as the cheapest ocean rates.

The United States' Congress, at its last Session, passed a law directing the bar in the mouth of the Mississippi to be removed or deepened to 30 feet, so as to allow all classes of ocean steamers and vessels to enter the Port of New Orleans, and thereby to thoroughly re-establish the export and import trade of this most important port in the North American Continent ; and for this purpose appropriated $7,000,000, and by the same law gave the contract to accomplish this great object to Captain Eads, the great American engineer and bridge builder. Mr. Eads has gone to work, and recent reports show that he has already deepened the Channel over this bar to more than 21 feet. Mr. E. J. Read, C.B.M.P., and able engineers of Europe, declare that Mr. Eads will make this a success. Even vigorous dredging will open up this channel.

In the speech of General Sherman at the Eads Banquet at St. Louis, in honour of his undertaking the improvement of ' the mouth of the Mississippi, the General said :—

" Mr. Eads has bridged the Mississippi, and he has undertaken to curb the mouth of this mighty river to make it fulfil the high office as the carrier of that vast commerce which must thence go to the markets of the world. The citizen of the United States who cultivates his farm on the Upper Alleghany, Wisconsin, or Yellowstone is as much interested as he who cultivates his cotton and rice, or sugar or orange grove in sight of the Balize.

" I have seen the steppes of Southern Russia, which produce the wheat exported from Odessa and Taganrog, and am satisfied they are identical with the plains of Western Kansas and Nebraska, now lying idle, and fed on by herds of wild buffalo.

" Let Captain Eads remove the bar at the South Pass even to the depth of 25 feet, so that sea-going vessels may at all times reach New Orleans, and I am certain that England and Ireland alone will give you a certain market for $30,000,000 (£6,000,000), that go now to the Black Sea for wheat alone. Then take the other European countries, Brazil, the West Indies, and other places, that need our cheap grain, and you have a single item of trade that amounts to hundreds of millions annually."

"The aggregate value of farm products for 1870, was $3,447,658,000; yet our country is in its infancy, and the amount of human food that this valley can produce, is only limited by the demand and the cost of carriage, and we all know that the Mississippi River itself affords the cheapest possible carriage, provided the necessary "ships are ready at its mouth to receive this freight."

"*If as industrious as their fathers, the surplus of food for shipment abroad from this valley will be simply infinite—plenty to give occupation to the Northern Lakes and Canals, and every railroad leading eastward, as well as the vaster amount that must flow down the Mississippi to go to the Ocean markets.*

"And I say to Captain Eads, *go in;* 'Work like a beaver' on your great dams and dykes, and may God spare your life and health to see the *Great Eastern* steam up to New Orleans for her 25,000 tons of St. Louis superfine flour to carry back to Sheerness for the hungry millions that want it in that human hive—London."

The *Times* of Sept. 21, 1875, published a portion of Mr. Jefferson Davis' address delivered at De Soto, Mississippi, on the 8th inst. He said, "No man, no course of policy, no deep designs of ambitious men, could ever dissever the people of the Mississippi Valley, in all the future they will surely stand together. The Great River bound them together by ties stronger than any politics could invent, and from its source to its mouth the people who dwell in the Valley must be united." "*He then spoke at considerable length upon the vast agricultural resources of the country, and the future development of the commerce of the Mississippi Valley, and its advantages and importance to the nation, and predicted that the time would soon come when fleets of iron barges would float down the mighty Mississippi bearing a commerce greater than that of the whole world.*"

Look at the Mississippi River system on the geographical map, and the barge navigation adopted?

The Report of the Committee of the National Board of Trade says :—

"The inland navigation of the West is of *immense expansion.* Official reports give the aggregate length of steam navigation on the Mississippi and its Tributaries at 16,674 miles. The flat-boat and batteaux navigation of the head waters and branches of these great Rivers increase this navigation more than 10,000 miles; and in the course of a short time slack water and canal improvements will swell the grand total of Western inland navigation to at least 50,000 miles."

"River navigation has assumed new importance of late by the inauguration of a cheaper and more efficient system of water transportation. On the Western Rivers they have introduced the system of Steam Tugs and Barges on a large scale.

"The effect is virtually to convert the river channels into railroads, the steam tugs being locomotives and the barges being freight cars. Incorporated Companies of large capital own the tugs and barges, and run them upon time Schedules, just as railroad companies run their trains—the trains picking up barges as they pass different wharves and leaving others. The expense is but a fraction of railroad transportation, and the river channels are prized as Nature's substitutes for long railways."

"By means of the Barge System, experience shows that it will make the Upper Mississippi, Ohio, and Missouri rivers the most continuous and effective inland water routes accessible to Western products.

"These steam tow-boats are of immense strength, they carry no freights, but fuel enough for the round trip. The management of barges, like that of freight cars, is independent of the motive power.

"The tug brings in a load of barges and without delay takes out another and proceeds. But few men are required, and the cost of transportation does not exceed that of Ocean freights."

The Convention of buyers and shippers held in St. Louis in 1873 declared the distance from St. Louis to New Orleans was the same as the distance from Chicago by the lakes to Buffalo. That the barge system was used on the Mississippi, and propellers on the Lakes, that one tow-boat with barges carries 200,000 bushels of wheat from St. Louis to New Orleans at 5 cents the bushel, with a profit to Transportation Company, and for the same expense that one Propeller will carry 40,000 bushels from Chicago to Buffalo. That "the tow-boat, moreover, gets sufficient up-cargo to bring for the home-trip, while the Propeller cannot." One member in Convention declared "that barge transportation could whip any other mode for cheapness of freights." (pp. 19 and 20.)

REPORT OF THE UNION MERCHANTS' EXCHANGE OF ST. LOUIS TO THE SENATE COMMITTEE.

"*What may be accomplished.*

"The introduction of barges on the Mississippi River from this port to New Orleans reduced the average freight rate at once, as will be seen by reference to the table of averages submitted. Thus, in 1866, the average on corn to New Orleans was 23 7-10 cents per bushel. In 1867 it was 28¾ cents. In 1868, the year the barges came in full operation, the average dropped to

10 cents, and the lowest rate attained was 5 cents per bushel.

"*The navigable rivers which drain the Mississippi Basin are best fitted for the cheap carriage of its products to the markets of the world. This is the only water route over which shipments of these products can be moved to the seaboard during the winter season . . . . and proceed to their destination by water, either to European ports, the Atlantic coast, Cuba, Mexico, South America, or any other part of the world.* Let these improvements be speedily effected, and the consumers of the Eastern States and of Europe, learning that they can obtain their grain at lower rates by way of New Orleans, will at once provide suitable vessels for moving it from that city, and whatever steamers and barges may be needed to move the surplus of the Mississippi Basin by the river will be quickly supplied. While all other routes will be freely employed, the broad river, the natural and free highway from the interior to the sea, restraining all by its constant competition, and offering cheap transportation for quantities absolutely unlimited, will confer upon the producers of North-west, and the consumers of all other sections, benefits which no human mind can estimate." (P. 25).

OTHER IMPORTANT FACTS ARE ESTABLISHED BY THE SENATE REPORT.

Another important fact is established by this Report beyond all controversy, that *climate influences* are not unfavourable on wheat, flour, Indian corn, and other "cereals" shipped to New York and Liverpool *via* "the Mississippi and Gulf route." The testimony of shippers and others, supported by numerous exhibits and statistics of actual shipments by this route for a series of years, settle the question that these cargoes arrive in Liverpool in as good condition as grain and flour shipped from New York and Canada, and always command as high a price in the markets. As cumulative evidence on this point, the commerical statistics show that years of actual shipments of wheat and flour from San Francisco, first down the Pacific Ocean, though the tropics, around Cape Horn, and thence north through the tropics again, on the Atlantic, always arrive in "first-class" condition in Liverpool and New York, and *command the* HIGHEST prices in those markets; and the large shipments of grain from Russia to England and other North-Western nations in Europe, by way of the Mediterranean Sea, is a further proof of the facts established.

"That the cereals and meat of all kinds are produced much cheaper in the Mississippi Valley than in any other portion of the world. With the Mississippi River improved so as to permit unrestricted commerce at the cities of New Orleans and St. Louis with the world, and the reduction of the excessive freights on the surplus productions of the Mississippi Valley to a proper paying and uniform standard of rates, this great valley can supply England and other countries with bread and meat cheaper than Russia or any other country. Indeed, through this cheap outlet, the cost of grain and meat will be reduced to a price which will enable the United States to *regain* and *permanently hold* the English and European markets for her surplus breadstuffs as against any competing nation."

From New Orleans, *via* the Atlantic and Gulf Ship Canal, wheat can be delivered at New York for 7 to 10 cents per bushel, and in Liverpool at 12 to 15 cents. From the Trans-Mississippi States, *via* the northern routes to New York at 68 cents per bushel, to Liverpool 79 cents, and *via* the Mississippi and Florida Ship Canal route to New York, and New England States from 12 to 15 cents, and to Liverpool from 20 to 25 cents per bushel. Twenty-five cents being equal in value to one English shilling—here is a saving of from 400 to 500 per cent. by the Mississippi route, and the time saved by the latter route is from 10 to 15 days.

The following official Reports on commerce and trade in the United States, from Her Majesty's Secretaries of Embassy and Legation and British Consuls, published by the British Government, fully corroborate the foregoing reports and statistics on the immense agricultural capabilities and productions of the Mississippi Valley and the Gulf States; the large surplus productions that are *wasted* for want of cheaper freights and adequate Transportation Routes, and the very cheap route, the Mississippi River and its tributaries afford for its outlet, &c.

Commercial Report, No. 13 (1874), part II. From the British Consul at the Port of New Orleans, pp. 648-654, *says :—*

"The following table presents a complete statement of the number of bushels of corn shipped to Liverpool and Queenstown, from this (New Orleans) port during the present year, 1873, and the names of the vessels. The bulk of the corn arrived *at its destination in good condition and obtained good prices.* Had *tonnage offered,* these exports during the past twelvemonths would have perhaps equalled those of 1871-72, as the idea that corn heats in the Gulf of Mexico, and reaches Liverpool in bad order has been exploded.

"A crucial test was made in the case of the British Steamer 'Memphis,' which, ladened with corn, was *detained* at the mouth of the Mississippi River during the hottest part of May and June for *thirty-nine days,* and, having

D

broken her screw, was obliged to return and discharge. Her cargo was found to be in *better order* than when *she started*.

" (Here follows the Table.)

" Statement of grain raised in certain States tributary to the Mississippi River in 1873—aggregate 1,069,660,000 bushels (or $26,741,500 tons). (This does not include the States of Ohio, Michigan, and Wisconsin, forming a part of the Mississippi Valley, which raise an average of 500,000,000 bushels per annum).

" It will be observed that these figures represent only bushels of grain. No account is taken of other productions of this wonderful Valley. These yet remain to be added to the computation :—

Hay	...	75,000,000 tons
Potatoes	...	60,000,000 bushels
Tobacco	...	300,000 hgds.
Cotton	...	2,403,000 bales
Animal food, surplus beef, cattle and hogs	...	5,135,600 heads

" And still we have made no computation of the crops of hemp, sugar, rice, fruits, and vegetables, nor yet of Mining products, such as lead, iron, copper, coal, and salt, all of which, with innumerable other articles, are to be added with grand totals given above." " The agricultural resources of these States *are all but unlimited*. With capital and labour the present yield of cotton and cereals might be doubled in a very few years."

Commercial Reports, No. 3 (1875). From the British Legation Office of Washington City, United States. Part II. Quotations from pp. 60—64.

" The question of Transport has during the year (1873) assumed considerable importance. Notwithstanding the building of new Railroads, the cheap transport of agricultural production from the West (Mississippi Valley) does not seem to be sufficiently provided for; and, as a matter of fact, *the country presents the anomalous condition of being the richest in the world in products useful to man*, and yet one of the poorest in proper facilities of distribution of those products.

" The price of products rises or falls in proportion to the accessibility to a market. Thus, in Iowa and Nebraska, corn is valued at 25 to 30 cents, and wheat at 90 cents per bushel, while in Michigan corn is worth 59 cents, and wheat 132 cents.

" Taking the entire products of some of the most promising States, as given in the Agricultural Report, and calculating the quantity required for the whole consumption, as well as for the live stock in each, the following is the *surplus production* in tons weight. The sur-

plus consists mostly of corn, wheat, oats, potatoes, butter, cheese, meats, tobacco, flax, and wool, and all of it should find its way to the Seaboard, but for the expense of conveyance. (See Revised Table).

Illinois	... ...	7,175,727 tons
Indiana	... ...	4,500,323 „
Michigan	... ...	1,851,206 „
Ohio	... ...	3,187,422 „
Minnesota	... ...	938,242 „
Wisconsin	... ...	1,286,513 „
Iowa	... ...	3,290,638 „
Nebraska	... ...	292,345 „
Kansas	... ...	946,328 „
Missouri	... ...	2,933,892 „
Total	... ...	26,402,636 tons

" Take the *total products* of the United States and Territories for 1872, as shown in the Agricultural Reports for that year, the result of accurate calculations, showing the amount unsold and unused for lack of transportation facilities is astonishing."

" The total cereal and meat products of the entire country, as shown by the Official Reports, is here given; the total consumption and the total exports, as evidenced also by Government Official Reports; *and beyond all these there is a surplus of* 663,811,340 *bushels in the aggregate of the varied products. Some of this aggregate is, doubtless, utilized, but there are no data or returns anywhere to show it.*

" *Inquiry from season to season only elicit the reply, that, when not burned, it lies over deteriorating, and is applied to some inferior purpose, or used for manure.*

" *Besides these cereal products, there are also* 481,531,389 *lbs. of meat in excess, and, whether these be in the living or slaughtered state, equally a waste.*

" *These products at the cash prices given in official returns of the export values, amount to the sum of* $517,935,405,"

Which amounts to an aggregate of 15,000,000 *tons, and all this is a practical loss to the farmers and consumers.* The opening of the Mississippi River and Atlantic and Gulf Ship Canal Route will collect and transport every ton of this surplus to the Atlantic Seaboard and to the markets of Europe, at least 400 per cent. cheaper than that which is now exported from this Valley.

Commercial Report, No. 10 (1875), of the British Embassy and Legation Office, at Washington, United States, pp. 312 and 313. Under the title of " Proposed Inland System of Navigation" this Report says :—

" As to relative costs of transport by water and railways an instance is given of a case in point. A Cincinnati steamer, with her tows laden with coal from Pittsburg, was passing down the Ohio River, bound to Orleans, distant from Pittsburgh about 2,000 miles. The cargo consisted of 336,000 bushels of coal (weighing 13,440 tons). This coal was being transported to New Orleans at 5 cents. per 100 lbs. At this very moderate rate the down trip brought to the boat and barges $13,440, considered a remunerative trip by the owners. Now, to have carried such a freight by rail would have demanded a force of fifty trains, or 1,344 cars, with 10 tons each. At $200 a car, with 10 tons freight, to be carried 2,000 miles (which is even lower transportation than can be profitable on the railroads), this cargo would have amounted to $268,000, *making a difference of more than $250,000 on the transportation of the cargo by one cheap steamboat and her barges..............strikingly* corroborating the statements made by Prof. Maury.

Cost by Rail ...		$268,000
„ Water		13,440
Gain by Water	...	$254,560"

RUSSIAN TESTIMONY.

Commercial Reports, No. 4 (1876). *Part II. Of the British Consul-General Stanley on the Trade and Commerce of Russia and Odessa. Presented to both Houses of Parliament by Command of Her Majesty. April* 1876.

" Memorandum sent by the Odessa Committee on Trade and Manufactures to the Council of Trade and Manufactures, at St. Petersburg, and translated by the British Vice-Consul at Odessa.

This Report says : (from pp. 437 to 440).

" The real danger threatens us not from those places which serve as depôts for the sale of Russian grain, but from other competitors for those foreign markets which have hitherto been the consumers of our produce.

"These threaten not only the grain trade of Odessa, but that of all Russia.

"The first rank among these competitors is, as is well known, held by the United States of America.

"In their Report for last year the Committee pointed out that the cause of the continued progress of the United States is the increasing abundance of their production. With a population half that of Russia, the United States produce nearly as much grain as the latter.

"Last year their produce was 175,000,000 hectoliters; that of Russia 210,000,000 hecto-

liters. The United States can export their surplus produce at prices ruinous to us.

"Only a few years ago the United States held a secondary position in the English markets, which is the most important for us, but after the civil war the state of affairs began to change.

"Of the 9,000,000 to 14,000,000 quarters of foreign wheat required by England, the proportions supplied by Russia and the United States have been as follows during the last seven years :—

				Russia. per cent.		United States. per cent.
1867	...	...	...	44	...	14
1868	...	...	...	32	...	18
1869	...	...	...	32	...	18
1870	...	...	...	38	...	21
1871	...	...	...	40	...	23
1872	...	...	...	51	...	24
1873	...	...	...	21	...	44

" The Committee has no positive information for 1874, but the result is probably less favourable to Russia than that for 1873.

"The total value of exports of grain from the United States has been as follows :

1871	...	...	...	$76,500,000
1872	...	...	...	80,700,000
1873	...	...	...	94,400,000
1874	...	...	...	145,300,000

" Of which the value of wheat and wheat flour was in

1871	...	...	$45,000,000
1872	...	...	38,900,000
1873	...	...	51,400,000
1874	...	...	101,400,000

" It must be remembered that the financial year in the United States begins on the 1st July, so the exports given as for 1874 are for the latter half of 1873 and the first half of 1874.

"*The above figures are to the highest degree instructive. They show that we have changed position with the United States. She has now our former high position on the English market, whilst we must put up with quite a secondary position.*

" What they chiefly prove, however, is the regular progressive movement of America.

" They show that we have to deal, not merely with an exceptional phase, depending on the state of the crops, but that the position acquired by the United States is beyond such influence, and not to be shaken.

" We cannot therefore indulge in the hope that even a most prosperous harvest in Russia will turn the scale in our favour and restore us to our former position, but we must rather believe that the United States will take a still higher position among the grain producers of the world.

" *Hitherto all the North American corn destined for Europe went by rail from Chicago to New York, and the costs of freights to England were so high as to amount to three times the value of the grain at Chicago.*

" This year they have begun the deepening the mouth of the Mississippi River, for which Congress has granted $2,000,000. (Corrected.—The Act of Congress donated for this purpose $7,000,000).

" On the completion of these Works there will be Cheap Water Carriage the whole way from Chicago, and the cost of transport to Europe will be diminished more then 50 per cent. The new way will moreover bring into cultivation many millions of acres of virgin soil on the banks of the Mississippi and its tributaries.

" *It is, in fact, impossible to calculate the amount of grain which America will be able to export, and which will render her absolutely the controller of the prices of the London Market; that we shall be utterly unable to compete with her.*

" The cheapness and fertility of her virgin soil, the favourable climate, the high class of agriculture, substituting, where possible, machinery for human labour, the Spirit of enterprise and aptitude for organising business of the Americans, are so many proofs that the fears of the Committee are well grounded.

" Witness, for instance, the struggle now going on between the Graingers' Association and the Railway Companies, in which the former have compelled the Companies to make important concessions in favour of grain," carriage, &c., &c.

(Here several reasons are given for expecting a largely increased exportation of grain from America.)

* * * * *

" The following will be the result :

" *The corn trade of Odessa and of Russia generally will share the fate of our wool trade.*

" *As Australia, South Africa, and South America have driven our Wool from the Markets of Western Europe, so will the United States drive from them our corn trade.*

" *Other competitors are comparatively unimportant.*"

SUMMARY OF CONCLUSIONS ON THE MISSISSIPPI VALLEY COMMERCE—THE IMMENSE ANNUAL LOSS SUSTAINED FOR WANT OF TRANSPORTATION FACILITIES, AND ADVANTAGES OF THE MISSISSIPPI, GULF AND FLORIDA SHIP CANAL ROUTE OVER THE NORTHERN LAKES AND CANALS THROUGH NEW YORK AND CANADA, AND THE RAILWAYS TO THE ATLANTIC—ALL COMBINED.

A COMPLETE SOLUTION TO THE WHOLE PROBLEM.

1. The Annual Commerce of the Mississippi

Valley and Gulf States, as shown by the official evidence of the United States, British and Russian Governments, fully sustained by the highest commercial evidence, has developed into gigantic amounts of tonnage and value, and the capabilities for *increased production* are practically unlimited.

2. The present Surplus production for export of grain alone amounts to about 25,000,000 tons annually; and the yearly increase to nearly 5,000,000 tons more.

3. That the Northern Lakes, with their connecting Canals through New York and Canada to the Atlantic seaboard, together with the through Trunk Railways, taxed to their fullest carrying capacity, only transport 7,000,000 tons of this surplus to the sea annually—that several million tons go by way of the Mississippi, while fully 15,000,000 tons of this surplus cannot get transportation at all by these Northern Routes, and remain in the farmers hands. And that the surplus export tonnage of all other productions, not grain, is also gigantic in amount, a very large portion of which cannot be exported to Ocean markets for the same reasons.

4. The actual loss to the producers, consumers, shippers, carriers, &c., on this surplus of grain which the farmers cannot get shipped, amounts to five hundred of million of dollars annually, as is shown by the Report of the Chamber of Commerce of the State of New York, and the Reports of the United States and Great Britain ; and that the losses in other productions, not grain, is also enormous in amount.

5. Disadvantages of the Northern route by the Lakes and Canals to New York and Canadian ports. Ice blockade and total suspension of lake and canal navigation, averaging six months each year. All vessels and watercraft tied up during this period earning nothing, and subject to heavy port charges, insurances, &c., wholly dependent upon railways to bring the crops to the city of Chicago and other Lake ports, at heavier freights than will deliver the same exports at Liverpool *via* the Mississippi route.

6. All commerce shipped by Northern Lakes and Canal routes is taxed extra freight, and extra tolls, to protect the shipping and canal capital during the six months of suspended navigation, and to cover all unavoidable expenses connected with this shipping stock and the canals during the same period, and this can never be avoided.

Also extra high freights from September 1st to April, covering the stormy months of Lake Navigation ; while it happens yearly that produce is locked up in Lake ports, or detained *in transitu.*

7. But above all, for six months each year the farmers can have no market. Suspension of navigation occurs just at this time when the farmers do most need the market, for the rail-

ways have no capacity to carry much of this surplus—and with no competition railway freights are put up to frightful rates. See Government Reports.

ADVANTAGES OF THE MISSISSIPPI RIVER, GULF AND FLORIDA SHIP CANAL ROUTE OVER THE NORTHERN LAKES AND CANAL ROUTES, OR OVER ANY OTHER POSSIBLE WATER ROUTE.

1. Not obstructed by ice, but open to navigation all the year round from the Mississippi Valley to Liverpool.
2. Its ships, steamers, and barges are not tied up on account of ice, but can carn freights every month in the year.
3. In winter no produce locked up in warehouses, or detained *in transitu*, nor shipped by railways.
4. The Mississippi and tributary rivers possess sufficient capacity to transport all the surplus productions of the Mississippi Valley.
5. Freights 400 per cent. cheaper than any other route, and down river by the barge system is as cheap as the cheapest ocean freights.
6. Farm products of the trans-Mississippi States, and all below the mouth of the Ohio River can be delivered in Liverpool *viâ* the Mississippi route for the same freight that railways can deliver it in Chicago.
7. All *ocean freights* from New Orleans to the Atlantic seaboard and to foreign countries, while from Chicago to the Atlantic seaboard for six months are 1,500 miles of lake and costly canal freights, and the other six months the most costly railway freights, and involving two extra transhipments.
8. The water route from New Orleans to Liverpool *viâ* the Florida Ship Canal is shorter than from Chicago to Liverpool *viâ* the Lake and Canal routes. (See Report, New York Chamber of Commerce.)
9. Shipments from the Mississippi Valley and Gulf States to Liverpool *viâ* New Orleans are from 10 to 15 days quicker than *viâ* Chicago routes.
10. Grain and flour ships in better condition by the deep-river waters than by the shallower canals, as the Erie and Canada Canals.
11. No tolls to pay as on all the Northern Canals. It is the great free high-way for all commerce to reach the ocean, and for importing into this Valley.
12. All classes of Ocean Steamers and Sailing Vessels can run direct to New Orleans— River 150 feet deep—Ocean Steamers of 2,000 tons can run from Liverpool and New York to St. Louis direct.
13. The United States Senate, after full investigation, came to a unanimous conclusion in favour of the Mississippi, as the first and most important of all the routes, affording the

cheapest freights and the most feasible and advantageous channel to let out the commerce of this vast basin to the Atlantic seaboard.
14. And, finally, the Congress of the United States, at its Session of 1875, passed a law and made liberal money appropriations of $7,000,000 to remove the bar in the mouth of the Mississippi River, to afford a channel of water 30 feet in depth over the bar, to allow all sizes and classes of ocean vessels and steamers to trade in the harbour of New Orleans and St. Louis, and also to improve the Mississippi River and its tributaries, in conformity with the Senate Report.

Capt. Eads, the great American engineer, is executing the work for the Government, and his efforts have demonstrated that he will succeed in thoroughly re-opening the port of New Orleans, which before the late war was the second largest exporting Port of the United States. He has already secured a depth of 21 feet over the bar.
15. More than three-fourths of the entire exports of the United States are the productions of the Mississippi Valley and Gulf States, and with the removal of this Bar in the Great River, often styled in History and Geography as the "Father of Waters," and upon the completion of the Florida Ship Canal, the Vast Surplus productions of bread stuffs, meat, 3,000,000 bales of cotton, and a vast list of other productions will reach the markets of the world, cheaper than by any other route.
16. These improvements, accomplished as they surely will be, must establish direct trade between Europe and this Great Valley, and it is probably not too strong to say the time is not far distant when New Orleans will not only become the Largest Exporting Port of the Western World, but of the Old World also.
17. This done, then there will be no more corn burned for fuel and beef cattle slaughtered on the Western Plains for their hides and tallow. The farmers will have a market all the year round. They will raise more, and all the world can go up and down this Great Commercial free high-way to carry this surplus to the world's markets at the cheapest rates of freights known.

Then the cheapest bread and meat can be supplied to feed the hungry millions of our own and foreign lands.
18. The six New England States import as much grain from this Valley annually as our whole foreign grain exports. The New York and the whole Atlantic seaboard will be greatly benefitted by this route.
19. The surplus commerce of the Mississippi Valley and Gulf States, as established by the cumulative authorities quoted, having no present outlet or cheap outlet to the seaboard, will be transported to the Atlantic seaports and foreign markets by way of the Mississippi River and the Atlantic and Gulf Ship Canal Route—

1st. Because this is the cheapest and best route.

2nd. Because the United States' Government is giving it strong aid to make this the proper outlet.

Barge Companies on the Mississippi and its Tributaries stand ready to contract to transport grain and other produce, through this great water route at one dollar per ton for every 1,000 miles. As the distance is less than 5,000 miles from the most remote regions of production to New York and Philadelphia, Baltimore, and Boston, *viá* New Orleans, it will be seen that from the most remote corners of production grain can be delivered in New York and the other cities named at $5 per ton, while all the grain in the Trans-Mississippi States cost over $22 per ton to New York by the Railway routes; and from St. Louis, the centre of this Valley, it can be transported to New York by this new route for $3½ per ton.

Russia fully comprehends the situation. Commodore Maury has truly said—" Here, upon this Central Sea (the Gulf of Mexico), nature has, with a lavish hand, grouped and arranged, in juxtaposition, all those physical circumstances which make nations truly great. Here she has laid the foundations for a commerce the most magnificent the world ever saw."

No Ship Canal can have the same geographical position as this in any other part of the world, for a gigantic commerce waiting now to pass through it with a developing commerce, that must for all time to come make it the greatest International improvement of the age.

AMOUNT OF NET TONS OF MERCHANDISE NOW READY TO PASS THROUGH THE SHIP CANAL.

		Tons.
1.	Present Commerce of the Gulf, &c.	10,000,000
2.	Exports from the Mississippi Valley and the Gulf States ...	15,000,000
3.	Imports into the Mississippi Valley and the Gulf States (large)	
4.	Freights *viá* the Three Trans-Continental Railways and the Darien Ship Canal (large) ...	
5.	Exports, Imports, and Internal Trade of the State of Florida	2,000,000
	Total (now)	27,000,000

Items 3rd and 4th will be large, as will appear self-evident from a little reflection upon the facts. Some of these improvements are now being constructed, and perhaps all may be completed within the next ten years.

It is an established fact that the Suez Canal is both a commercial and financial success, and is bound to become more so every year.

The Report of the Yearly Meeting and Exhibits in the Appendix hereto, published in the *Economist* of July 22, 1876, shows it was earning a net dividend, after payment of all preferred claims, of 6½ per cent. on its capital shares of £8,000,000.

			Tons.
Its traffic in	1872 was	... ...	1,430,000
„	1873 „	... ...	2,085,000
„	1874 „	... ...	2,424,000
„	1875 „	... ...	2,800,000

Compare the traffic of these two great ship canals.

REMARKS.

According to English papers, England imports annually about 11,000,000 tons of grain to supply her deficiency.

She can supply this annual demand from the Mississippi Valley, by direct trade with the ports of New Orleans, St. Louis, Cincinnati, Louisville, and other shipping centres, at from 40 to 75 per cent. cheaper than from any other part of the world. *It ought to cost her in freights not over a shilling per bushel from the place of production, and in return she can sell her manufactures to this valley, in payment for this grain. Here is reciprocity of trade at once. Why not foster it?*

Practice, however, is different. England sends most of her ships to New York, Boston, Philadelphia, Baltimore, and Canada, and thereby compels the Mississippi Valley farmer to transport his grain to these Atlantic Cities over the costly lake and canal routes, or the still more exorbitant railways over an average distance of 1,500 miles. The amount of these freights, tolls, insurance, transhipments, and all middlemen's charges is 82 bushels in 100, or for every 18 bushels the farmer sends by these routes he must send 82 bushels along to pay the expenses. (See Maury's Report.) More than three-fourths of these enormous charges can be saved to the farmer and consumer, besides paying handsome ocean freights to carry this trade direct from New Orleans to Liverpool.

Again, why does England carry her exports required in the Mississippi Valley to these North Atlantic Cities, and thereby compel the Mississippi Valley consumer to pay these enormous freights and middlemen's charges?

Direct trade with the Mississippi Valley will at once avoid all this, and afford England cheap bread and grain, and the Mississippi Valley farmers cheap manufactures.

Again, three-fourths of all the exports of the United States is the production of the Mississippi Valley and Gulf States, and most of this is forced to New York and the other Atlantic

Cities to be purchased there by the English consumer, saddled with these exorbitant transportation costs, &c. This is a gigantic business for these Atlantic Cities. They have grown wealthy and powerful out of this circuity of trade, and this entirely at the expense of England and the Mississippi Valley.

Why not sent half the foreign ships now running to the Northern ports to New Orleans? This would greatly benefit shipping capital, and at once correct the evil.

From Europe to New Orleans, through the Florida Ship Canal, we have one of the finest ocean ship routes in the world, and that all the year round, without ice, fogs, or other obstructions.

CHAPTER II.

THE ATLANTIC AND GULF SHIP CANAL OF FLORIDA.

The following named Official Maps show the location of the Ship Canal, and also the Tide Water Route—Gulf Stream— The Straits of Florida—The Gulf of Mexico and Caribbean Sea, and the contiguous Countries.

1. THE UNITED STATES' OFFICIAL MAP OF THE STATE OF FLORIDA, made by the Bureau of Topographical Engineers, by order of Hon. Jefferson Davis, Secretary of War, in conformity with a Resolution of the United States' Senate of the 11th February, 1856, calling for a "*General Map of the Peninsula of Florida, illustrative of the recent Surveys for a Canal*, executed by virtue of the appropriations made for that purpose, and reproduced in 1873."

2. UNITED STATES' OFFICIAL MAPS AND REPORTS OF COAST SURVEYS—of the whole Peninsula of Florida and its Coasts—of the Gulf of Mexico—and of the inland Tide Waters, Rivers, Sounds, Lagoons, Bays, and Harbours, accurate, full, and complete.

3. NEW OFFICIAL MAP OF THE STATE OF FLORIDA IN 1875, showing the Counties and Townships by the United States' Surveys—all the Inland Waters, Improvements, Railways, Cities, Towns, &c., &c.

4. COLTON'S MAP OF FLORIDA, to the same effect.

5. OFFICIAL FRENCH MAP (Paris, 1862), showing Mexico—The United States on the Gulf—The West Indies—Central America—South America —The Atlantic and Pacific Oceans—The Gulf of Mexico and Caribbean Sea—The Peninsula of Florida—Gulf Stream and the Straits of Florida —and minutely showing the Coral Reefs, Rocks, Sandbanks, and hidden dangers to Navigation through this "*Pass*," all quite complete.

6. BRITISH MAP OF MEXICO AND CENTRAL AMERICA, showing nearly the same matters as the above French Map, by James Wyld, Geographer to the Queen and H.R.H. the Prince Consort. London, &c.

7. PRIVATE MAPS OF THE COMPANY.

LOCATION.

The Ship Canal commences in the harbours of Fernandina and Nassau Inlet, in the Atlantic; thence by way of the inside tide waters and connecting Canal into the St. John's River; thence by way of the St. John's and Doctor's Lake; thence overland into the Suannee River (at tide water); thence by way of the Suannee River into the Gulf of Mexico. Length of this route 165 miles. Nearly one half of this distance is through deep tide waters, which need but little improvement.

Under the Charter Act of 1874 the Company has the right to go up the St. John's, and thence cross by the Ocklawaha River, Lake Orange, and overland to the River and Bay of Wacassasse into the Gulf, or by way of Silver Springs and the Withlacoochee River into the Gulf. The two latter routes for the *West Division* afford more natural *water mileage* and less overland distance, but a *proportionate* longer route.

Neither the land or water section presents a single engineering difficulty.

There are no mountains, or hills, or swamps, hard rocks, or quicksands to encounter on the whole line; geography describes the surface of the State as being generally " low and level."

The *East Division* runs through the St. John's River and the inside tide water and Fernandino, with their connecting canal. The St. John's River is a magnificent tide-water stream like the River Thames, but it is three times as long, and averages more than five times the width of the Thames from London to the sea.

It is frequently called the "Peerless River of the South," and both history and geography describe it as an " arm of the sea," or " ocean frith."

The following short description of this great river is found in the Official Land Office Report of the United States' Government for 1870 :—

" The numerous rivers of Florida afford great facilities for internal navigation, giving free access by steamers far into the interior, and rendering available extensive tracts of rich country, which would otherwise remain unsettled for many years to come. The St. John's River, the principal river of the State, rises in Lake Washington, and flowing in a *northerly direction*, through an *exceedingly level country*, empties into the

Atlantic near the north-east corner of the State. For 150 miles from its mouth it has an average width of nearly two miles (in some places over five miles), *and is navigable for large sea-going steamers as far as Pilatka*, and for smaller steamers to Lake Washington. Many of its tributaries are also navigable for considerable distances, and it is estimated that this river and its branches afford 1,000 miles of water navigation."

The broad part of the river, for the distance above mentioned, is called the Lower St. John's, and the upper part, passing through a series of beautiful connecting lakes, to Lake Washington, is called the Upper St. John's. The Atlantic tide is perceptible to Lake George, and from Lake Harney, 250 miles to its mouth, it has a fall of only 3½ feet, showing the country is almost a *dead level*.

This river, from the junction of the Canal to its *débouchement* into the ocean, a distance of nearly 90 miles, may be properly considered as a vast bay and harbour of quiet, land-locked water, with anchorage extension and holding ground of the best description, and of sufficient capacity to accommodate the combined navies and merchant ships of the United States, England and France.

Here ships can lie in safety at nominal harbour dues, receive unlimited supplies of first-class coal from the near coal-fields of Alabama at the lowest rates, make repairs, and receive other supplies. These are great advantages.

The *Connecting Canal* can be completed with an additional expenditure of £20,000, so as to allow ocean steamers and sailing vessels to pass through from the harbours of Fernandina and Nassau Inlet into the St. John's River. The mouth of the St. John's is wholly impracticable to keep open, on account of drifting quicksands.

FERNANDINA HARBOUR.

The *Alabama Statistical Register* of 1871 publishes a description of this noble harbour, from the Report of Senator Yulee, of Florida.

"The port of Fernandina, next to Norfolk and Pensacola, is the best in the United States.

"The entrance to this port is easy with all winds; the channels (of which there are three) are straight; the harbour deep, varying from 20 to 50 feet, and almost completely land-locked; the anchorage extension and the holding-ground of the best description. The deep-water line reaches close to the shore for a length of two miles, so that a continued wall, but little advanced from the line of shore, will give wharfage for two miles, with a depth of 20 to 30 feet at low water, and warehouses can line the whole wharf-front. The entrance from the sea to the wharves is about two miles, and from the plateau of the town the approach can be observed seaward as far as the telescope can sight. The depth of water on the bar varies from 20 to 23 feet at low water, and high tide 30 feet."

The *Official Guide* of Florida of 1873 says:—

"This is the best harbour of the Atlantic south of Norfolk, and is spacious enough to shelter the fleets of the United States, and to admit over a good bar and through a straight channel, at ordinary high tide, all classes of ocean vessels. Its port, Fernandina, is a small city, and, though stunted by the check its young growth received during the war, is now surely advancing towards its natural destination—the outlet for the products of the whole of Florida; the centre for its lumber trade and naval stores; and the Atlantic shipping port for the largest share of the Gulf commerce.

"From its insular position, Fernandina, fanned by

the constant sea breezes, cool in summer and mild in winter, is entirely exempt from the malignant and contagious fevers that visit annually nearly all the larger and many of the smaller towns of the South. Thus she offers to the far-seeing capitalists the chance of building up a wide-spread and lucrative trade; to invalids in search of health, a mild and salubrious climate; and the pleasure-seeker will find in her *unrivalled beach*, with its invigorating surf-baths, and its 15 miles of smooth, unbroken race-track, sufficient attraction for a lengthy stay. With a liberal policy pursued by those who control her destiny, the future of Fernandina must be great and bright."

THE WEST DIVISION.

The evidence relating to this part of the route is voluminous and interesting.

1. Reports of United States' Topographical Engineers and Land Surveyors.
2. United States' Senate Report on Transportation Routes to the Sea-board (important evidence).
3. Other Official and Private Reports and Showings.

This evidence establishes the following facts :—

1. That a grand ship canal is feasible across this land section.
2. That the surface of the country is nearly on a dead level, with a small ridge or elevation, requiring a *deep cut* through it.
3. That the geological formation is mostly clay, deep down with rotten limestone at the bottom.
4. That this excavation can be done at 10 cents (fivepence) per cubic yard.
5. That the sloped banks and bottom will be firm, and not any part of the whole canal will require dredging.
6. That the Suannee River is a deep-tide water river, far above the point where the canal enters into the river, and but little improvement will be required in that river.
7. That the harbour in the gulf will require some improvement, but the cost will not be large.
8. That there is ample water on the land section for a cheap canal with locks; but a tide-water canal, without locks, is practicable from ocean to gulf.
9. That a re-survey, with accurate estimates, is recommended of this division.
10. That the canal, from ocean to gulf, runs through one of the most beautiful, interesting, and healthy countries in the world.

The entire canal will have ample capacity to allow all sizes and classes of Ocean Steamers and sailing vessels to pass and repass freely, with numerous turnout stations, depôts, and wharves constructed at proper points along the whole line.

Sailing vessels will be towed through by the Company's powerful tow boats.

The proposition is to make this

A TIDE-WATER CANAL

from the Atlantic to the Gulf, without any locks. This is entirely feasible, and although the cost is much greater than one with locks, yet its superior efficiency and shipping capacity, with the immense amount of commerce which will immediately pass through it, at once justifies the additional cost; and even then the cost will be small compared with the cost of the Suez and other ship canals now constructed, and those proposed to be constructed, such as the Darien Canal.

ESTIMATED COST FOR A TIDE-WATER SHIP CANAL,
WITHOUT LOCKS

Total	£4,000,000
(Cost of Suez Canal	£19,000,000)

We have already seen that the traffic will be ten times as large per annum as the Suez Canal from the beginning.

One Engineer estimates the cost by way of the most southerly and longest route as follows:—

	Miles.
From the mouth of the Withlacoochee River to Fort Clinch	9
„ Fort Clinch to Blue Spring ...	12
„ Blue Spring to Silver Spring...	24
„ Silver Spring, through Lake Kerr, into the St. John's ...	28
Down the St. John's...	90
Through the Sisters and Tide-Waters to Fernandina	20
	—
	Total 186
Length of Excavation	67
Natural Waters, requiring no Dredging	119

	Feet.
Average Depth of Canal	30
Width at Top	210
„ at Bottom	150
Total Excavation, cubic yards ...	74,337,185
Cast at 10 Cents	$7,433,718 . 50
Excavation at the Mouth of Withlacoochee	$250,000 . 00
Construction of Four Locks ...	$800,000 . 00
Total Cost of Ship Canal ...	$8,438,718 .50
Or Sterling (nearly)	£1,684,000

In the second volume of United States' Senate Report, &c., p. 807, a crude estimate of cost is put at $7,000,000. (See Evidence, same volume, pp. 954 to 964.)

The chartered and corporate rights to construct this Ship Canal are derived under the "Act of the State of Florida," approved February 19, 1874.

The rights, franchises, privileges, and powers of the Company under this charter are ample, liberal, and complete. (See Act and Charter.)

THIS COMPANY HOLDS THE KEY TO THE SITUATION.

No ship canal across the Peninsula can possibly reach the Atlantic coast, except through the Company's ship canal from Lake George to the harbour of Fernandina. This point is settled by the inevitable laws of nature, viz.: as the Company's canal and route is the only possible outlet to the Atlantic from the Gulf.

On this point the United States' Senate Report is clear. It says:—"One fact may be taken as conclusive, and that is that Fernandina harbour is the natural terminus of any canal through Florida, connecting the Gulf with the Atlantic."

There has been a project talked of to promote the construction of an Inland Steamboat and River Barge Canal from the Rio Grande, by way of the cities of Galveston, New Orleans, Mobile, and Pensacola; thence across the upper end of Florida, terminating at Savannah in Georgia, and partial organization was made for this purpose. Its length would be about 1,000 miles. But a recent Report of the United States Chief of Engineers to the National Government, dated April 4, 1876, for ever settles this scheme as wholly impracticable.

The concluding Report of C. W. Howell, Captain of Engineers, U.S.A., says:—

"I have this to report: 'So long as the port of New Orleans is open it is preposterous to think that Savannah can draw over the route here reported upon any portion of the commerce of the Mississippi River, either export or import.'"

Again, Report of Mr. A. N. Damrell, Captain of Engineers, United States' Army, to Brig.-Gen. A. A. Humphreys, Chief of Engineers, United States' Army, says:—

"Such a route would, in my opinion, be feasible as a work of engineering; but, with its proposed terminus, it possesses no commercial advantages as long as the ports of New Orleans and Mobile are kept open."

The Annual Report of the Chamber of Commerce of New York, page 45, remarks:—

"No commercial city of any importance has ever flourished, except where there occurs a break in the grand lines of transport from the land to water course of the interior, and from the latter to the ocean."

The very object of such Canal would be to carry the commerce of the Mississippi River and other rivers directly past the ports of Galveston, New Orleans, Mobile, and Pensacola, to the Atlantic seaboard, and to make them simply *passing and not transhipping ports*. Will these important gulf cities permit this, and allow their business throats to be cut by a private Canal Company. The United States' Government has appropriated $7,000,000 to open the mouth of the Mississippi River, and to improve the same, in order to export the commerce of the Mississippi valley through the gulf. Is that undertaking also to be defeated?

This, if carried out, would be a merely local internal improvement. It would not accommodate any part of the commerce of the Gulf of Mexico or Caribbean Sea, nor the trans-Continental trade from the Pacific, going by the Darien Ship Canal, or the Pacific Railways. It will cost more money than will build the ship canal across the Peninsula of Florida. It will not cheapen transportation as much as the ship canal, and the construction of the ship canal will for ever keep from it all through commerce required at the Atlantic seaboard. Hence it is impracticable.

THE GREAT TIDE-WATER CANAL ROUTE

FROM FERNANDINA THROUGH THE PENINSULA TO KEY WEST AND CUBA.

Commences in the harbour and bay of Fernandina, running thence southerly, and by the Company's canal connecting with the St. John's River, near its mouth; thence south-westerly up the St. John's River and connecting lakes to Lake Washington; thence by short canal to Indian River, Musquito Lagoon, and Halifax River; thence down Indian River, Jupiter Narrows, and connecting canal to Lake Worth; thence down through Lake Worth and canal to New River; thence southerly through New River and connecting canal to Biscayne Bay; thence south-westerly on Biscayne Bay and Channel, Barn's Sound, and Florida Bay to the harbour of Key West, on the Gulf of Mexico; thence across the channel to the city of Havana, in Cuba, 84 miles. Length of the route through the Peninsula, 450 miles.

E

The great commercial importance of this route to the United States and to the State, in order to establish direct trade with Cuba, and to carry on export and domestic commerce of this State, induced the Federal Government to commence the construction of these canals, and to improve the channels of these waters where required, having in view the establishment of this magnificent steam route from Fernandina, through the Peninsula to Key West, and thence to Cuba. As the State was so directly interested in this improvement, the United States' Government made a liberal and unconditional donation of a portion of her national domain to the State, to enable the State, or any company it might charter, to continue and complete these works.

On the 28th day of July, 1868, the State granted a charter, incorporating "The Southern Inland Navigation and Improvement Company of Florida," with liberal franchises, rights, concessions, and powers, thereby authorizing and empowering this Company to connect the waters above described by a series of canals, also to improve these waters by dredging or otherwise, and to complete and perfect these canals, and maintain this route.

The State also made a liberal donation to this Company of 2,300,000 acres of lands in aid of and to enable the Company to complete these works and improvements.

Under this charter the Company organized and carried on these improvements. Since the American financial crisis no work has been done for want of means to go on.

A large amount of work has been done on the canals and waters described. The amounts still required to be done are detailed in the Report of the Engineer for the Construction Company.

The Company has extended its route from Indian River, by way of Halifax River, to the City of St. Augustine, and thence North into the St. John's River. This will make a straight route from Fernandina to Key West, nearly the whole distance of tide waters by connecting canals. It possesses so many advantages that the additional costs become inconsiderate.

ESTIMATED COST OF CONSTRUCTION AND FULL EQUIPMENT OF THIS ROUTE.

State Engineer and Company's Engineers' Estimates $5,000,000
Sterling £1,000,000

Of this amount there is a margin of 25 per cent. for contingencies. With ready means the work can be completed within eighteen months.

HARBOUR AND CITY OF KEY WEST.

The "Official Guide" of Florida thus describes this harbour:—

"The Island of Key West is about six miles long and one wide. The City of Key West is situated at the westerly extremity, where there is a LARGE AND COMMODIOUS HARBOUR OF GREAT DEPTH OF WATER (from 30 to 70 feet deep), and of incalculable importance in a commercial point of view. It is the principal coaling station for the Gulf trade, an army and naval depot. The markets of New York, and other Northern cities, and Havana, are supplied from its port with immense quantities of fish, oysters, turtle, sponge, and numerous other commodities. It has a large commercial trade with the West Indies, Central and South America. It exports from Florida large quantities of lumber, timber, cattle, hogs, and sheep to Cuba. Five steam-ship lines—three from the Atlantic and two from the Gulf—trade regularly with its port. It also receives large amounts of imports, chiefly from Cuba and San Domingo. Fort Taylor is located here, and commands the entrance to the harbour. This is a fine structure, with castellated walls, bastions, and towers, mounted with 140 guns; 80 15-inch Rodman guns are mounted on its massive walls. Along the beach, at intervals of a mile, are several martello towers of great strength; and these, with Fort Taylor, give the island prominent features."

There is an excellent ship route of deep waters from the harbour of Key West across the channel to the City of Havana, in Cuba, entirely free from keys, coral reefs, or sandbanks.

"The City of Key West has a population exceeding 12,000, is rapidly increasing in population and wealth, having trebled both since the late war. Thrift and industry characterize the city. New houses are building in large numbers; and the prospects are that with the improvements now going on, and the completion of the canals connecting the great inland water route from Fernandina, through the Peninsula, to Key West, and the establishment of a daily ship ferry from Key West to Havana, the limits of the city will soon be extended over the whole island on which it stands.

"The island of Key West is the most important of the Florida Archipelago; has long enjoyed a very high reputation as a resort for invalids, and its claims are undoubtedly of the first order; reports from the United States' navy and army physicians show 'that the extreme equability of the temperature, and the benign influence of the tempered sea-air, suit the delicate breathing organs of the consumptives. Thousands are permanently cured. Intermittent fever is never known here; pneumonia, and affections of like nature, are exceedingly rare; diseases of the alimentary canal are remarkably unfrequent.'

"Frosts never occur; while in the winter months the average temperature is about 70°, and the average of the summer is never above 92°.

"The island is well wooded. The vegetation is entirely of a tropical character. Tall cocoa palms rising to the height of 60 or 80 feet, with their immense feather-like leaves, and laden with fruit throughout the year, delight the eye at every turn; the date palm is also found here growing to perfection; the almond tree, with its horizontal branches, grouped in whorls like an umbrella, and the tamarind tree, the orange, lime, lemon, guava, sapadillo, custard-apple, shaddock, maumee-apple, sour-sop, and all tropical fruits flourish here in great luxuriance and beauty. Besides these, there is a great wealth of flowering shrubs, plants, and vines; oleanders, roses of every hue, night-blooming cereus, jasmines, and, in short, an epitome of all the rare and beautiful vegetation of the tropics are to be found here."

The following is from the British Reports on Commerce and Trade of 1875, Part II., made by the British Vice-Consul at Key West:—

"AS A NAVAL STATION.

"Key West has long been one of the principal naval stations of the United States, and it is said to possess more advantages for the same than any other port in the union.

"1st. For its susceptibility of fortifications.

"2nd. For ease and number of approaches with all winds.

" 3rd. The difficulty of blockade.

" 4th. The ease in which supplies may be thrown in in spite of the presence of an enemy.

" 5th. Abundance of wood and water.

" 6th. The facility of communication with and deriving all the advantages by water, of supplies from the northern and southern sections of the Union, provisions from Louisiana, spars and live oak from Florida and Georgia, cordage, iron, canvas, powder, and shot, &c., from the north.

" 7th. It commands the outlet of the trade from Jamaica, the Caribbean Sea, Bay of Honduras, and Gulf of Mexico.

" 8th. It holds in subjection the trade of Cuba.

" 9th. It is a check to the naval forces of whatever nation may possess Cuba; it is to Cuba what Gibraltar is to Ceuta; to the Gulf of Mexico what Gibraltar is to the Mediterranean."

WORK DONE.

The work done by the Company on the line between Fernandina and Lake Washington and money expended in land purchase are covered by the sale and issue of 1,250,000 dollars of Capital shares.

£100,000 expended in construction-works will open up the connecting Canal between the St. John's River and Inside Tide Waters to Fernandina, and will cut the Canal connecting Lake Washington with Indian River at the City of Aeu Galla, and thereby establish steam navigation from Fernandina to the south end of Indian River—a distance of 350 miles, traversing the whole of the St. John's and Indian River Valleys.

COMMERCIAL IMPORTANCE OF THIS ROUTE.

1. It will open a short, safe, steam route to Cuba, at Havana, and promote direct trade between the United States and the West India Islands.

2. This commerce already exceeds 172,000,000 dollars per annum (see U.S. Senate Transportation Report. p. 196). Key West is an important Ocean Port for the commerce of Florida, and this trade is rapidly increasing. So great is this commerce becoming, that a scheme for building the Great Southern Railway, through the Peninsula to Key West, is now projected, but if built it can never compete with this Water route.

3. On the full completion of this route the smaller ocean steam ships and small coasting vessels carrying Gulf commerce can pass directly through this route to the North Atlantic, and avoid the heavy losses through the " Florida Pass."

4. In time of peace it will furnish the United States' Government many facilities to provision her forts, carry her mails, naval supplies of ship-timber, lumber, stores, &c., at the cheapest freights; and in time of war a land-lock channel, and secure passage.

5. This great tide-water Canal line, with the Ship Canal, will make nearly all the rivers and lakes of the State available for steam navigation. More than 1,500 miles of internal navigation, permeating every section of the State, will thereby become utilized to carry on a vast inland and export commerce. Much the heaviest commerce of Florida is on the Atlantic coast side. This coast south of St. Augustine is wholly impracticable to afford facilities to this commerce, which is bound, before many years, to increase

to a great extent. The dangers from the coral reefs, rocks, sand banks, and currents of Gulf Stream will not permit shipping ports being established on this coast. This commerce, both export and import, is now forced through the Gulf Stream and the Straits of Florida at an immense loss.

6. The surplus productions of the State are practically all ocean commerce, viz., timber, lumber, Sea Island and short cotton, sugar, tobacco, rice, Indian corn, live stock; and to the North Atlantic cities will be furnished regularly the tropical fruits, winter and spring garden vegetables, melons, sweet and early Irish potatoes, fish, oysters, turtles, and numerous other valuable products, almost without limit, which can all be shipped direct on this route at the cheapest freights possible for all time to come, and without transhipments, and in the best condition for markets. The Northern Cities consume annually nearly $200,000,000 of vegetables and fruits, obtained from the temperate and tropical zones. Florida can supply all the winter and early vegetables, and the semi-tropical and tropical fruits now so largely imported from the West Indies and Central and South America. (See United States' Reports on this point, also The Times, and British Legation Report of Mr. Watson).

7. Italy is the charming climate and resort for the people of Europe. Florida is the Italy of North America, and when the severe winters set in, then the invalids and pleasure-seekers of the North flock to Florida, and an average of 50,000 to 60,000 visitors spend their winters in the valley of the St. John's, and along the water line of this Company. On the opening of this line from Fernandina to Key West, this population will be constantly travelling on this most charming route of the world, and will annually increase. This will bring immense and annually increasing revenues to this Company.

8. On the completion of these improvements the Consolidated Atlantic and Gulf Ship Canal Company will possess 630 miles of Canal and improved watercourses, on which the Company will collect tolls for the commerce and vessels that pass and repass over them; besides, 870 miles of tributary rivers and lakes will pour their commerce through the Company's routes, as the only way to reach the ocean. This tributary commerce paying tolls to the Company.

9. The area of Florida is about 60,000 square miles, or nearly equal to the area of the six New England States. She is capable of supporting a population of 10,000,000, and can then export surplus products of the soil annually of a greater amount in value than any other State in the Federal Union.

The ultimate amount of this State commerce may be properly measured by the annual commerce of the States of Ohio, Indiana, Illinois, Michigan, Iowa, or Missouri, which the official statistics show to be enormous.

The amount of local traffic is vast in all the States. In Illinois the local earning on the 5,000 miles of her Railways is over 85 per cent. of the total earnings.

The value of local traffic created is also strikingly illustrated in the following case of the Pacific Railroad from Omaha to San Francisco, whose earnings (see the Report of General William J. Palmer, one of the most practical railway engineers and thorough railway managers in America, published in 1874) were as follows:—

" Gross earnings, $14,137,192, or about £4,800,000.
Nett   "   13,504,838,   "   2,700,000.

"Its construction," he says, "has reversed, to a great extent, the course of the world's trade with the Indies, so that teas and other Asiatic merchandise now come from the West instead of the East, and England sends her mails to Australia by way of New York and California, yet the bulk of the revenue of this railway is derived from local transportation, originating between the two termini of Omaha and San Francisco. Immediately prior to the construction of this highway (in 1866), a single coach line, an occasional emigrant train from California, and the supply of the interior Government military posts, constituted the entire movement. Nearly the whole of this enormous transportation represented by the above figures was simply *created* by the construction of this railroad. It did not *exist before*, and could not have existed till the railway was built."

EARNING, EAST DIVISION.

It is estimated that the nett earnings on through freights, per annum, will be at least $1,000,000
The local freights given by items in a small Report 3,535,000
Sale of lands and timber, to be added, which will be, at least 500,000

Total $5,035,000

Half of this amount may be safely relied on before the "West Division" shall be completed.

CHAPTER III.

The maximum of the share capital shall not exceed $40,000,000, or £8,000,000, and will represent and own the canals, franchises, real estate, and all other property and rights of the Company, subject to the proposed Bonded Mortgage Debt of not over £5,000,000 on both Divisions.

The Stock and Bonds will be limited to the lowest amount required to raise the money necessary for the entire construction and equipments, and to pay for all property purchased.

The commercial and financial character of the Ship Canal and Tide Water Canal route, and their immediate and future possible earnings, have been fully shown from unquestionable authorities; and it is respectfully submitted their great intrinsic value and nett earnings will be a perfect security, guarantee, and solid basis to support the amount of share capital and the bonded debt, and to make them safe and desirable investment securities.

But in addition the Company owns a vast and most valuable real estate, which forms a DOUBLE SECURITY— AN ABSOLUTE SECURITY OF ITSELF, WITHOUT THE CANALS AND THEIR EARNINGS—to pay every pound of the capital shares and bonded debt, and from this source leave a large margin of profits, exclusive of the canals and their earnings.

The Company is not without authority and precedent for coming to this conclusion.

The United States' Government granted land endowments to the St. Mary's Ship Canal Company of Michigan and to twenty-five railway companies up to 1872.

The Reports and Exhibits of these Companies, and Summaries of some of them published by the United States' Government, are of real financial interest.

The St. Mary's Ship Canal Company obtained a grant of 600,000 acres. From the proceeds of sale of a portion of these lands the Company constructed the required improvements, and then turned the Canal over to the Government; whilst, from further sales, the Company has paid its shareholders an annual dividend of 12 per cent. for the fourteen years last past, and still owns the most valuable part of the grant—the present value of which is estimated at $4,000,000 cash. (See Company's full Report.)

The annexed table shows the names of four of the railway companies above referred to, the average price per acre of the sales, and the rate per mile realised on their grants:—

Names of Companies.	Average per acre.	Realising per mile.
	$ c.	$
Grand Rapids and Indiana	13 98	50,967 [50]
Burlington and Missouri River ...	11 70	15,000
Illinois Central	11 35	41,854 [30]
Hannibal and St. Joseph............	11 00	42,500

The average price per acre received is $12. Most of these roads run through the timberless prairies, and these lands as a rule had no forests to be realised.

The real cost for construction of portions of these roads through the level prairies was only $15,000 per mile. Taking all the twenty-five companies and their grants, some running thousands of miles through the great American desert, destitute of both trees and good soil—the surface being covered with sand, sage-bush, and alkali—and taking a fair average of these lands, they will not compare favourably at all with the poorest and most indifferent lands of the Company; and yet the fact is officially published to the world—

"*That the average price of all the sales made of all the land grants, good and bad, was over $7 per acre up to 1872.*"

For a fuller exhibit, take the case of the Illinois Central Railroad Company, which has a large share of its stock held in England, and is well known.

The Official Report by the United States of the result from this Company's grant is given and published in the Land Office Report of 1870, p. 209.

The Report says:—

"The aggregate amount of land donated under the Act was 2,595,053 acres, which at the minimum Government price was $3,243,750. The double of this sum represented the aid to be given thereby to the railway, viz., $6,487,500. The total of the sales made have realised to the Company an average of $11·85 per acre, amounting to $23,968,786. The balance undisposed of now averages $12·55 per acre, at which rate they will swell the actual pecuniary aid derived from the land endowment to $30,000,000, which is equal to the entire cost of the road and the equipment, entirely reimbursing the stockholders for their investment, while the profits remain undiminished."

Now be it known that these lands were chiefly prairie, and not an acre of timber lands on the whole route. The lands are not better in quality, and can never bring as much nett profit per acre from cultivation as the Florida lands. They are also farther off from the Eastern markets.

It is a fact not to be lost sight of that, as a rule, Land Grant First Mortgage Bonds are safer securities than the same Company's Franchise Bonds, inasmuch as they have a *double basis of security*—1st, the land and its values; 2nd, the liability of the Company, its franchises and assets.

American Land Grant Bonds are held in high estimation in America and Europe, and are now more sought after by investors than Railway Bonds.

The Union Pacific Railway Company's Land Grant First Mortgage Bonds command 97 to 98 per cent. cash in sterling in the London Market. They are esteemed as perfectly safe, and yet the fact is well known that the grants of this line are the poorest lands of any grant in America, destitute of timber, the larger part poor and unproductive soil, *and the most remote from the markets.*

	Acres.
The Company owns by grants and by perfect fee simple titles, free of all incumbrances	2,300,000
And controls, and will obtain complete title to, further grants and purchases	6,000,000
Total acres	8,300,000

These lands are largely covered with valuable forests for all kinds of timber and lumber uses. The lands will return larger nett profits per acre from agricultural and horticultural productions than any other lands in the United States outside of Florida, and these are handy to home and foreign markets. The State of Florida is also filling up more rapidly, both in regard to population and capital, than did the regions in which the above "Railway grants" are located.

VALUATION OF THE LANDS ON THE ABOVE BASIS.

8,300,000 acres at $12 per acre (being the average that *has been* realized by the four Companies referred to) ...	$99,600,000
But 8,300,000, even at $7 per acre (official average of all Land Grant lands sold)	$58,100,000

The Company has created £1,000,000 sterling Land Grant Bonds, and has secured the same by 1st Mortgage, covering 2,300,000 acres of the above lands, to which the Company holds perfect grants and titles. These lands are valued and scheduled in the mortgage by the State at $23,000,000.

With this solid property, the franchises and improvements in hand, the Company proposes to commence its basis of financing, the money to be applied first in completing the "EAST DIVISION," and its further proceeds on the "WEST DIVISION."

The following Government Official Reports fully describe the Lands of Florida and of the Company, their soils, productions, climate, &c., &c.

TITLES.—Parties desirous to purchase or loan money on real estate, must have reliable business evidence, showing the character, resources, and value of the property, and good titles.

The United States' Government has, in this case, itself furnished this evidence.

The title to all the lands in Florida, except private valid grants, vested in the United States' Government. Under Acts of Congress, the United States' Government, through her official land surveyors, had the Florida lands surveyed into townships, ranges, sections, quarter-sections, and 40 acre lots.

At the same time these surveyors also made topographical reports, showing the character, quality, and productiveness of the soils, the timber forests, and all other valuable resources on every tract so surveyed.

The Official surveys, maps, and topographical reports were filed and recorded, according to law, in the General Land Office of the United States at Washington. These officers are great experts, and possess accurate education, and these surveys and reports are made conclusive evidence, by which the United States' Government, the States, and the people are governed. Lands are sold and bought only on these surveys and reports.

Their accuracy is unquestionable.

The law further requires the Commissioners of "The General Land Office" annually to compile these topographical reports, surveys, and maps; and the United States' Government publishes these annual volumes, called

"LAND OFFICE REPORTS."

These Reports for 1868, 1869, 1870, 1871, 1872, 1873, 1874, contain the topographical reports, surveys, and maps of the Company's lands, and furnish all the evidence desired.

The United States' Government also issue annually, from the National Bureau of Agriculture, official evidence in volumes called

"DEPARTMENT OF AGRICULTURE REPORTS."

These Reports furnish the highest evidence attainable on all the subjects treated of therein; and foreign Governments make frequent quotations therefrom as containing the best evidence on these subjects. As examples, see the British Reports on Commerce and Trade made by the British Legation Office and British Consuls in the United States, for frequent quotations. The volume of 1862 has an exhaustive report on the "Soil, Climate, and Productions of Florida"—the volume of 1867 on Horticulture and the Fruits of Florida; and the Reports of 1871, 1872, and 1873, are explicit on the productions and profits of farming in Florida, rapid increase of population, and the great rise in the price of lands, &c.

Further, we have the official evidence published by the state of Florida, in annual reports from her Land Office Department, for the years 1869 to 1876, fully covering and elaborating the whole subject. (All the above reports are in hand for inspection.)

These reports impart reliable information on the climate of Florida, the variety and productiveness of her soils (yielding the largest variety of agricultural and horticultural productions of any State in the Union), profits in farming, planting, fruit and vegetable culture, the immense forests of Florida, large timber and lumber industries, live stock raising, fish, oysters, naval stores, and other important resources of the

State, rapid increase of population and wealth, internal improvements, &c.

All these reports describe the Company's property and lands, soils, timber, and all other resources, and for greater assurance they are made a part of this statement.

QUOTATIONS FROM THESE REPORTS.

(For fuller description see also Appendix hereto.)

" By far the finest lands in Florida, denominated ' Rich Lands,' are: 1st. The 'Swamp Lands;' 2nd. The Low and High Hummocks; 3rd. The Prairies, or ' Savannas;' and 4th. The first-class Pine Lands.

"**The 'Swamp Lands'** are unquestionably the most durably rich lands in the State; they are intrinsically the most valuable. They are formed entirely of humus, or decayed vegetable matter, of extraordinary depth, and, from long use in portions of the State, show evidence of inexhaustible fertility. They occupy natural *depressions*, or basins, which have been gradually filled up by deposits of vegetable *débris*, &c. Drainage, which is practicable, is, however, necessary, to *render the greater portion* available for purposes of agriculture. In the United States' Survey's Reports they are called ' Marsh Lands : *the richest of all*. Alluvial deposits, full of decayed vegetable matter ; indeed, most of them are little less than beds of peat. They only require to be drained to become inexhaustible mines of agricultural wealth ; they furnish never-failing stores of muck to enrich thin pine lands ; they will produce abundantly anything that can be put into them. But the great crop, and that which is destined to be one of the main interests of the State, and a great source of wealth, is sugar-cane. On these lands it grows luxuriantly, tasseling out at the top, which it does not do in other States.'

" It has been demonstrated that these lands will yield four hogsheads of sugar to the acre, a most convincing proof of their value. Sugar cane is here instanced as a measure of the fertility of the soil, because it is one of the most exhaustive crops known, and is generally grown without rest or rotation. It is, however, not the only criterion by which to judge of the *relative fertility of lands situated in different climates* ; for we find on the richest lands in Louisiana (the great sugar-growing State) the crop of sugar per acre is not more than one hogshead, or about one half that of Florida.

" This great disparity in the product of those countries is accounted for, not by inferiority in the lands of Louisiana or Texas, but by the fact that the early incursions of frost in both these States render it necessary to cut the cane in October, which is long before it has reached maturity, while in Forida it is permitted to mature without fear of frost. It is well known that it ' tassels' in Florida, and it never does so in either Louisiana or Texas. When cane 'tassels,' it is evidence of its having reached *full maturity*." The words " Swamp" Lands may seem objectionable to people not informed. As has already been observed, immense amounts of the richest and highest-priced farming lands in America were once called "Swamp Lands," which have been *drained*. Fully one quarter of the State of Illinois has been thus reclaimed, and the United States' Land Office Report of 1869 says :—

" It will be observed that originally fully one-third of what is now the State of Louisiana was in the condition of swamp, or overflowed land. Much of it has long been reclaimed, and under a high state of cultivation. Being an alluvial deposit, the lands, when reclaimed, became the most fertile and productive farms and plantations in the State, and have for many years yielded immense crops of cotton and sugar, and before the war commanded from $100 to $150 per acre in gold." (And will do so again).

" **Low Hummocks** rank next, and are not inferior to the swamp lands in fertility, and like them consist chiefly of decomposed vegetable matter deep down. They are always moist, and some of them require drainage. They are always covered with a heavy growth of live, water, and other oaks, cypress, ash, gum, bay, cedar, &c., and when cleared and brought under cultivation they are very productive, and practically inexhaustible."

" The growth of trees, shrubs, and vines upon these low hummocks is most surprising, and so dense as to present an almost impenetrable vegetable barrier to all ingress. They are immensely fertile, indeed, almost incredibly so, as is sufficiently shown by the fact that from one acre has been produced 4,000 *pounds of sugar*, and other crops in proportion."

" **High Hummocks** are in the highest repute in Florida for purposes of agriculture. These differ from low hummocks in occupying higher ground, and in general presenting a gently undulating surface, covered with a heavy growth of great variety of lumber, of hard woods, already described, and composed of deep and rich soil, underlaid with marl, clay, or limestone. The very richest variety of hummock is the ' cabbage hummock,' so called from the cabbage palmetto trees with which it is covered. These trees grow sometimes to the height of 100 feet or more, this soil being composed of shell and vegetable matter mixed, is of rare fertility." " It will be readily understood by anyone acquainted with agriculture, that such a soil, in such a climate as Florida, must be extremely productive. This soil scarcely ever suffers from too much wet, nor does drought affect it in the same degree as other lands. High hummock lands produce, with but little labour of cultivation, all the crops in the country in an eminent degree. Such lands do not break up in heavy masses, nor are they infested with pernicious weeds or grasses. These lands are very abundant, whilst their extraordinary fertility and productiveness may be estimated by the. fact that three, often four, hogsheads of sugar are made per acre, on lands which have been many years in constant cultivation."

" All these varieties of hummock are frequently enhanced in value by the presence of *wild orange trees*, sometimes singly, or in small groups, and again in large groves."

"**Prairie and Savanna Lands.**—The rich alluvials bordering on the streams, and known as Savannas are subject to inundations, and are highly valuable for the production of sugar and rice. The low savannas, like the prairies of the more elevated portions, are mostly rich vegetable mould, or loam, like the rich prairies of Illinois ; others have the appearance of clay, but upon close inspection, it is muck, mixed with marl.

" These lands are destitute of trees, but covered with luxuriant growth of nutritious, tall, perennial grasses, and of green savannas, covered with flowers, on which vast herds of cattle and sheep graze, both summer and winter, and grow fat without other food. Some of these herds are very large, as many as 30,000 to 40,000 head of cattle being marked by the brand of a single owner. These stock growers are amongst the wealthiest men in the State, and acquire it easier than those engaged in any other industry."

" **The Pine Lands** are divided into first, second, and third class.

"**The First-rate Pine Lands** in Florida have nothing analogous to them in the other States. The top is a deep, vegetable mould, beneath which, to the depth of several feet, is a chocolate-coloured, sandy loam, mixed, for the most part, with limestone pebbles, and resting on a substratum of marl, clay, or limestone. This land is also extremely fertile, producing splendid yields of all the most exhaustive crops for many years. Large portions have been cultivated in short cotton for many years, yielding from 500 to 1,000 lbs. of seed cotton, and some have produced 400 lbs. of Sea-Island cotton for fourteen consecutive years, and are still as productive as ever, so that the limit of their durability is still unknown."

"**The Second-rate Pine Lands,** which form the largest proportion of Florida, are all productive. They rest on a basis similar to that of the first-class. These lands afford fine natural pasturage, like the first-class. They are heavily timbered with the best species of yellow and pitch pine; they are for the most part high, rolling, healthy, and well watered; they will produce the finest crops of Cuba tobacco, oranges, lemons, limes, bananas, and other tropical productions, also Sea-Island and short cotton, sugar-cane, and every variety of garden vegetable, which make them more valuable than the best bottom lands in the Northern and Western States.

"The prevalent forest growth of Florida is yellow pine, and of course the soil may be in general characterized as 'light,' and is either sandy or loamy; but owing to peculiar climatic or atmospheric influences they are of far more intrinsic value where 'light' than is usually attributable to the same character of light soil at the North or West, as is evinced by the fact that a bale of cotton or 3,000 pounds of sugar have not infrequently been made from an acre of these pine lands. Indeed, many of the pine lands are so underlaid with marl or clay as to give all the strength of clay soils without their stiffness and difficulty of cultivation."

"**The Third-rate Pine Lands,** or most inferior class, are by no means worthless: the greater portion of them is covered with valuable timber, and with luxuriant vegetation and good pasturage. A small portion is high, rolling, sandy, and sparsely covered with a stunted growth of 'Black Jack,' and some good pine."

"Besides the everglades, there is but a very small proportion of worthless lands compared, with any other State. There are no mountain wastes, barren plains, nor deserts, and the land with this soil, whilst it is unfit for the culture of cotton, sugar-cane, corn, and tobacco, may always be made available for the culture of different kinds of cereals, fruits, or vegetables."

"In the poorest pine barrens, the peach is a vigorous grower, and an abundant bearer, and the grape succeeds equally well. From the great and continually increasing demand for grapes and pure wine, for peaches, and other fruits, either dried, canned, pickled, or preserved, no more promising undertaking can be entered upon than the orchard and vineyard business in the pine districts of Florida. These fruits grow to great perfection on these lands. The most inferior class of these pine lands is the best adapted for the culture of Sisal hemp, which is one of the most remunerative crops produced in the State. It will yield this product, worth $300 per acre, with less cost than any crop that can be grown, and therefore these poorest lands in Florida will yield larger profits per acre than the richest lands of the Mississippi Valley can possibly produce from their staple crops."

"Every district in the State abounds with fertilizers of muck, marl, and phosphates in quantities sufficient to fertilize the poorer lands, when necessary, for ages to come."

Again, 1868 Report—"The great fertility of the soil is everywhere evinced by luxuriant crops produced, including those of the temperate and torrid zones, the latter predominating. Sea-Island cotton succeeds well in all parts of the Peninsula, with a productiveness rivalling the best portions of the coast of Georgia and South Carolina, while the sugar-cane thrives even better than in Louisiana or Texas, owing to the absence of frosts. The ordinary yield of sugar per acre in Florida is nearly twice that of Louisiana, and the cultivation much easier. The area in Florida suitable for the culture of this staple is amply sufficient to supply the demands of the United States. The sandy soil is well adapted to the cultivation of Cuba tobacco, which yields an average of 700 pounds per acre, and, in South Florida, admits of two cuttings per annum. Silk culture must become a leading branch of industry in Florida, since every species of mulberry grows profusely in this latitude as far south as 27°, and experiments in the production of silk have proved highly satisfactory. Indigo was formerly the principal staple of Florida, and, with the exception of sugar, is one of the most certain and profitable crops, admitting two cuttings annually. It is found growing wild throughout the State, and around old fields where a century ago it had been cultivated. *In this genial climate all the tropical and semi-tropical fruits, such as the orange, lemon, lime, olive, fig, citron, pine-apple, banana, guava, the palm, with all the other tropical fruits, are produced in as great perfection as in the more tropical climate of the West Indies, Central America, and Brazil, and with far less attention and greater immunity from injury by insects or vicissitudes of climate, than the common fruits of Northern orchards. These fruits are celebrated for their great size and superior flavour. Grapes thrive luxuriantly, and the peach is at home here.* Sisal and New Zealand hemp, jute, and all the cereal crops of the Northern and Western States are grown here."

"Every description of garden vegetables of the temperate and the torrid zones is raised here with great success. Owing to the fact that vegetation grows all the year round, the winter vegetables required in the markets of the Northern cities can be supplied from Florida for four months each year, when no other State in the Union can produce them during this period. Tomatoes, peas, beans, cucumbers, potatoes, melons, cabbage, beets, asparagus, and, indeed, the whole list of spring vegetables, can be shipped to Northern ports, from two to three months earlier than from any other State; and both in respect to tropical fruits and the earliest garden vegetables, Florida possesses a monopoly of the markets for the northern cities over any other State, which must build up an industry of gigantic extent, and immense profit to the people of the State.

"Experiments made on the soil along the Atlantic coast, from Indian River to Cape Sable, embracing several millions of acres, prove the soil well adapted to the culture of coffee."

What is called Middle Florida possesses all the conditions of soil and climate for the production of the best teas, and tea will grow over the whole Peninsula.

The superior climate of the State has much to do with the growth of all vegetation.

"The maximum temperature in summer is near 85° Fahrenheit, and in winter ranging 45°, rivalling the favourite climate of Italy."

The "Official Guide of Florida," by the Hon. J. S. Adams, says:—"The wealth of Florida *at present* mainly consists in her timber, and, as a consequence, the leading industry will for some time be the manufacture of timber. But as the forests give way th agriculturalist will push forward, and increase the crops of cotton, sugar, tobacco, rice, Indian corn, sweet and Irish potatoes; the gardener will grow the early and winter vegetables for the Northern markets to an enormous extent; while the *fruit grower* will become a main element of prosperity in the future. No other State or country can present such an extensive list of fruits capable of being grown as Florida. And no State can exhibit a fruit grown on its soil which cannot be cultivated with more or less success here. The following is only a partial list of the fruits of the State:—Oranges of all kinds, lemons of every variety, limes, citron, mango, sour-top, custard-apple, cocoanut, shaddock, paw-paw, date, fig, peaches, nectarines, apricots, plums, bananas, plantains, *pine-apples*, sweet almond, bitter almond, pomegranates, maunée apple, sapodilla, alligator pears, cherries, apples, pears, tamarinds, guavas, grapes of great variety (the forests abound with wild grapes), currants, mulberries, *strawberries* of every kind in the greatest perfection, blackberries, dewberries, huckleberries, &c. In this list it will be seen that not only are all the fruits of the northern latitudes represented, but many others in which the State enjoys a monopoly; add to this the water-melon, and the musk-melon, of whole citrous family."

"*In the growth of the tropical and semi-tropical fruits Florida enjoys a monopoly which, when fairly developed, will make her one of the richest and most important of the United States. Oranges, lemons, pine-apples, bananas, and various other tropical fruits will yield an average profit of at least one thousand dollars per acre yearly.*" "*It is the adaptability of the climate to grow these productions that makes even the inferior lands of Florida susceptible of producing crops more valuable than those of the best lands in other parts of the Union. It is the appreciation of this fact that is awakening such an interest in the business, and bringing to our shores large numbers from nearly every State.*"

When the fact is borne in mind that the Atlantic cities and their contiguous population consume annually $200,000,000 of vegetables and fruits, including the tropical fruits and early vegetables imported from the West Indies, the Bahamas, and other tropical countries, all of which Florida can supply to meet the demands of the whole nation, it must be seen that this great and most profitable industry will be pushed forward to meet this immense demand, and that the fruits and vegetables of Florida will be produced and shipped on a scale beyond even our present conception.

(UNITED STATES' LAND OFFICE REPORTS, 1868, 1869, 1870 —UNITED STATES' AGRICULTURAL REPORT, 1862— FLORIDA LAND OFFICE REPORT, 1869, 1873).

FORESTS.—TIMBER AND LUMBER.

Florida Land Office Report, 1862, says:

"Florida is, beyond question, the best timbered State in the Union. Out of about 38,000,000 acres, only some 3,000,000 or 4,000,000 is now included in farms; of the rest nineteen-twentieths (exclusive of the area covered by rivers and lakes) is covered with heavy forests. On all the least moist, and more level portions, the pine is the prevalent forest tree, either the yellow or pitch pine. It grows with great beauty, and attains a large size, furnishing some of the handsomest pine lumber to be found in the markets of the world. The extent of the pine lands and the possible amount of lumber that could be manufactured, would be almost incredible to one who has never visited Florida. There are probably more than 30,000 square miles of heavy pine forests within the limits of the State.

"In the moister lands, along the rivers and creeks, and on the margins and swamps, an almost indefinite variety of trees are to be found, of which the most valuable for timber and lumber are live oak, white oak, the hickory, the ash, the birch, the cedar, the magnolia, the sweet bay, and the cypress. Of all these varieties a great abundance is to be found throughout the State. Of pine of the best quality, of cedar, and cypress in particular, the supply for any purposes of manufacture may be said to be inexhaustible. *The larger proportion of what has loosely been called swamp in Florida, is simply low hummock, with a soil of inexhaustible fertility, and covered with a dense growth of mainly cypress, magnolia, and sweet bay.* The timber of the cypress more nearly resembles that of the northern basswood than anything else; can be used for all purposes to which basswood is applied, and for railway ties and sleepers, for durability, has no equal in any other variety of wood. It is more easily split than basswood; can be warped and bent into desirable shapes. For clothes' pins, for fork and rake and broom handles, and for pails and tubs, cypress furnishes a superior material, while the red cedar yields the best known material for pails, tubs, and chests of a nicer and more costly description.

"The timber of the magnolia, also, is susceptible of a variety of uses, and is now being extensively used for the nicer and finer kinds of wheelwright and cabinet work. *Of this timber the supply is very large.* The wood of the red or sweet bay, in fineness of texture and in its other valuable qualities, stand equal to mahogany, and most persons cannot distinguish it from mahogany. It is coming into great demand for cabinet work." "It abounds in the State."

"The resources of Florida in the direction of the manufacture of the wooden ware, tools of all descriptions made from wood, and fine cabinet work, are very great." "An inexhaustible abundance of material, at the cheapest possible rates, and very great accessibility by water communication, offer inducements for the manufacture of lumber, wooden ware, and all kinds of tools made of wood."

Also United States' Land Office Report, 1868, p. 19:

"The principal forest trees of this State, some of which are eminently adapted for ship-building, are live oak, mahogany, magnolia, pine, cedar, and cypress. Mangrove, boxwood, mastic, satinwood, crabwood, and lignumvitæ, abound on the keys, and generally in the southern part of the State."

United States' Land Office Report, 1869, p. 103, speaks of the timber of Southern Florida; also the timber of the Middle and North Florida:—

"The flora of this region embraces a great number of species, including many found in the tropics, as well as those indigenous to the temperate zone. Among the most important forest trees are the live, red, white, and water oaks, cedar, cherry, cypress, hickory, elm, pine, ash, gum, magnolia, birch, walnut, mahogany, and dogwood. The other varieties, found principally in the southern portion of the State, and on the keys, are lignumvitæ, boxwood, mastic, satinwood, palmetto, and crabwood. Large quantities of live oak are annually sent to various foreign and domestic ports for ship-building, and other purposes. THE LUMBER PRODUCED IS ESTIMATED AT TEN MILLION DOLLARS ANNUALLY (IN 1869), and this interest is rapidly increasing. Florida is nearly all timbered; yellow and pitch pine form the basis. The undergrowth embraces an extensive variety of plants and vines, while flowers exist in the greatest profusion."

Present product is over $25,000,000 per annum.

(41)

From "Florida Settler" and "Official Guide," 1873.

"Lumber.

"First on the list of State productions we place lumber, as it holds at present the first rank among the industries of Florida, whether we consider the amount of capital involved, the value of the material produced, or the extent of the resources from which it is drawn. It can be asserted with confidence, that over no other State in the Union is valuable timber so extensively and uniformly distributed, and ere long the lumber business of this State will rival in extent that of any other. Within the last few years the manufacture of lumber has received here an enormous impetus, consequent upon a knowledge and recognition of the vast timber resources of the State, and *now the trade begins to assume gigantic proportions, with an almost unlimited power of expansion.* When anyone contemplates, in the light of knowledge, the astonishing wealth of the State in timber, the question at once arises, Why has it remained so long almost untouched, and less favoured portions of the country sought after for the supply of lumber? Hitherto, nearly all the yellow-pine flooring consumed in the great cities of the North was been obtained from South and North Carolina. But at no time in their history have these States contained a tithe of the pine timber of superior quality to be found in Florida. It is by no means an exaggerated estimate when we put the heavy pine forests in the State as covering an area of 30,000 square miles.

Values.—The quality of the lumber is attested by the fact that it commands in market 10 per cent. more than that of any other section. The *New York Mercantile Journal,* in an article on the lumber market, states as to values:—

"Yellow-pine flooring and step-plank from Florida are in fair demand at $30 per 1,000 feet, while the inferior lumber made in North and South Carolina moves slowly at $23 to $25. The yellow pine, so called, growing in the Carolinas, is objectionable for many reasons. In the first place the tree is of a different and less enduring species, has a greater proportion of sap-wood and black knots; and in the second place it is from these trees that the manufacturers of pitch and turpentine procure their material, depriving them of the elements which give the durability and peculiar excellence of this kind of wood for building purposes. *Architects and owners should always require in their specifications that the yellow pine to be used in first-class buildings should be of the growth of Florida.*"

"The highly deserved reputation of the pine lumber furnished by the forest of the State, is attracting the attention of capitalists in all parts of the country; and besides those mills already established, some most gigantic enterprises are constructing to take advantage of the resources of the State."

Florida Land Office Report, 1873, says:—

"In 1871, Mr. Judah, the well-known and highly competent railway engineer, was employed by the Jacksonville, Pensacola, and Mobile Railroad Company to survey their route from Appalachicola River to Pensacola city. This company had a land grant of 600,000 acres, and Mr. Judah and his associates made a full Report on the value of these lands and the forests and timber thereon.—Extracts from Judah's Report.

"Nearly the entire body of these lands (600,000 acres) is covered with a dense growth of yellow pine of a quality unsurpassed by that of any other State in the Union. Some of the largest and finest lumber-mills anywhere to be found in the United States are located upon the Blackwater River in the vicinity of the town of Milton, in Santo Rosa county. The amount of lumber annually shipped from this district is about 50,000,000 feet, yielding upwards of $500,000 to the manufacturers, and costing the millowners, delivered in the log, upwards of $40,000. . . .

"Quantity of Lumber on these Lands.

"Allowing twenty trees per acre fit for cutting into saw-logs, averaging 500 feet Board Measure per tree, and the quantity amounts to 6,000 million feet of lumber, which is worth, manufactured, at only $12, $72,000,000. At only five trees per acre, the quantity is 1,250,000,000 feet of lumber, worth $18,000,000. Allow it worth 82·50 per thousand feet standing (a fair estimate), and it will pay the whole cost of the road."

"It is a fact that timber makes anew again in twenty-five to thirty years; so that after going over a body of timber, cutting off that large enough for saw-logs, *leaving* the smaller timber, this smaller timber will have grown sufficiently in from twenty-five to thirty years to yield another supply equal to the first."

"Spar-timber exists nowhere in greater abundance or of better quality than upon these lands. Heavy European contracts have been filled from this locality, and contracts can be obtained to any extent that can be filled. Good spars bring from $100 to $300 each. Reliable associates have traversed these lands and report that they have seen lands where twelve spars could be cut from an acre. Allowing that *one spar* can be cut from each five acres, and it gives 125,000 spars, which at only $100 each are worth $12,000,000 at tide-water."

"It is not unlikely that the land may yield an average of one spar per acre, which would give us the value of spar-timber alone, standing, of $62,500,000. The spars of Florida are well known in Europe, and are believed to be equal to any in the United States."

"The value of such a domain as this can scarcely be estimated. The value of the lumber alone on these lands will exceed the total aggregate cost of the Illinois Central Railroad."

Mr. Judah's Report has been adopted as correct by the United States. See "Agricultural Reports," 1871.

"These railroad lands are nothing more than a fair sample of the lands throughout the State in respect to their capacity for lumber. But besides the pine, great varieties of the most valuable timber are to be found distributed all over the State, and capable of being worked up and put upon the market with highly remunerative results. The live and the water oaks of the State have a world-wide reputation, and though the demands of ship-building throughout the entire country, and in some parts of Europe, have for many years been supplied from the forests of the State, its resources in this are apparently untouched. The cedar swamps of Florida are at the present time supplying most of the pencil manufactories on this continent, while the immense quantities of cypress to be found scattered all over the Peninsula promise to furnish the most desirable railroad ties that can be found. Then for the manufacture of furniture, sashes, blinds, waggons, and wooden ware of every description, there is an unlimited supply of red bay, cherry, white oak, ash, birch, hickory, gum, elm, and a number of other equally valuable species of timber."

The Florida pine differs materially from the Northern. It is the tropical *long-leafed* variety, only

F

grows in an exceedingly mild or warm climate—admits of a very fine finish and polish, much of it being well adapted for fine cabinet furniture. It has also a preservative quality, not found in any but the long-leafed kind. The yellow pine of Florida is probably not excelled anywhere. It justly commands a premium of 10 per cent. over other pine lumber.

SHIP-TIMBER.

Florida has more first-class ship-timber and lumber for naval construction, and of better quality, than *all* the balance of the United States put together. This fact is established by the Congressional Report on Forrestry of 1874. The Report says, p. 38 :—

" The amount of public lands reserved by authority of law is now very nearly as follows :—

	Acres.
" In Mississippi	26,218
„ Florida...	208,824
„ Louisiana	9,170
„ Alabama	240 "

Live and water oaks only grow in the Southern States. The Government having the power to select her lands for naval construction, made her chief and almost exclusive selection of her Florida lands for this purpose. If she could have selected any better elsewhere, *she would have done so.*

The " Florida Official Report," 1873, says :—

" Within the last year or two some fine saw-mills have been erected in Appalachicola, and immense quantities of lumber are manufactured and shipped to various quarters of the globe, and the city is again reviving."

The Pennsylvania Tie Company have erected a large mill, nearly completed, for the purpose of manufacturing the cypress railroad tie and sleeper. It is one of the most extensive establishments of the kind on the continent.

This cypress timber has proved to be the most durable railroad timber known. Ties and sleepers will last on and in the ground for 15 years, or equal to two or three sets of good oak ties. This timber abounds on the Company's " hummock " lands. It is used for many purposes, and will yield the Company large profits.

ESTIMATE.

Estimating the Company's forests and their values on the 8,300,000 acres at a minimum in quantity and in price, it is safe to say—

	Acres.
The pine forests cover at least	3,000,000
And other timber	1,000,000
Total timber lands	4,000,000

The common selling price of lumber is $15 per 1,000 feet Board Measure (B.M.), equal to 83½ cubic feet of hewn or squared timber.

But put this price at the present low, depressed rate, $12.

	Feet B.M.
Minimum yield per acre of pine lands at	4,000
„ „ „ cypress „	10,000
„ „ „ other lumber	4,000

Then

	Feet B.M.
3,000,000 acres pine lands at 4,000 feet yield...	12,000,000,000
500,000 acres cypress at 10,000 feet yield	5,000,000,000
500,000 acres cedar, mahogany, &c., at 4,000 feet yield...	2,000,000,000
Total ...	$19,000,000,000
At $12 per 1,000 feet yield ...	$228,000,000
Deduct one-half for cost of manufacturing and marketing (high estimate)	114,000,000
Net profit	$118,000,000
On 2,300,000 acres ...	$16,000,000

This amount is independent of the timber cut and shipped in the log, such as ship-spars, live oak, water oak, and all timber for mines, of which this property can furnish many millions of dollars' value in the aggregate, and *all this variety* is needed, and has a ready gold market in England and elsewhere.

By examination of the Timber and Lumber Reports of Florida, Michigan, Wisconsin, Maine, and Pennsylvania, it will be seen the above estimate is below the minimum there reported.

Estimating the value of the trees " standing " at only 4,000 feet B.M. per acre, and $2½ per 1,000 feet (a low average price, as shown from the Timber Reports of the Great Timber States), and we have a profit of $10 per acre,

or 4,000,000 acres at $10	$40,000,000
or 2,300,000 „ „ „	12,000,000

It will be seen by comparison that the estimates are far below those of Mr. Judah reported above. He gives a maximum value on 600,000 acres of $72,000,000, and a minimum of $18,000,000, besides spar timber alone at $62,500,000.

It is proper to remark here, that the rapid exhaustion of timber in America, and in all countries accessible by water-way, is fully shown by the Government Reports of Great Britain and the United States, briefly noticed in the Appendix hereto. (Note B.)

It is proper to remark further, that a large quantity of Florida timber is now being shipped to the English and other European ports. Much of it is worked up into cabinet furniture, and for such use is highly appreciated in the markets. London timber merchants now offer to this Company to purchase heavily of its Florida timber. Large quantities of it are supplied to the West Indies and South America. Here the Company possesses an immediate source of large income.

THE LOCATION OF THE COMPANY'S 2,300,000 ACRES, AND FUTURE PROFITS THEREFROM.

To obtain an intelligent idea of the importance of the ready market and value of these lands, it should be borne in mind that they are located in East Florida, mostly in a solid body on each side, directly along and contiguous to the Company's " Great Tide-Water Canal Route," in the most desirable portion of the State, and handiest to water-navigation and markets.

They are shown on the official maps of surveys.

The N. boundary commences a few miles above the city of Pilatka, on the Lower St. John's ; thence S. on both sides of the Lower and Upper St. John's River and series of connecting lakes; thence again S. on both sides of Indian River, Lake Worth, and New River, terminating north of Biscayne Bay; thus extending N. and S. of each side of this magnificent chain of navigable waters and connecting canals, for a distance of 234 miles, extending E. to the Atlantic coast, and commanding that coast for this great distance; embracing a large portion of the rich St. John's and Indian River Valleys. The largest part of the immigration into the State is rapidly populating these valleys, and, as a consequence, the lands are rising greatly in value.

The present Executive Governor Stearns, who was formerly Surveyor-General of the United States for the District of Florida, Ex-Gov. Reed, and the Hon. M. A. Williams, one of the United States Surveyors, engaged for over twenty years in surveying Florida lands for the Government, have all made a written appraisal of the first-named 2,300,000 acres, and they put the valuation at $8, $20, and $25 per acre. Now it so happens that there are private plantations and large farms held and owned by sundry individuals at intervals through this grant; and large portions of these private plantations and farms have been sold for cash during the last three years, and during the year last past, land has been sold on the St. John's for $50, and as high as $150 per acre; and much has been sold on the Indian River and Halifax River, the lowest at $10 per acre. Population is pouring into this part of the State very rapidly. United States Senators and other wealthy men of the Northern States are buying locations on these waters, and are building magnificent residences, and laying out beautiful tropical gardens, to spend their winters in this charming and salubrious climate, and thereby avoid the rigors of winter.

Accurate admeasurements shew that Lake Washington is 13 feet higher than Indian River. It is proposed to cut the Company's 6 mile canal deep enough to drop the surface of the lake about 4 feet. This would leave a fall, still, of 9 feet from the lake, which will afford magnificent and most valuable water powers, sufficient to drive a large number of mills and manufactories all the year; and a large industrial city will accordingly grow up on this favoured site, bound to result in great profits to the Company.

Here the new and beautiful City of Eau Gallie is located, with its broadly laid-out streets, and beautiful natural parks of tropical groves and perpetual blooming flowers, having Salt-water Rivers and Ocean on one side of it, and Lake Washington—15 miles length of fresh water—on the other side. Above this latitude the frost line ceases. The fresh ocean breezes and trade winds continually fan and cool this charming spot.

The State Agricultural College, an Institution founded by the State and endowed by the United States, has been located on this new city site, with 5,000 acres of fine land as endowment.

South of Lake Harney, along the St. John's River, the Company owns 450,000 acres of land, which require special notice. There are no richer lands on the earth, —they are covered with perpetual green pastures, on which tens of thousands of heads of cattle feed winter and summer, and grow fat. These lands will abundantly raise any vegetable or fruit sown or planted on them. They will raise 4,000 pounds of sugar to the acre, and for Sea Island Cotton no better lands exist in America.

On the completion of the Company's Canal, these lands will be all thoroughly drained, and will then readily rent for $10 per acre, which will ultimately bring in a rental revenue to owners of $4,500,000 per annum. The whole tract is richly worth $100 per acre. (See official reports, &c.) The Mississippi River cotton

and sugar lands sold readily for $100 to $150 per acre, in cash, before the late war, they will do so again.

But the Company's lands here located have the advantage in climate and soil, and will raise crops of greater value per acre.

A large body of her land granted will front on the great Ship Canal, and for a full description and location of the other grants, see official surveys, maps, and inventory.

CITY, TOWNS, AND VILLAGE SITES ALONG THE SHIP CANAL, &c.

At the Terminal Harbours of the Ship Canal, in the Atlantic and Gulf, and at Key West, large commercial cities must grow up under the control of the Ship Canal Company, and on the 630 miles of canals and improved water courses, the Company will establish depôts and wharves every 8 or 10 miles, and also lay out town and village sites. Railway and Canal Companies in America and other countries have done so, and have realised immense revenues and profits therefrom. The population settle upon and improve those points, and the Company should realise profits enough from this source to pay the whole construction cost of the works.

A highly respectable firm of English solicitors has fully examined and reported upon the legal status of this Company, upon all its papers, documents, titles of real estate, bonds, mortgage, &c., &c., and upon the value of the 2,300,000 acres mortgaged, and have delivered a statement of facts and legal conclusions therein to the following effect:—

1. That the charters and the organization of the Company thereunder are in due legal form.

2. That the bonds and mortgages securing the same, together with all the necessary intermediate steps, are all in due form of law, and that the Company is now in legal shape either to sell or borrow money on its property and securities.

3. That the titles to real estate are perfect. On this point they say, "It seems clear that the three grants mentioned (2,300,000 acres) are valid, and vest the title thereto in this Company, and that neither the United States nor the State of Florida can annul or withdraw either of them, and that by the deed of conveyance a free, clear, perfect, and absolute legal title is evidenced and vested in the Company in fee simple, without conditions whatsoever."

4. They lastly find the following official evidence relating to the value of these lands, and come to the conclusion that these lands are worth now in the market from $5 to $100 per acre, and are ample security for a loan of £1,000,000.

The following is their full report on this point:

VALUE OF THE COMPANY'S LANDS.

These lands are located, in what is called "East Florida," in the Counties of Marion, Putnam, St. John's, Orange, Volusia, Brevard, and Dade, along and on each side of the Company's Tide Water Canal line, for a continuous distance of over 230 miles (see Official Map, Grants, and Deed), including a large portion of the rich valleys of the St. John's and Indian Rivers. It appears also that interspersed through this body of land are occasional plantations, which, since the late Civil War in the United States, have been subdivided into smaller tracts, and sold, and now occupied; while several of these counties, possessing lands outside of the Company's grants, have each a considerable population, which is rapidly increasing yearly.

(44)

POPULATION OF THESE COUNTIES.

Marion	... ...	16,000
Dade	... ...	10,000
Putnam and St. John's	... each	6,000
Volutia and Brevard	... about	5,000

A full description of the lands of the State and of this Company—variety of soils—agricultural and horticultural productions—extensive heavy forests, &c., &c., is contained in Official Reports, issued by the United States' Government and by the State of Florida, named as follows :—

United States "*Land Office Report*," 1870, pp. 44 to 53.
" " " " " 1868, pp. 17 to 23.
" " " " " 1869, pp. 100 to 105.

United States "*Department of Agriculture.*"
Report, 1862, pp. 59 to 65.
" " " " 1868, pp. 140 to 147.
" " " " 1872, pp. 160 to 171.
" " " " 1873, pp. 510 to 511.

United States' "*Special Report on Immigration*," Statistics, &c. 1872, pp. 138 to 147.

Annual Messages of the Governor of Florida, with accompanying Documents from the State Land Office Department, &c., from 1869 to 1875.

In full corroboration of these Official Reports, it appears there are numerous Geographies, Histories, British and American books, periodicals, and papers, also showing the value of the Florida Lands.

It will also be found that, since the late American war Florida has been rapidly increasing in population and wealth. *The chief immigration and settlements appear to be into the St. John's and Indian River Valleys ; besides, this portion of Florida has become a great national resort for pleasure-seekers and invalids*, who leave the Northern States during the severe winter months, and spend their winters in the salubrious climate of Florida. It is reported that from 40,000 to 60,000 visitors spend their winters annually in East Florida.

In the Annual Survey Report to the United States' Government, by M. L. Stearns, United States' Surveyor-General in Florida, dated August 31, 1870 (see U.S. Land Office Report, pp. 331 to 333), this officer reports that "*The Eastern portion from the St. John's River to the Coast, and including Indian River, is settling up very rapidly, perhaps more so than any other part of the State*, and consequently that section presents a greater variety of interests than any other. The lumber trade is very important. There are on the St. John's River some twenty steam saw-mills, three-fourths of them at or near Jacksonville. The richest sugar lands in the State lie in various localities along the Indian river, and offer an inexhaustible mine of wealth to the industrious and enterprising farmer. The natural advantages of the State are ample."

The Official Agricultural Report of the United States for 1871, page 164, says:—"One great advantage which these (Florida) Lands possess over Western lands lies in their ability to produce six great staple productions, the most valuable known, and of which the supply cannot equal the demand, while the western lands produce but two great staples, viz., wheat and corn. These staples are yellow pine lumber, the best timber for naval construction, house-building and cabinet work. Cotton (both Sea Island and short staple), tobacco, sugar and rice, in addition to which may be enumerated, among other products, hay, corn, oats, potatoes (sweet and Irish), all kinds of vegetables, oranges, bananas, figs, peaches, quinces, and many other tropical fruits, which can be grown nowhere else in the United States as well as here."

From the foregoing official Government authorities it appears quite clear that the Florida lands, *including those belonging to the Company*, contain a very large amount of valuable forests for a great variety of timber and lumber, of *yellow* and pitch pine, live oak, water-red and white oaks, cedar, cherry, cypress, hickory, elm, ash, gum, magnolia, birch, walnut, mahogany, satinwood, and in some portions lignum vitæ, boxwood, mastic, palmetto, crabwood, &c.

That the soil and climate are specially adapted to the culture and growth of all tropical and semi-tropical fruits, viz., the orange, lemon, lime, citron, fig, banana, plantain, mango, soursop, custard-apple, cocoa-nut, shaddock, paw-paw, date, nectarine, apricots, pine-apples, plums, peaches, cherries, apples, pears, tamarinds, almonds, grapes of great variety, strawberries, blackberries, currants, mulberries, &c., &c.

In addition to this list add all the garden and field vegetables of the Temperate and Torrid zones, which grow there summer and winter. In the culture of these fruits and winter and early vegetables, Florida claims a monopoly over any other part of North America. The Northern cities and States import vast quantities of these fruits and vegetables annually from foreign countries, which Florida can supply.

Very many cases are mentioned of the large profits realized per acre in the cultivation of the *staples*, as compared with other States, and extraordinary profits are shown in the raising of the orange, banana, fig, grape, strawberries, and other fruits, and in the winter and early vegetables. These features are attracting a large immigration to Florida from the Northern States since the war, and it is claimed that the Florida Lands possess a special value over other rich lands in other States, because of their adaptation to the growth of the tropical fruits and winter vegetables, for the Northern States and cities will afford a continual market for these products.

VALUE PER ACRE OF COMPANY'S LANDS.

The following letter and valuation is entitled to consideration, viz. :—

"OFFICE OF SURVEYOR GENERAL,
"Tallahassee, Fla. *Aug.* 25*th*, 1870.
" Sirs,
"From our knowledge and information, which we have of the land ceded and granted to your Company by the Trustees of the Internal Improvement Fund of the State of Florida, we would appraise their value at from $8 to $10 per acre, upon the completion of the Canals and Improvements contemplated by the Charter of the said 'Southern Inland Navigation and Improvement Company.'

" HARRISON REED, Governor and President of the Board Internal Improvement Fund."
"M. S. STEARNS, United States' Surveyor General.
" J. S. ADAMS, Commissioner of Lands and Immigration.
" T. H. OSBORN, and others."

In appraisements and letters, dated January 28th and March 29th, 1871, by Mr. M. A. Williams, one of the United States' Land Surveyors of Florida for twenty-five years, he says :—

" I have, within the last twenty (20) years, either surveyed for the United States' Government, or examined for the State of Florida most of the lands granted to 'The Southern Inland Navigation and Improvement Company.' I have no doubt that a very large portion of these lands would be worth and would sell for from $10 to $25 per acre upon the completion of the Company's Canals," &c.

He says he has spent more than twenty-five years in surveying public lands in Florida for the United States' Government, that the Company's Lands extend from Palatka on the St. John's to Biscayne Bay, that he is "Well acquainted with the character of these lands on the entire route," that he "selected a very large portion of these lands" for the State from the United States' Lands, that they are among "the richest and most valuable in the State." Part require *draining* (see Judge Fry's Synoptical Report, p. 15, and Engineers' Reports, "cutting the canal from Lake Washington to Indian River, so as to drop the surface of the Lake 4 feet, will drain the Company's Lands"). Williams further says :—"Your line of improvements will open the only available tropical portion of Florida, and will unquestionably be the most *attractive portion of the State*, and the most desirable for the thousands of visitors who annually seek this climate for health and pleasure, and it will also be the most desirable for the production of all the tropical fruits," &c.

The United States' Agricultural Report for 1871, and the United States' Special Report on Statistics and immigration, show the value of the lands of the Southern Slave States in 1860, and the large decline of price during the late American war, as the result of that war. Of Florida they say—"In some sections of the State lands declined during this period from 20 to 50 per cent., but on the St. John's River and Indian River they have advanced *one-third in value* since the date named," and on page 165 of the first-named report, the Government says: "The price of wild land in Dade County is about $50 per acre. Cultivated lands at Key West and Boca Chico can be sold at prices varying from $500 to $1,000 per acre, according to the stock of fruit growing."

The large amount of construction work performed, and the rapid increase of population in the last few years, have fully demonstrated the above valuation of the Governor, Land Commissioners, and the United States' Surveyors.

"The message of Governor Harrison Reed to the Legislature, delivered January 4, 1872, claims that the *increase of population during the last three years* has been 40,000, mainly as a result of the labours of the Immigration Bureau in exhibiting systematically the peculiar resources of the State. He especially calls attention to the fact that 1,200 miles of sea-coast, prolific of oysters, fish, and turtle, almost beyond parallel, with bays and inlets, and inland navigable waters of an equal extent; offer the richest inducements to enterprise and capital."

In the "Annual Message of Governor Stearns to the Florida Legislature, with "Accompanying Documents" of his Cabinet officers, for the year 1875. Land Office Department, p. 5, it is officially declared that:

"The past year has marked the commencement of a new era in the history of our State, in the unexampled influx of population which has taken place. We are in possession of sufficient data to be able to state that the accessions of weal' 1 and population have been greater during the past twelve months than in any three previous years ; and the consequence is a very perceptible effect on the material property of the State.

"This influx of immigration has been more apparent in the Eastern portion of the State, and is seen in the extraordinary advance in the price of lands ; in the extensive purchases that have been made for the

purpose of tropical fruit culture ; in the springing up of new and enterprising settlements, and the spirit of life and activity which is observable throughout regions where solitude hitherto reigned supreme. "There is, perhaps, no State in the Union about which there is so much enquiry at present as Florida."

This last-named Report shows, that in *Marion County* "very good unimproved farming land can be bought for $50 per acre."

In *Putnam County* the "*price of land varies from a Government Homestead to* $100 *or more per acre,*" and "*First rate orange land on the East side of the St. John's River is held as high as* $100 *per acre.*"

St. John's County varies about the same.

Volusia County (where the Company owns a very large body of land). "*Private lands in small lots can be purchased at from* $5 *to* $100 *per acre.* (The lands of this County are very superior in quality).

Brevard County "is fast showing the effects of energy and capital," and lands sell outside of the Company's grant at from $10 upwards per acre.

The United States' Agricultural Reports of 1873 shows :

"That *Orange County* is making rapid progress in population and wealth. It unites the advantages of diversified and beautiful scenery, a remarkably healthy climate, a productive and well-watered soil, and easy access to market. The climate and soil have proved by trial to be well adapted to the growth of oranges, lemons, and almost every other variety of semi-tropical fruits, as well as the principal vegetables. These attractions having become known are drawing immigrants from almost every State in the Union.

Lands which five years ago could be bought at 25 cents to $1 *per acre now bring* $50 *to* $150 *per acre.*"

The Trustees of the Internal Improvement Fund, who made these grants, appraised and fixed a schedule price $10 per acre (see Deed of Trust, p. 10, sec. 2). The law required the Board to "fix the price of the public lands granted in the Trust" (see Act 1855, sec. 22, "Bush's Digest" 375).

From the foregoing Official authorities, both of the United States' Government and of the State, we have a full exhibit of the character, value, and market price of the lands granted to the Company.

Large portions of these grants are worth from $5 *to* $100 *per acre, and in our opinion the evidence shows, that the average price of* $10 *per acre, as estimated by the Board of Trustees, is a fair valuation.*

Another mode of valuation is given by the United States' Government, in the numerous grants of lands, donated by the Government in aid of Railway and Canal construction. An Official Report is published by the Government, showing that all land grant lands, sold by the Companies to the year 1870, realized an average price of $7 per acre. In some instances the grants averaged from $8 to $12 per acre. The Hannibal and St. Joseph Railway Company sold their lands at an average of $11 per acre. The Grand Rapids and Indiana Railway Company realized an average of $13.98. The Burlington and Missouri River Railroad Company, averaged $11.70 and the Illinois Central (well-known in London) averaged $11.35 per acre. This Company's grant contained 2,595,000 acres. The sales made to 1870 amounted $24,000,000 cash, and the residue is selling since at an average $12.50 per acre. The whole grant will net to the Company $30,000,000 cash. (See United States' Land Office Report, Sept. 1870.)

The LOAN of £1,000,000 *secured by the Company's First Mortgage Bonds*, under the Trust Deed, covering two million three-hundred thousand (2,300,000) acres of lands, with other property, improvements, franchises, and rights, is and must be sufficient, safe, and most ample security for this Loan.

The *value* of these *lands alone* at the appraisement and scheduled rate in the Trust Deed is *four times the amount of the required Loan.*

At the *average rate of* $7 *per acre* for all land grants sold to 1870, they will be nearly *three times* the Loan.

Mr. Bennock, of London, after examining the evidence of their value, states they are worth "over 50 times the amount of the Loan required."

An important consideration to the Lender is found in the ability of the Company to pay the interest and principal of this Loan as they mature.

1st. From Tolls.
2nd. From the sale of Timber and Lumber.
3rd. From the sale of Lands.

The Company is in position now to collect tolls on the vessels and Commerce passing over its improvements.

It seems the Commerce on the St. John's River, Indian River, and Lakes, is quite large, and increasing rapidly.

It is reported in the United States' Land Office Reports that the annual export of timber and lumber from Florida in 1869 was $10,000,000, besides home consumption. This timber it is reported commands a premium of 10 per cent. in the City of New York over lumber from other States. Liverpool, London, and other British ports receive and furnish a ready market for this timber and lumber. Letters have been shewn from lumber merchants in London to this Company, offering to purchase from the Company amounts up to nearly £200,000. The Company's forests are readily accessible, and most favourably situated for shipment of timber and lumber. It has already been shewn that there is a large immigration into the St. John's and Indiana River Valleys, where the Company's land is situated, and that these lands have risen rapidly in value. Taking into consideration these facts, together with Reports of the large annual sales of land grant lands made by the Illinois Central, Grand Rapids, and Indiana, Burlington, and Missouri River, and numerous other Railway Companies, it would seem clear that the Company can from this source commence to receive large returns immediately."

SHIP CANAL.

It appears that The Atlantic and Gulf Ship Canal is incorporated and located under the Act of the State of Florida, entitled "An Act to provide a General Law for the Incorporation of Railroads and Canals," approved February 19th, 1874.

This Act is the Charter right of the Company—the franchises, rights, and powers it confers are complete and very liberal, and it would seem that the franchise is perpetual, and the Company has power to fix the rate of tolls and compensation for the use of the Canal, and to collect the same, to purchase, hold, use, and sell and convey real, personal, and mixed property, take and hold voluntary grants of land to aid in construction, powers to borrow money and execute Trust Deeds or Mortgages on the Company's property to secure such loan, &c., &c.

The provisions are comprehensive, and seem to guard the rights and privileges of the Company well.

To anyone wishing to become interested in this enterprise (financially or otherwise) it will be interesting and well worth the while to read and study the provisions of this Charter. Legislation so favourable to a Company is seldom obtained in England.

The commercial and international character of this Ship Canal, its importance, necessity, benefits, &c., are fully exhibited in the full and Synoptical Reports compiled by Judge John H. Fry, principally from Government authorities. We recommend that these Reports and the authorities quoted from be well read and studied.

"In conclusion, it is our opinion that the propositions and terms offered for the loans are an inducement to capitalists, and that the security for the loan seems safe and ample in amount."

Important Leader in the *Times* and the Official British Report on Commerce and Trade—On the Thrift of Florida—Increase of Population—Immense Profits in Tropical Fruit—Culture and rapid rise in the price of Lands in the St. John's Valley, right in the heart of the Company's Grants of 2,300,000 acres.

*Leader in the "*Times,*" London, June 23, 1876.*

"The latest volume of the Reports of the Secretary of Legations, which has been recently presented to Parliament, includes a contribution of more than ordinary interest. This is a careful analysis of the 'trade and some resources of the United States for the year 1875," and, apart from its general value, it embraces the first impartial review of the economical condition in the South that has been published in this country since the re-election of President Grant to the Presidency. The period of four years, which is now drawing to a close, was marked by a few startling events; but it is all the more likely that it was fruitful in steady, if silent, progress among those communities which, after the desolating convulsions of the war, could only hope to repair their strength by rest. The writer of the Report, Mr. Grant Watson, was First Secretary of Legation at Washington, until, on the nomination of Lord Lytton to the Indian Viceroyalty, he was promoted to the Lisbon Legation. His conclusions are sober and inobtrusive; his survey of facts is wide and searching, and, upon the whole, his Report is a most praiseworthy addition to our knowledge of the United States.

In Mr. Watson's judgment the South had, at the close of last year, reached a turn in its fortunes at which the abiding consequences of the war were being overcome by the strong permanent elements of industrial prosperity. The worst days clearly were past. The riches of the soil, the generosity of the climate, and the abundance of labour had begun to tell, and wealth was being recreated with amazing rapidity. The Civil War had rent the old fabric of society from top to bottom, but some of the fragments fell into new relations, and others obtained scope for free growth by the ruin of the rest. The slave-owning aristocracy of former days has wholly disappeared. But there were other slaveholders who were no aristocrats, who worked with their own hands—the 'mean whites,' as their betters used to call them—and these, recovering from the shock of the conflict, are now becoming steadily prosperous, while, in spite of some political disturbances and consequent suffering, there is 'a general diffusion of means for ease and comfort unknown before.' By the side of this class the Negro freedmen cultivate for the most part their own holdings. 'Cotton culture has been democratized by emancipation.' No single estates now yield 1,000 or 2,000 bales for individual owners; but the small farmers, white and black, "raise cotton for their own profit individually, and the aggregate of their little crops nearly reaches, and will soon exceed that which was produced before the war.' Mr. Watson reckons the production of 1875 at

3,800,000 bales, and the value of this quantity is ' diffused among many thousands, or, perhaps, millions of persons or families." Wealth begets wants, and the elevation of living among the "mean whites" and the freedmen has developed an immense increase in the consumption by the South of Northern manufactures. Of this development there are no precise statistics, but Mr. Watson calculates that the Southern consumption of Northern commodities is now at least quadruple, and may possibly be tenfold that of the period before the war, while it is known to be constantly augmenting. The condition of the freedmen, who are now politically enfranchised as well as emancipated, is, of course, not wholly bright; but some have amassed "wealth," many thousands, "own houses and pay taxes," and Mr. Watson does not hesitate to say that they will ultimately become "a Conservative element" in the State. "Their labour is adding largely to the wealth of the South, and is essential to its further development."

Energetic efforts are being made in various directions to hasten and to guide this process of renovating growth.

As an example Mr. Grant Watson points to *the case of Florida, which the war and the consequent ruin of the planters may be said to have first brought to the knowledge of the North, and opened to the influx of Northern enterprise and capital. The " Land of Flowers," where Ponce de Leon placed his fabled "fountain of youth," has in late years attracted, by the charm of its climate, crowds of invalids from the Northern States, and this communication has at length disclosed to the shrewd Northern mind the capacities of this fertile peninsula. Especially since the crisis of 1873 paralyzed trade and industry in the North, setting capital seeking after investment and labour for employment, the development of the resources of Florida, which, as a fruit-producing country, has not a rival in the world, have received a great share of attention, and whenever the crisis at the North comes to an end, reviving speculation, as Mr. Watson predicts, "will turn thither, and give a still greater impetus to this already rapid movement." The orange groves of Florida are in themselves sources of wealth as rich as the most famous lodes of Nevada. The fruit is "cultivated as easily, and produces as quickly as the apple, and yields in full bearing from 1,000 to 2,500 per cent. per acre to the owner on the ground, at present prices, and with but trifling labour." The Florida orange ripens deliciously, and will certainly supplant, in the markets of the Northern Cities, the half-matured foreign fruit of which at present New York alone consumes 500 millions annually. The land fitted for this profitable and pleasant occupation has, of course, gone up rapidly in price. A large tract was purchased on the St. John's River eight years ago at about one dollar an acre, and has lately been re-sold for orange planting at prices varying from 50 to 120 dollars ; while other estates, bought some four or five years ago at 25 dollars an acre, and planted with orange trees, brought a couple of years since not less than 1,000 dollars an acre.* In this neighbourhood, a Swedish colony has been established, it is stated, with the most encouraging results. The most severe frosts do not touch the fruit trees, though on the glowing shores of the Lago di Garda, as travellers in Lombardy and Venetia will remember, the tender lemon has to be carefully covered during the winter. It is plain that a new industry of great value has been opened, and that it possesses attractions to win the Scandinavian settlers from Ohio and Wisconsin. This, however, is only a typical instance of a movement which, according to Mr. Watson, is progressing in many parts of the Southern States—wherever, indeed, the natural advantages of climate and soil, set free by the break-up of the old social system, invite Northern capital and enterprise. Unless this progress should be unexpectedly checked, the calamities of the Civil War will quickly be obliterated by the rising tide of a prosperity almost without parallel, even in American experience.

British Commercial Trade Reports, No. 6 (1876), Part II., by Her Majesty's Secretaries of Embassy and Legation, &c., &c. Presented to both Houses of Parliament, by command of Her Majesty, May, 1876.

REPORT BY MR. WATSON ON THE TRADE AND SOME RESOURCES OF THE UNITED STATES, FOR 1875 ; WITH A PREFACE ON THE MATERIAL CONDITION OF THE SOUTHERN STATES.

WHILE the Northern States of the Union, especially in their commercial and manufacturing interests, are greatly suffering at the present moment, a turn would appear, finally, to have been reached at the South, whose soil, climate, and abundant labour are now telling upon it in rapidly augmenting prosperity.

The class of former slave-owners have been, for the most part, ruined and permanently impoverished; but the lower strata—those who themselves work—have recovered from the devastation of the war, and a general diffusion of means for ease and comfort, unknown before, may be observed, although certain localities are still agitated, and are suffering by reason of political disturbances.

Cotton culture has been democratized by emancipation. While no longer crops yielding from 1,000 to 2,000 bales are raised to enrich single families and develop luxurious and extravagant tastes in these, the negroes whom they formerly owned, and who as slaves were scantily and coarsely clothed, having few wants, now raise cotton for their own profit individually, and the aggregate of their little crops nearly reaches, and will soon exceed, that which was produced before the war ; and its result—for last year, about 3,800,000 bales—is diffused amongst many thousands, or perhaps millions of persons or families, and goes to supply the increasing wants of this numerous class of new consumers ; and, while no statistics are published, the consumption by the South of articles manufactured at the North has probably more than quadrupled (it may be tenfold) that of before the war, and it is constantly augmenting.

The former slave, now a freeman (voter), as well as freedman, has become very generally an owner of the soil which he cultivates; in many instances he has amassed wealth ; many thousands own houses and pay taxes, and will eventually become a conservative element thereby of society, though now greatly under the lead of political adventurers. Many are naturally lazy, thriftless, and, in some towns where they swarm, a pest of society ; but it cannot be doubted that their labour is adding largely to the wealth of the South, and that it is essential to its further development.

Florida would, like Texas, appear especially to have been favoured in rapid development of its resources and increase of wealth. Its remarkably fine climate has attracted invalids in crowds, and these have brought more particularly to the attention of the North the advantages of its soil and peninsular position for semitropical fruit-culture, especially the orange, which is now taken hold of there with northern energy and a great deal of northern capital. The almost fabulous returns from it are attracting crowds who are thrown out of employment by the crisis at the North, and their money "s well, no longer to be profitably employed there ; and, while the present movement is owing mainly to the necessities of the people which make Florida's harvest, it is probable that when the reaction comes at the North, with the passage of the present crisis, speculation will turn thither and give a still greater impetus to this already rapid development. Amongst other things that might be cited as instances of the latent wealth of this favoured region may be especially mentioned—

Oranges, which are cultivated as easily, and produce as quickly as the apple, and yield in full bearing from 1,000 to 2,500 per cent. per acre to the owner, on the ground, at present prices, and with but trifling labour. This superior ripe fruit must end ere long in supplanting the half-ripe foreign fruit, of which now (oranges and lemons) there are nearly 1,000,000,000 imported into the United States annually (to New York alone 500,000,000, or half of the entire amount).

To give an illustration of this increase of prosperity in the State of Florida, in this one direction, some facts, the correctness of which may be relied on, may prove of interest, relating to one property on the St. John's River, the " Sanford Grant," of twenty-five square miles, which was purchased in 1868 at about one dollar per acre. Lands for orange culture upon it have been sold in the past year at an average of 50 dollars, and up to 150 dollars per acre. Land there purchased four years ago at 25 dollars an acre and planted in orange trees, has been sold three years later at 1,000 dollars per acre, and its neighbourhood in Orange County abounds in similar instances.

SANFORD'S GRANT, ORANGE COUNTY.

"The undersigned," says a widely circulated advertisement, "offers for sale to actual settlers, or improvers only, and in lots to suit buyers, the lands embraced in the above property, consisting of about twenty-five square miles.

"A portion of this tract—about 6,000 acres—is believed to be the choicest orange land in Florida. A Swedish Colony, established for four years on the centre of the grant, and rapidly increasing, furnishes reliable, intelligent labour, and an incontestible proof of its unsurpassing healthfulness.

"A settlement from Wisconsin, and another from Ohio, with a post office ('Twin Lakes'), at either extremity of the grant, demonstrates in the most striking manner the large profits derived from orange-culture when well directed. Full bearing groves in the neighbourhood abundantly testify to the large and certain income resulting from such labour on a small outlay. It is beyond the line of injurious frosts. The unusual severe cold on the 15th instant, which blighted the banana tops even so far south as Enterprise, left no trace on the grant opposite, protected by the warmer waters of Lake Monroe on the north ; and at General Sanford's large grove (Belair)—sixty-five acres—with many hundreds of tropical and thousands of semi-tropical and imported plants, not a leaf was touched. Green peas, strawberries, tomatoes, &c., can be grown the winter through in the open air, in profitable union with the orange-culture.

"The Swedish Colony will undertake to clear fence, plant, and cultivate (on guarantee) lands for orange groves, of which eighty are already in different stages of development.

"Besides the Sanford House, which will open on the 1st January, be open for 150 guests, and which, when completed next year, will be the largest hotel in the State, boarding-houses, churches, schools, post and express offices, saw-mills, stores, &c., present the usual conveniences to settlers on and near the grant.

"Steamers, ten times weekly to Jacksonville, offer the indispensable facilities of direct water communication with market to fruit and vegetable-growers.

"The prices of land are from 5 dols. to 100 dols. per acre, according to quality and location. Special rates for villa sites upon high banks of lakes.

On the lower pine lands, unfit for orange-culture, five acres will be given to each of the first twenty families who settle upon them.

"L. M. MOORE,
"Land Agent for the Grant (and Postmaster),
Sandford, Florida."

Amongst the produce of Florida may be mentioned many varieties of fruit, such as the banana, the guava, the bread-fruit, &c., the sugar-cane, starches, medicinal roots and herbs, cotton, tobacco, paper, grapes, endless variety of fishes, and lime-sand.

A most interesting book, of 806 pages, and illustrated, has been published in Glasgow in 1875, entitled, "**The Southern States of North America,**" by **Mr. Edward King,** and sold by W. G. Blackie and Co., in which a valuable chapter of 65 pages is devoted to Florida : its Climate, Fruits, Culture, &c., &c.

[Extracts.]

"The wealth of Northern cities is erecting fine pleasure houses in St. Augustine, surrounded with noble orchards and gardens. A brilliant society gathers there every winter, and depart reluctantly when spring comes on. Hundreds of families have determined to make it henceforth their winter homes."

"In December, the days are ordinarily bright and sunny, a salt, sea wind blowing across the peninsula ; from ten until four o'clock one can sit out doors, bathed in floods of delicious light."

"The number of persons whom I saw during my journey, who had migrated to the Eastern or Southern sections of the State, 'more than half-dead with consumption,' and who are now robust and vigorous, was sufficient to convince me of the great benefits derived from a residence there."

"Physicians all agree that the conditions necessary to insure life to the consumptive are admirably provided in the climatic resources of the peninsula. The European medical men are beginning to send many patients to Florida."

"For the healthy, and those seeking pleasure, it will become a winter paradise ; for the ailing it is a refuge and strength."

"The mornings of December, January, February, and March, the four *absolutely perfect months of East Florida* are wonderfully soft and balmy ; the sun shines generously, but there is no suspicion of annoying heat. The breeze gently rustles the enormous leaves of the Banana, or playfully tumbles a golden orange to the ground."

"*The Indian River Valley* is difficult of access, *but swarms of travellers are now finding their way there.* Hardly 1,000 miles from New York, one may find the most delicate and delightful tropical scenery, and may dwell in a climate which neither Hawaii, nor Southern Italy, can excel."

"Among the cocoanuts and the mangroves here, invalids may certainly count on laying a new hold upon life ; and the invalid who comes here pale and racked with a harrowing cough is, after a few weeks, seen tramping about in the cool of morning with gun and fishing-rod, a very Nimrod and Walton combined. It can be made one of the richest garden spots in America."

"*When the necessary dredging and building of canals has been accomplished, so that the* INDIAN RIVER ORANGE *may have an outlet, viâ St. John's River, the North will be* SUPPLIED *with oranges of* MORE DELICATE TEXTURE THAN IT HAS YET SEEN; THE NUMBER OF GROVES ALONG THE RIVER WILL BE LEGION.*"

"The fitness of Florida for the growth of tropical and semi-tropical fruits is astonishing. Not only do the orange, the lemon, the lime, and the citron flourish there, but the peach, the grape, the fig, the pomegranate, the plum, all varieties of berries, the olive, the banana, and the pine-apple grow luxuriantly. Black Hamburg and white Muscat grapes fruit finely in the open air; the Concord and the Scuppernong are grown in vast quantities. The guava, the tamarind, the wonderful alligator pear, the plaintain, the cocoanut, and the date, the almond and the pecan, luxuriate in southern Florida and the Indian River country. Within these boundaries a tropic land, rich and stranger, will one day be inhabited by thousands of fruit-growers, and where beautiful towns and perhaps cities will spring up."
—"A good tree will bear from 1,000 to 3,000 oranges yearly. Some trees at Mandarine have produced 5,500, many of the oranges weighing nearly a pound."
—"One young grove on Indian River, with 1,350 trees, produced in a season 700,000 oranges. They were sold for $25 to $68 per 1,000 case, and netted to its owner over $20,000."—"Col. Heart's grove nets him from $12,000 to $15,000 yearly."—"Dr. Moragne has a grove that nets him over $20,000 per annum."—"Only one man is required to attend one of these groves, who requires one or two negro men to help pick and market them."—"The culture of oranges will certainly become one of the prime industries of Florida."

Such well-known men as Mr. Astor, A. T. Stewart, Col. John P. Howard, General Sanford, Hon. Mr. Anthony, U.S. Senator of Rhode Island, and others, have embarked capital in these valleys for tropical fruit culture, or winter residences.

Another Report says:—

"The celebrated Dummitt and Burnham plantations on Indian River are yielding very large returns to their owners."

"At a fair estimate ten acres will yield a gross revenue of $15,000 to $20,000 per annum, which is *life long.* These estimates can everywhere be substantiated. The products of a single grove of *five* acres on the St. John's River were sold last year for $15,000."

"*Bananas pay equally well.* An acre will yield 1,500 bunches, many of which will bring $3 per bunch."

Mr. King (page 403) also shows the class of men who are engaging in this class of industry :—

"Property is becoming exceedingly good, yearly rising in value."—"In a few years those of Mr. Stockwell, of Maine, with 400 bearing trees, Mr. Burr, of Morristown, N.J., the Estate of Mosten (200 each), Mr. Brown, of New York, 2,000 young trees, Dr. Parsons, the Long Island Nurseryman, and others, will yield fortunes to their owners. Col. Dancey has a lemon grove of over 200 trees. Among noticeable groves are those of Mr. Cowgill, the State Comptroller; Dr. Mays, at Orange Mill; a number of New York gentlemen at Federal Point; Captain J. W. Stark, and the fine estate of Captain Rossignol. There are also many successful orange groves scattered from Rawlestown to San Matteo, Murphy's Island, Buffalo Bluff, Welaka, and Beecher. There are many groves on the Ocklawaha River and neighbourhood."

Besides such leading men of wealth, numbers of men, who have not over £100 cash, are engaging in these industries. They purchase a few acres, plant

them in orange and other fruit trees, and between the rows of trees they cultivate enough vegetables to pay all their expenses for living and for making further improvements, and in a few years their fruit will yield them larger returns than their capital and labour can bring them in other industries.

The Land Office Reports of Florida, for 1875, p. 18, in speaking of the character of immigrants settling in Florida, says :—

"They are men of the same type as those who have made that belt of country, extending from the Atlantic to the Pacific, and from the Ohio River to the Lakes, the grandest theatre of industrial activity on the continent. They are men possessed of cunning hands, resolute hearts, and clear heads; and to such no finer field then Florida was ever presented for occupancy. It is a field overflowing with the elements of wealth and substantial enjoyment. It has an abundance of raw material and rich soil, upon which all the fruits, all the crops, and all the animals necessary to man's subsistence, comfort, and convenience, can be cultivated and propagated, and a climate so congenial to his physical nature that the very exuberance of his spirits doubles his pleasures and robs adversity of half its woes."

Harper's New Monthly Magazine, No. 308, January, 1876, in an article on "Florida," p. 290, says :—

"*Orange County, without railroad help, or metal, or minerals, has by its orange groves alone increased in wealth from twenty to a hundredfold in six years.*"

In a new work just published (1876), entitled, "Camp Life in Florida," by Hallock (whose books on American subjects are considered high and reliable authority), says :—

"Now, more than ever, is attention being directed to the Land of Flowers. Winter visitors in vast numbers migrate thither as regularly as birds of passage. Twenty thousand people visited St. Augustine last winter, and will be multiplied in the next. The hotel accommodations there have been trebled within five years, and are still increasing, not only at Jacksonville, Green Cove Springs, and other favourite resorts on the St. John's River, but also on the *Eastern Seaboard* and the South West Coast hotels are being erected for use in the approaching season. Now steamers have been added to the St. John's River Lines, and increased facilities opened for communication with the North.

"Agricultural resources have been developed beyond expectation, lands have been opened that are richly adapted to the cultivation of the orange, banana, guava, and pine-apple, while the Northern markets for green peas, cucumbers, strawberries, tomatoes, and melons, offer pecuniary temptation to gardeners that cannot be overlooked. Agricultural and Emigration Societies have been established, and newspapers devoted to the economic interests of the State.

"Lands for well located farms have appreciated *five times their value in three years,* and real estates has advanced to fancy prices at the principal watering-places. Northern merchants have built princely residences there; settlements have been made at numerous points on the coast and in the interior; old familiar places are no longer recognised. Such changes have a few years brought.

"There is no place on this continent like Florida for both *game and fish.*

"Frost seldom, if ever, injures the sugar-cane, it tassels, and *grows from 15 to 20 feet high.*

G

"The settlers find much profit in the culture and sale of fruits and vegetables for the Northern markets. Even in the interior of the State, notably at Lake City, many of the citizens are speaking of giving up the cultivation of cotton, and turning their attention to English peas and other vegetables for shipment to Northern States.

"A few years ago, with the exception of Welaka, scarcely anything was to be seen but the *interminable forests along the St. John's River.* There was scarcely a settlement or clearing to mark the advance of civilization. What a change now appears ! Landings, clearings, houses, and orange groves map out to the eye of the traveller the rapid improvement now going on.

"There seems no doubt that the population and developed resources of Florida are destined to double in ten years. Those who have some prescience will do well now to take time by the forelock, that they may reap coming advantages."

Mr. Ledyard Bill's late published history of "Florida and the St. John's Valley," after describing the young city of Jacksonville, with its ocean commerce equal to some cities in the north of three times its population, with the steamers, brigs, and schooners in its harbour, and towns and noted mineral springs, hotels, and social life on the St. John's, concludes, "that the banks of St. John's will in time be as famous for their vineyards and wine as are those of the Rhine in Europe," and the almost endless productions of the tropical fruits of every variety that grow in the tropics, and the early vegetables required in the Northern cities, now mostly imported from the West Indies, Central America, and the Bahamas to an enormous extent, will make the St. John's River, with its lakes and lagoons, a tropical orchard, vineyard, and garden from end to end."

He further says :—

"*Even the pine lands of the poorest quality suit the grape, and more wine can be made from an acre of this land than from any two acres of the ordinary wine-growing in Europe. The highest yield in Europe is not over five hundred gallons to the acre, whereas, in Florida, over fifteen hundred gallons is a common yield. When these facts become known fully, it must excite the grape-growing population of worn-out France and Italy to try their fortunes in our most favoured land.*

"There is no sort of necessity for America importing the miserable adulterations that she is now doing, and sending her gold across the ocean by the millions in exchange, when within her own boundaries she is favoured beyond all lands in soil and climate adapted to the production of superior wine, and in such quantities as not only to supply the home demand, but have a surplus for exportation.

The orange of Florida excels the fruit of any other country, both in size and sweetness. This the general testimony of competent judges, and we unqualifiedly concur, *especially when we remember those grown in what is known as the Indian River country. These seldom reach any of the Foreign markets, the home consumption being sufficient to require them all.*

"The orange is the longest lived fruit-tree known to us; it will flourish and bear fruit for more than 100 years.

"*The present groves will run an average yield of 2,000 per tree; they can be marketed at 25 dollars per 1,000. This would give a return of 50 dollars per tree, or to an acre of about 500 trees 5,000 dollars.* The labour of one man is quite sufficient to tend the largest grove in Florida, except the time of gathering, when two are required.

"Mr. Howard, from New York, has within a year past (1869) invested nearly 50,000 dollars in St. Augustine in real estate, which is feeling the effect of the healthy influx, property having already risen to fourfold its value five years ago, and still not high. The residence of Senator Gilbert was bought by him at the close of the war for $8,000, and we judge it worth $40,000 now."

M. Lanier, a Frenchman, has just published (1876) a Book on Florida, somewhat after the style of Murray's Guide Books.

On page 132 he furnishes a list of towns and stations on the St. John's River. There are 42 towns and stations from Jacksonville to Salt Lake on the St. John's. Five years ago there were less than ten. He describes the St. John's and Indian River Valleys fully. He says :—

"Green-Cove-Springs is one of the most popular winter resorts on the St. John's. The Springs, with the Clarendon Hotel adjoining, are but a short distance from the river. Connected with this hotel are hot and cold baths, and swimming baths of spring water.

"*These waters contain sulphates of magnesia and lime, chlorides of sodium and iron, and sulphurated hydrogen, and have a temperature of 76° Fahrenheit.*

"*They are used for the cure of rheumatism, gout, Bright's disease of the kidneys, and such affections. Beside the Clarendon, the Union House, a charmingly erected hotel offers accommodation to visitors; and there are good private boarding houses.*" * * *

"Melonville is on the right hand side of Lake Monroe, and is in a neighbourhood which is beginning to exhibit much activity in settlements and improvements. Hereabouts are many orange-growers, the flourishing Swedish Colony brought over by General Sanford in 1871. Euroka, Eau-Clair, Wekiva, Lake Jennie, Lake Maitland, Lake Conway, Fort Reid, and other settlements. Extensive interests have been established here in orange-groves. Adjoining General Sanford's lands are those of Mr. William Astor, consisting of 8,000 acres of timber and orange lands. Not far off is the Fort Butler Grant, in which Mr. Aster is said to be interested, on which are numerous groves of wild oranges, and the charming little Lake of Schermerhorn." At Enterprise he says :—

"Consumptives are said to flourish in this climate, and there are many stories told of *cadaverous persons* coming here, and turning out successful huntsmen and fishermen, of ruddy face and portentous appetites after a few weeks."

Of the Indian River Country he says :

"The general character of the lands in the Indian River Country appears to be a strip of high rich soil, lying immediately on the Western shore, from a half-mile to a mile in width, then coming Westward a belt containing "hummocks and savanas" of great fertility from one to two miles in width, then ridges of light hammock, then still Westward rich grazing lands."

"Upon these lands, oranges, sugar-cane, bananas, pine-apples, lemons, limes, guavas, strawberries, blackberries, grapes, figs, nectarines, apricots, corn, indigo, sweet-potatoes, mellons, and all manner of garden vegetable grown and yield profusely."

"Along this Indian River country is a marvellously bland air, and I have been told of many over-worked men and incipient consumptives who have here found new life. The waters are full of fish, oysters, and turtles of the best varieties for table use ; the woods abound in deer, wild turkeys, and other games, and the whole land amounts to a perpetual invitation to the over-worked, the invalid, the air-poisoned, the nervously-prostrate people to come down with yacht and tent, with rod and gun, and re-build brain, and muscle, and nerve. *The price of lands ranges from 5 to 50 dollars per acre.*"

"*The largest sized and finest flavoured oranges grow in this charming Valley. Many persons hold the Indian River Orange to be typic fruit.*"

"Judge Du Pont informs me that he has raised from Pine Land 69 barrels of syrup per acre, bringing the handsome sum of $400 per acre."

"As to the profits, you can make $300 an acre sure."

"Figs are yielding a profit of from $1,000 to $1,200 per acre, and instances are reported of Banana yield of $5,000 per acre."

The Indian river valley lies south of the frost-line, and all the official and private Reports on Florida speak of this locality as possessing the finest climate, and altogether the best fruit and vegetable-producing region of the whole State.
The Company owns about 1,000,000 acres in this productive valley.

Without elaborating further, it must appear self-evident to any thinking mind that to appraise the Company's Lands at ten dollars per acre is to set a low price, and that the Company may confidently expect to realise an average of, at least, ten dollars.
This will make the mortgage security in lands over $23,000,000 cash basis. Mr. Conover, one of the United States Senators from Florida, telegraphed to London, in answer to inquiries from London parties, that the lands belonging to the Company "will sell, now, in cash at from $8 to $30 per acre, making an average of $16.50 per acre, cash now."

SUMMARY CONCLUSIONS UPON THE COMPANY'S REAL ESTATE—ITS GREAT VALUE—WITH AN ESTIMATE OF ANNUAL INCOMES THEREFROM.

The official Reports of the Governments of the United States, Florida, and Great Britain, together with the Reports and Statements from men of unquestionable high character, quoted and referred to, established the following facts :—

1. That four-fifths of the area of the lands in Florida are covered with magnificent forests, furnishing timber and lumber of the most superior quality, for ship and house construction, cabinet and ornamental work, &c., of which many millions of dollars worth are annually shipped to the Northern Cities, to Europe, the West Indies, South America, and to other markets. These timber resources alone are bound to make the State rich, as the timber in the States of Maine, Michigan, and Wisconsin, made them rich.

2. That the soil of Florida is varied, rich, and very productive, successfully growing all the variety of staple crops of the United States; that all the tropical fruits grow there to perfection; that the garden vegetables grow all the year round, winter and summer; that the markets of the Northern and North-Western Cities and States, and Canada, which are bound up in ice and winter four or five months each year, can be fully supplied with these tropical fruits, and winter and early spring vegetables, and that in these respects Florida can control and monopolize the Northern markets, which now consume over $200,000,000 annually in fruit and vegetables.

3. That the State is rapidly increasing in population and wealth; that great progress is making in developing and utilising her timber, agricultural, and horticultural resources; and as a consequence and fact, her lands are rising rapidly in price.

4. That this population is chiefly settling in the St. John's and Indian River Valleys along the lines of the Company's Canals and Routes, and the principle development is taking place in these Valleys.

5. That this Company owns and has perfect grants and titles to 2,300,000 acres of rich lands located in the St. John's and Indian River Valleys, along the Company's Canals and Water Routes, and in and about all the settlements, which are now making the remarkable demonstrations in tropical fruit and vegetable culture, showing larger profits per acre than any other lands in North America can produce. It is in the central region of the Company's lands in Orange County, where the wonderful development in tropical fruit culture is reported upon by the British Legation Office at Washington in 1876, and so aptly treated in an able leader in the *Times* of June 23rd, 1876, showing that lands were purchased there, eight years ago, at about one dollar per acre, and the same are now selling for fifty dollars to hundred-fifty dollars per acre, and that the profits from Orange culture is from 1,000 to 2,500 per cent. per acre yearly, and that Northern capital is flowing into that region, &c.

6. The evidence and common history of that country show, that the INDIAN RIVER VALLEY, on account of its being south of the terminal frost line, its unsurpassed favourable climate, and its great adaptability of soil, IS FAR SUPERIOR FOR THE SUCCESSFUL CULTIVATION OF THE ORANGE AND ALL THE TROPICAL FRUITS, than the St. John's Valley is, or any more northerly portion of the country, for in the latter Valley and more northerly regions, not ALL the *tropical fruits can be successfully raised*, and the quality of the fruit is not so good, as is shown by the fact that Indian River Oranges and fruits command a premium price in the markets, and 1,000,000 acres of the Company's lands are located in the Indian River Valley.

7. Tens of thousands of people from the Northern States annually spend their winter season in Florida for pleasure or health, and to avoid four to five months of the severe rigors of winter, ice, and chilling atmosphere of the North; and on account of the superior climate of the St. John's and Indian River Valleys, the conveniences, improvements, and attractions of those Valleys, nearly the whole of this visiting population go to the different cities, towns, villages, mineral springs, and settlements in these Valleys, and spend their visiting seasons there.

8. *That the market value of the Company's lands is from $5 to $100 per acre, cash. The value of the Company's lands in hand, 2,300,000, exceeds $30,000,000. The 6,000,000 acres will run a much less price per acre.*

9. THE ESTIMATED ANNUAL INCOMES FROM THE COMPANY'S LANDS.

Taking into consideration the annual sales and incomes heretofore realized by Railway and other companies from their Government land grants in aid of their enterprises, &c., and the demand for the Company's timber and lands, it would seem safe to estimate, from the sale of timber, from sale of lands for agricultural and horticultural purposes, from the sale of town and village lots, from ground rents and other issues, and profits from the realty and buildings, an aggregate of $8,000,000
On the east division, before the completion of the west division 1,000,000
On the east division, by its completion from Fernandina to Lake Worth ... 500,000

From this must be deducted 15 per cent. to cover all expenses.

CHAPTER IV.

CANAL PROPERTIES CONSIDERED.

Canals as Financial Enterprises.

Considering for a moment steam and horse canals, we may deduce a few practical conclusions.
1. Canals cost less than railways.
2. Their commercial results are unquestionable.
3. The cost for operating and maintaining are nominal compared with railways.
4. Financially their net earnings are more certain, and greater in proportion to cost.
5. There are proportionally less failures of canals than railways.
6. They afford the cheapest freights for all heavy articles of commerce, of all systems of internal improvements.

These conclusions must be inferred from the fact that nearly all commercial nations have resorted to this system, and still cling to it, and we are now entering upon a period of great expansion of the system.

"If there is any part of the world that could discard canals and rely solely upon railroads, it would be the British Islands and France, because they are surrounded by water, and from the interior to a seaport is comparatively a very short distance. But yet we find an aggregate of about 12,000 miles of canal and improved navigation in these two kingdoms, whose territory combined does not greatly exceed that of the four cotton States of the Atlantic seaboard. Yet all these canals find profitable employment, and more extensive works of the kind are contemplated. While in England, it is said no acre of land is now distant more than fifteen miles from navigable water.

"These canals are not owned by the State, and having been thus extended by private capital, show they are financially feasible. Norway and Sweden, and other European countries, add largely to this aggregate. The canals of China and Holland are historical.

"Of the great canal system in North America the benefits of this class of improvements are fully appreciated. Nearly every canal is overtaxed with freights beyond its capacity, and more than ten canals are complete and great financial successes.

"We will name but one, as an illustration, to show the financial success and commercial results produced by the Erie Canal.

"If it be true that 'one well-attested experiment is worth ten thousand untried theories,' we have the experiment here long and well tried, and the result also.

"From a statement made by the Auditor to the Legislature of the State of New York, dated March 20, 1873, it appears that, during the twenty-six years ending with the fiscal year 1872, the total receipts from the Erie Canal amounted to $81,952,010; and that the total expenditures for superintendence, repairs, maintenance, damages, and collections, amounted to $22,075,570; showing a net income of $59,876,440, or 73 per cent. of the gross income during the period mentioned.

"The net annual profits realized from operation of the Erie Canal amounted to $2,302,940. The financial results of the Erie Canal are, however, of small moment in comparison with its commercial results, the grandest of any material enterprise of modern times. Connecting the ocean with the great lakes which interlace the heart of the continent, it developed the possibility of the most productive area on the face of the globe, the value of the merchandise transported on this Canal to the end of 1872 having amounted to the enormous sum of $6,065,060,698."—(*United States' Senate Transportation Report.*)

The Erie is a horse Canal of 363 miles long, and closed by ice five months each year.

THE SUEZ UNIVERSAL CANAL is a practical illustration of a grand international improvement. M. Ferdinand de Lesseps has immortalised himself in the clear, certain knowledge he had of the feasibility of this canal, and in the untiring energy and the gigantic efforts he displayed in raising the capital, constructing the canal and making it a grand financial success, and all this in the face of opposition at first, and apathy of one of the greatest of commercial nations, which was forced to come to M. de. Lesseps at the 13th hour.

Full Reports of the Annual Meetings of the Company, with its financial exhibits, &c., for the years 1875 & 1876, are published in the *Economist* of London, March 6th, 1875, and July 22nd, 1876, with elaborate comments by the *Economist*.

These reports are full of interesting matter, and well worth a careful perusal.

From these reports it seems the Share Capital of 400,000 shares of £20 each, amounts to £8,000,000. The total costs of construction, equipment, &c., &c. is £19,000,000.

"RETURN OF THE NUMBER AND TONNAGE of SHIPS PASSING THROUGH THE SUEZ CANAL FROM 1870 TO 1875.

	No. of Ships.	Gross Tonnage.	Net Tonnage.	Increase of Net Tonnage.	Per Cent. of Increase on Previous Year.
1870...	489	654,911	436,609	...	...
1871...	763	1,142,200	761,467	324,557	74
1872...	1,082	1,744,481	1,158,582	397,115	50
1873...	1,173	2,085,421	1,367,777	209,194	18
1874...	1,264	2,421,803	1,631,650	263,872	19
1875...	1,494	2,940,708	2,009,984	378,333	23

"In the *second* place, the report and correspondence clearly show that the property is a rapidly-improving one, while there are some features of a peculiarly satisfactory character in a question of profit. One or two tables, which we extract from the report and subjoin, show very clearly what is now very well known, and we need not, therefore, dwell upon—the progress of the traffic and the gross receipts since the opening of the Canal. But the effect of this growth on the net income of the Company is also very striking, and we have now the means of exhibiting it for the last three years.

"Taking the figures of receipts and expenditure for these years, we have the following comparison :—

	1873.	1874.	1875.
Receipts...	£991,000	£1,056,000	£1,233,000
Expenditure	225,000	248,000	248,000
Net earnings	766,000	808,000	985,000
Proportion of net to gross income.	77 %	75 %	80 %

"The accounts of 1875, summarised in the manner we adopted in dealing with the accounts of 1873 and 1874, exhibit the following results :—

RECEIPTS.	£	EXPENDITURE.	£
Interest received ...	25,000	Expense of administra-	
Revenue from domain	34,000	tion	39,000
Receipts from transit service and naviga-		Management of domain	23,000
		Transit and navigation	
tion...	1,165,000	service...	63,000
Receipts from main-		Maintenance	113,000
tenance service ...	5,000	Water service	10,000
Supply of water and			
miscellaneous ...	4,000		
Total	1,233,000	Total	248,000
Receipts as above			£1,233,000
Expenditure as above			248,000
Net earnings			985,000

—showing a gross income of £1,233,000, earned at a cost of £248,000, or about 20 per cent. And this £985,000 of net income is more than sufficient, after defraying all preferential charges, to pay 5 per cent. on the share capital of £8,000,000. These preferential charges are as follows :—

Interest of obligations	£321,000	
Sinking fund obligations	81,000	
Interest of Trentenary bonds	37,000	
Sinking fund of Trentenary bonds	14,000	
Annual charge of obligations and bonds ...	4,000	
Control of Egyptian Government	1,000	
Annual charge of coupons and shares ...,	500	
Commissions, &c.	4,000	
Total	462,500	

Deducting which sum from the above net revenue of

£985,000, leaves £522,500 available for division, in one form or other, among the holders of shares out of the earnings of the year. As 5 per cent. on the shares only absorbs £400,000, there has been manifestly a considerable surplus over 5 per cent. for division.

In fact, the sum distributed and the mode of. distribution has been as follows :—

Interest of the consolidated arrears of coupons £68,000	
„ on share capital	81,000
Sinking fund of shares for 1875	3,200
Statutory reserve	2,200
Net profit, so-called, divided in the propor-	
tions of 71 per cent. to Shareholders, 15	
per cent. to Egyptian Government, 10 per	
cent. to Founders, 2 per cent. to Directors,	
and 2 per cent. to *employés*	42,400
Total	515,800

—the difference between this amount and the above total of £522,500 available for division, arising from certain arrears of receipts and expenses which are dealt with in the accounts. Roughly speaking, the original owners of £8,000,000 of share capital have received about £520,000 for the year 1875, or at. the rate of 6½ per cent. Allowing for the circumstance that £68,000 of this sum is paid in respect of capitalised arrears of interest, which are represented by certificates now detached from the shares, and that £2,000 more is set aside as statutory reserve, the actual sum divided in the form of sinking fund or interest out of the last year's earnings, among the holders of shares in the Suez Canal is about £445,600, or a little more than 5½ per cent.

"In reality, the Shareholders have received even more than this for 1875. The position of the Company being now established, a sum of £18,660 has been taken from a balance brought forward from former years, amounting to £85,932, and has been applied by way of sinking fund to redeem the shares —the application being to make up for the omission to apply the sinking fund in the years 1870 to 1874, when the earnings was insufficient. This is a windfall to the Shareholders for the year, and will not be repeated in precisely the same form ; but there is still an undivided balance of about £70,000 which will be available to increase or equalise dividends in future years.

"Altogether the facts appear to us fully to bear ont the statement with which we began, as to the remarkable nature of this property, which has now (1875) been introduced to the London Stock Exchange. It seems quite probable that it may become another illustration of the great value of an absolute monopoly of an article of increasing use, of which the shares of the New River Company, which supplies North London with water, and which has had all the benefit of the vast growth of London for 200 years, have, perhaps, been the best illustration hitherto known. The position of the Suez Canal Company appears to us a commanding one of the same species." (The New River Stocks are the most valuable known in the world).

"The Company has an absolute monopoly of a certain route, the business of which must increase with the growth in numbers and wealth of nations which are served by it," &c.

OTHER CANALS.

McCulloch's "Commercial Dictionary" of 1839 gives a short history of the systems of canals in Europe and other countries.

He says of the

"Dutch Canals.

"No country in Europe contains, in proportion to its size, so many navigable canals as the kingdom of the Netherlands, and particularly the province of Holland. The construction of these canals commenced as early as the twelfth century, when, owing to its central and convenient situation, Flanders began to be the *entrepôt* of the commerce between the north and south of Europe. Their number has been astonishingly increased. Holland (says Mr. Phillips, in his "History of Inland Navigation,") is intersected with innumerable canals. They may be compared in number and size to our public roads and highways; and as the latter with us are continually full of coaches, chaises, waggons, carts, and horsemen, going from and to different cities, towns, and villages, so, on the former, the Hollanders, in their boats and pleasure barges, their treckschuyts, and vessels of burden, are continually journeying and conveying commodities for consumption or exportation from the interior of the country to the great cities and rivers. An inhabitant of Rotterdam may, by means of these canals, breakfast at Delft, on the Hague, dine at Leyden, and sup at Amsterdam, or return home again before night. By them, also, a most prodigious inland trade is carried on between Holland and every part of France, Flanders, and Germany.

"The Yearly Profits

Produced by these canals are almost beyond belief; but it is certain, and it has been proved, that they amount to more than £250,000 for about 400 miles of canal navigation, which is £625 per mile, the square surface of which mile does not exceed 2 acres of ground; a profit so amazing, that it is no wonder other nations should imitate what has been found so advantageous."

"The canal from Amsterdam to Nieudiep, near the Helder.—The object of this canal, which is the greatest work of its kind in Holland, and probably in the world in 1825, is to afford a safe and easy passage for vessels from Amsterdam to the German Ocean. It was completed in 1825, and proved a great success to Holland, and in 1867 a new canal, still larger, was in course of formation."

McCulloch further says:

"It is a well-known fact that canals, which connect places that have an extensive interconrse, and when no very extraordinary difficulties have to be surmounted in their construction, they most commonly yield very large profits."

The Hon. C. C. Andrews, United States' Minister, resident at Stockholm, made an official Report to the United States' Government on the canals of Sweden and Norway.

This Report says:

"These canals have all been constructed by private companies, which, in some cases, have received aid from the States. The Government is not the owner of any canal. The rate of tolls is fixed, however, by the Government, and it is not the policy of the Government that the canals shall yield any further revenue than is sufficient for their maintenance, and for a fair interest on the private capital actually invested in them.

"Steamers and sailing vessels navigate a part of these canals. The business of the canals, as a whole, is increasing at the rate of about 4 per cent. a year. Several important new ones are projected, and will, no doubt, be constructed."

"If the tolls were not regulated by Government the earnings of these canals would yield large dividends upon the construction capital."

The *Economist* of February 20th, 1875, says:

"The construction of canals is beginning to absorb public attention both in Germany and Austria, more than it ever did before. At present the construction of a canal between the Oder and the Danube is much spoken of. German shipping is likely to be greatly improved by the new measures adopted affecting the canal trade, &c.

The aggregate mileage of canals in the United States is more than that of any other nation. They are generally owned and controlled by the several States in which they are located. Their great utility and commercial benefits have been thoroughly demonstrated. The amount of commerce transported by these canals is gigantic, and its value in money simply enormous. The net earnings over all costs for operating and maintaining them show a large percentage of profit on capital expended in construction. The facts have been demonstrated that canals can earn a liberal profit on construction capital, and afford rates of freight over 300 per cent. cheaper than the American railways. The National and State Governments have determined that the American canal system must be greatly enlarged and increased. A number of private companies have been chartered to contruct the most important canals of the country, while the Federal Government contemplates constructing other important lines, and from recent history it would appear that nearly all commercial nations are contemplating the increase of canals; and the history relating to internal improvements shows that capital has suffered less, and produced surer satisfactory returns than the railway system has been able to do.

CHAPTER V.

RECAPITULATION OF INCOMES.

Expenditures.

It is estimated that 15 per cent. of the gross earnings of the Ship Canal and Through Route will fully cover all administration charges, services of transit, towing, pilotage, maintenance of canals, magazines, and repairs on all other improvements; that 10 per cent. will be a large deduction from sale of Lands, Timber, and Lumber not manufactured by the Company; that 25 per cent. of the earnings of the Company's steamers and other water craft will cover all deductions on that account, and that 50 per cent. of the gross receipts from sales of timber, lumber, and other forest products, will fully cover all expenses for manufacturing and marketing the same.

By turning to the Annual Account and Exhibits of the Suez Canal Company for the year 1876, as published in the *Economist* of July 22, 1876, it appears that "the maximum of 10 francs per ton on the official net tonnage would be raised" *after the Surtax is extinguished.* Ten francs nearly equal two dollars American coin. The maximum tariff on through net tonnage will not exceed one dollar per ton. All local freights must have special rates, similar to American Railway and Canal Company's charges.

Estimated Gross and Nett Earnings annually from the Ship Canal and Tide Water Canal Route, and the Profits from the Company's Lands and Forests, &c., &c.

Ship Canal.

25,000,000 tons nett, at $1	...	$25,000,000
Deduct 15 per cent.	... ...	3,750,000
Nett earnings ...	...	$21,250,000

Tide Water Canal Route Traffic.

Gross $4,000,000 nett ...	...	$3,400,000

Forests.

Timber, Lumber, &c., nett	$1,000,000

Lands.

Sale of Lands, Town Lots, Rents, Issues, and other Profits, nett ..		$2,550,000
Total nett	...	$28,200,000

These results seem almost fabulous, but it must be remembered that they cannot be fully attained for several years after the full completion of the works, and the outlet of the commerce of the Mississippi Valley into the Gulf of Mexico, which the United States' Government has undertaken to do, and will accomplish. It is quite reasonable that these results will be realised fully within less than ten years after construction.

Even 50 per cent. of these net results will make this one of the most successful financial enterprises of the age, and from the beginning the net incomes will pay all costs for operating and preferential charges, and also pay a liberal annual dividend on the share capital.

Again, a number of railway companies, both in the United States and in England, severally exhibit nearly as great an amount of gross earnings annually. The Pennsylvania Railway Company has exhibited over $22,000,000 net annual earnings. There is one instance in American Railways where the first year's net earnings paid back the whole construction capital, and 5 per cent. dividends on the capital shares.

Conclusions.

From the foregoing elaborate Report and cumulative evidence in support, the facts are submitted, in confidence and assurance, that the capital required to complete this consolidated enterprise is absolutely secure.

1st. From the certain earnings of the enterprise.

2nd. It is secured by the timber and lumber alone on the Company's lands.

3rd. The 8,000,000 acres of grants of the richest and most valuable lands in the State are good security for this capital.

4th. The franchises, rights, improvements, real, personal, and mixed property, form an aggregate security for the Bonds and Stock proposed to be issued by the Company, which are most ample and first-class for the investment of Capital.

JOHN H. FRY,

Attorney for the Company.

APPENDIX.

FLORIDA.—Note A.

CAPTAIN TOWNSEND, 2ND LIFE GUARDS, LONDON, spent a season in Florida, and wrote his " Wild Life in Florida," in which he says :—

" It was not until A.D. 1565 that Florida was permanently settled by the Spaniards, but she did not long retain her nationality. Ceded to Great Britain in 1763, with a population of only 600, she was re-ceded to Spain in 1784, sold to the United States in 1819, received a territorial government in 1822, and was admitted to the Union as a State in 1845. From 1815 to 1858 the country was harassed by repeated Indian wars, and in 1861 Florida joined the Southern Confederacy. Then her soil was for four years the scene of many bloody fights, until 1865, when the ordinance of secession was repealed, and in 1868 she was re-admitted to the Union.

" Thus for three centuries and a half constant changes of nationality and desolating wars have so depopulated and retarded the progress of Florida, that she has to-day all the characteristics of a newly settled territory, notwithstanding the fact that on her soil was built the first permanent town erected by Europeans on the continent of North America."

The question might be asked, Why is Florida, with such a desirable climate, rich soil, and wonderful natural resources, in a vigorous country like the United States, still a practical wilderness ?

The answer is correctly given above by an Englishman.

Immigration was practically prevented till within the last few years. Now we see from 40,000 to 50,000 Northern people visit Florida every autumn, and spend their winters in her balmy climate, for health and pleasure. And now every industry has sprung into life and activity. Social order and goodwill between the Northern capitalists and immigrant have joined hands with the Floridians; all are welcomed. Churches, schools, internal improvements, little cities and towns, are springing into life all over the State; and soon Florida will become the Italy and garden of the United States.

The geographical position of this State is unique, and of special interest. She is divided into East and West Florida. The whole peninsula constitutes East Florida.

The whole peninsula is fanned by the Gulf winds on the west, and the Atlantic breezes and trade winds on the east side, giving a pleasantness and salubrity of climate, and a power of vegetable production on her soil, so wonderful as to be almost incredible.

FINEST CLIMATE IN THE WORLD.

I quote from history :—

" The climate of Florida is one of its chief attractions; mild in winter, and not excessively hot in summer.

The temperature is more equable than that of any other State of the Union. The thermometer rarely falls below 40 deg. or rises above 95 deg.

" The records contained in the Spanish Archives at St. Augustine (on the Atlantic coast of Florida) show that the mean temperature of the winter months for 100 years averaged a little over 60 deg., and of the summer months 86 deg. Fahrenheit. The days are much shorter and the nights much longer in Florida in the summer than in the more northerly latitudes, hence the daily absorption of moisture and heating of the earth are constantly counteracted by the long cool nights. " Constant mention is made of the daily recurring sea-breezes, which cool off the after part of day, and gave a delightful atmosphere for nightly rest." History records the climate of St. Augustine as the most beautiful and healthy in the world, and " the climate of St. Augustine is the climate of the whole peninsula."

General Rawson, Surgeon-General of the Army, in his official Report to the Government, of the climate, diseases, &c., of Florida, reports : " The climate of Florida is remarkably equable and agreeable, being subject to fewer atmospheric variations, and its thermometer ranges much less than any other part of the United States, except a portion of the coast of California." He gives the facts, and concludes : " In the summer season the mercury rises higher in every part of the United States and even in Canada than it does on the peninsula of Florida. This is shown by meteorological statistics in this Bureau." In the summer it is hotter in New York, Boston, and Montreal, than in St. Augustine, Tampa, and Key West. " In the former cities the *thermometer frequently ranges as high as* 100 *deg. to* 109 *in the shade*, and that too without any breeze to relieve it, whereas it but rarely reaches as high as 90 deg. at any of the latter places." At Key West the mercury in fourteen years rose but three times to 94 deg. in the shade.

The History of Florida declares : " Indeed it would be difficult to find a climate in any part of the world so agreeable as on this peninsula." " The winters are delightful, five days out of six being bright and cloudless, and of the most agreeable temperature. In the larger portion of the peninsula *frost never occurs*, and even in the northerly portion frosts or ice are seldom felt, and the cold does not continue over an hour or two at a time." Carver's History says : " So mild are the winters there, that the most delicate vegetables, plants, and flowers of the Caribbee Islands experience not the least injury from that season ; the orange tree, the banana, the plantain, the guava, the pine-apple, &c., grow luxuriantly all the year. Fogs are scarcely known there, and no country can be more salubrious." " *Rain but rarely falls during the winter months in Florida ; three, four, and not unfrequently five weeks of bright, clear, and cloudless days occur continuously. This is one of the greatest charms of the winter climate in Florida; and in this respect it forms a striking contrast with almost every State in the Union, and especially with Texas, California, and Oregon." The latter States have but two seasons, the wet and the dry; six months corresponding to the winter being almost constant rain, like London in the fall of 1872; and six months, the summer or hot season, almost entirely dry.* These States require extensive summer irrigation to grow fruit and crops, which is very expensive. *The rains of Florida come in the spring and summer, when they are wanted to grow the crops.*

Thousands of travellers to Florida, who have visited Italy and Sandwich Islands, pronounce the Florida climate the best known.

The superior and exhilarating climate is produced by her peninsular position, which "causes it to be fanned on the east by the Atlantic breezes, and on the west by those of the Gulf of Mexico, both of which can be distinctly felt in the centre of the State. *Besides this the north trade winds play over the whole peninsula. The summer nights are invariably cool, and even the hottest days are seldom oppressive in the shade.* This is more than any State north of Florida can boast."

HEALTH.

As respects *health*, the climate of Florida stands pre-eminent. That the peninsular climate of Florida is more salubrious than that of any other State of the Union is clearly established by the medical statistics of the army, and also by the last Census Returns. These records show that the ratio of deaths to the number of cases of remittent fever has been much less among the troops serving in Florida than those serving in *any other* portion of the United States.

The proportion of deaths of remittent fevers in the U.S. Army

in the Middle Division	is 1 in	36
„ Northern „	„ 1 „	52
„ Southern „	„ 1 „	78
„ California „	„ 1 „	122
„ New Mexico „	„ 1 „	148
while in Florida it is but	1 „	**287**

The general healthfulness of Florida is proverbial. The average annual mortality of the whole peninsula from official Returns is 2·06 per cent., while the other portions of the United States is 3·05 per cent. (previous to the Mexican war).

The statistics of the United States' Census of 1860 show the proportion of those who died from consumption in the various States of the Union during the year ending May 31, 1860, viz :—

One in	254 in	Massachusetts.
„	289 „	Maine.
„	404 „	Vermont.
„	473 „	New York.
„	580 „	Pennsylvania.
„	671 „	Ohio.
„	727 „	California.
„ ·	757 „	Virginia.
„	797 „	Indiana.
„	878 „	Illinois; and only
One in **1·447** in		Florida.

These facts speak volumes in favour of the good health of Florida. Thousands of consumptive invalids go to Florida, and many, advanced beyond cure, die there; and this has increased the ratio of deaths beyond the true proportion. Dr. Warren, p. 209, asserts that 40,000 people die annually in the State of New York, and the six New England States, of con-

sumption. Large numbers from these States go to Florida to regain their health, and many become actual settlers. Ledyard Bill's book of 1870, on Florida, says that "30,000 people now annually go to Florida for health, pleasure, or settlement." Page 171, he says, "The number of strangers in the city of Jacksonville and other points greatly exceeded our expectations. They thronged in every street and public place. The fashionable belle of New York and of Saratoga, and the pale, thoughtful, furloughed clergyman of New England, were at all points."

For 100 years Florida has been the resort of invalids. Her noted mineral springs have been highly prized. History states that the 9th Regiment of British Infantry was stationed at St. Augustine, Matanzos, Picolato, and St. Marks, and during a period of twenty months not a man was lost by natural death. Another important fact is shown by the Report of the State Agricultural Society of 1870. It says: "*It is a fact worthy of note that a case of 'sun-stroke' has never occurred in the country, nor has an instance of 'rabies' or 'hydrophobia' ever been known.*" Every city in the north of the United States is annually suffering from both these evils. Governor Gleason, author of the 'State Constitution,' has written much on the climate and resources of the State. In his Report, September 8, 1868, he says: "*There is a constant sea breeze, commencing about 8 A.M., and lasting until nearly sundown. The climate is very exhilarating, and a white man can do as much labour in a day as in any portion of the United States.*"

The diseases so prevalent and destructive of life in the Northern, Middle, and Western States, induced by frequent and violent changes of atmosphere and contagion, either do not exist at all, or but rarely occur in individual cases, such as diptheria, scarlet fever, congestive fever, pneumonia, coughs, colds, pulmonary complaints in all their forms, bronchitis, rheumatism, and many others; whilst those occurring to childhood mostly are not known to exist there, such as croup, whooping cough, measles, mumps, &c.

Surely, on the score of health, Florida is a blessing to mankind.

United States' Agricultural Report, 1871, says :—

"Perhaps no other State has of late attracted so much attention as Florida. Its peninsular position, low latitude, almost tropical temperature, and its peculiar shape, which gives a sea-shore border to twenty-one of its thirty-nine counties, combine to give this State a character *sui generis*. Its uniformity of temperature makes it the Italy of America—a *sanitarium*, especially for consumptives and others unable to endure the rigours of Northern winters; and its semi-tropical climate allures the adventurous who desire a wider range of rural industries than northern farming or fruit-growing affords. Not only do ocean or Gulf waters lave a majority of the border counties, but inland seas furnish water transit and modification of climate to most of those in the interior. The climate of South Florida resembles those of Madeira and Barbadoes, both esteemed as resorts for invalids, having a temperature warmer than that of the former, and cooler than that of the latter."

Captain Townsend, 2nd Life Guards, says, in his book on Florida: "Many Englishmen now visit Florida in the winter, both for health and for the sake of sport and adventure, and to them I trust the following account of our tour may be of some interest; while to those who have not yet visited Florida, but who may chance to read these pages, I say,'' Visit Florida *between the months of October and February, and you will enjoy one of the most perfect climates, and see one of the most interesting countries in the world.'*"

Mr. Ledyard Bill's book on East Florida describes the climatic effects produced upon visitors entering the St. John's River, and the beautiful tropical scenery of that country. He says: " May Port is the first landing where we catch the first glimpses of a tropical growth—a small grove of palmettoes; though not over 25 feet in height, yet their peculiar character attracts the attention of the northern traveller. Casting your eye farther inland, and the green forests tell of a perpetual spring, and we now realize that we have passed from the chilling winds of a northern winter to the genial skies of that sunny land of which we so often hear, but seldom or never experience in any other of the Southern States. The abrupt turn of the river south already stated, produces curious atmospheric phenomenon of balmy air, denoting this the gateway to that tropical land where perpetual summer reigns. In the winter months the air seems redolent with the odour of balsam and wild flowers, wafted over the waters by the constant breezes; while on either shore the foliage is bursting into freshest and tenderest green, contrasting finely with the dark verdure of the perennial laurels, live and water oak, and magnolia, which line the river's sides. The banks of the river are mostly low, and except where under cultivation in orange groves, vineyards, gardens, and small plantations, dotted along with houses, are densely covered with the primeval forests, live oaks, water oaks, bay, gum, magnolia, hung with the long waving drapery of solemn moss; while the beautiful palm, with its crested crown, sentinels its shores. Beneath and interwoven among these, are the wild jessamine and creeping vines, lacing the undergrowth over with an unbroken verdure, and rising from the water to the tree-tops. Then a dell appears, festooned with climbing and overarching growth, gracefully curtaining its entrance, and tempting the beholder within the half-hidden sylvan retreat : occasionally a broad savanna is seen, bounded by the distant forest, while here and there a solitary palmetto stands alone like a plume. Then we enter Lake George, which, with its islands, looks like a fairy land. Passing into the Upper St. John's, we are transferred from lagoon to river and from river to lagoon. On either hand glimpses are had of bays and mirrored waters, whose shores are covered with wild birds, of variegated plumage and beauty. Again the river seems lost in a bewildering perspective of silver streamlets, separated by narrow meadow land covered with flowers, but up them they are all verdure-banked and moss-hung, and vine-curtained, and flower-bedecked; the very picture of tropical profusion and summer loveliness. On these shores were the beautiful homes of those brave red men who were so cruelly hunted by the bloodhounds of General Jackson, the story of which is dark and cruel."

Travelling is a national characteristic in the American people. Show them a place of pleasure and attraction, and they flock—swarm to it. Florida is becoming a great national resort in the autumn and winter. It is stated that, during the winter of 1874, just passed, not less than 50,000 people from the United States, and a considerable number of foreigners, spent most of the winter in the valley of the St. John's. Upon the completion of the Company's water route through the Peninsula to Cuba, and a thorough equipment of fine, luxurious steamers to run over this route, this visiting population will travel up and down this beautiful water route.

From the United States' Bureau of Statistics, 1872 :—

" WIDE RANGE OF CROPS.—Usually, at least within the borders of the Union, whatever may be the attractions and inducements that are offered by any particular State or section, the immigrant will be confined within the comparatively narrow limits of the usual range of crops characteristic of that section; and the offer of even a slight enlargement of the usual range of ordinary crops would be recognised as an inducement of great power. Other things being nearly equal, if the immigrant have the option of continuing the cultivation of crops to which he is accustomed, or of reaching out to the peculiar productions of different zones, he will feel the force of the attraction.

" To a resident of Canada, or of the Northern or Western States, it seems hardly possible in any one locality, and then without the variation of temperature often given in the vicinity of elevated mountains, that there may be successfully cultivated within an enclosure of ten acres, the oats, rye, and wheat of Canada ; the peach, quince, and sweet potato of the Middle States; the coffee, indigo, and ginger of the West Indies ; the orange, the lime, and the lemon of Central America; the olive, the grape, the coffee, and the spices of the East ; the date and palm of the desert, and the sugarcane, pepper, tea, and silk of Asia; but the citizens of Orange, Sumter, Hernando, and Manatee counties in Flori la know that they can do this; and when to the above are added rice, bananas, plantains, guavas, cocoanuts, pine-apples, and paw-paws, the infinite range of the productions of Florida is made fully manifest.

" ABUNDANCE OF WATER.—The State is bountifully supplied with the best water in every part. Lakes, ponds, springs and rivers are curiously frequent, and no sections can be found where ample supplies of water cannot be obtained by wells of little depth and at slight expense. Springs of mineral and salt water abound ; some of great magnitude. In Wakulla county, the Wakulla River, a stream of very considerable size, bursts forth at once from a single spring. The Chipola river has a similar origin in Jackson county. Silver Spring in its first outburst forms a spacious basin, into which the Ocklawaha steamers find easy admission."

The field crops, garden, vegetable and fruit culture, are fully shown in the United States' Agricultural and Florida State Reports. For further details I refer to them, and will only give a short list here.

"AGRICULTURAL FIELD CROPS.

(NOTES FROM OFFICIAL REPORTS.)

" All the field crops, vegetables, and fruits that grow in the temperate and torrid zones will grow successfully in Florida.

" COTTON.—Product in 1860 was 63,322 bales. No State exceeds Florida in this production, either in quality or quantity per acre.

" 200 to 300 lbs. of short cotton per acre is a fair yield upon ordinary soils, but 300 lbs. is not an unusual yield on strong lands.

" The celebrated Sea Island, or long cotton, is raised all over the State: 200 lbs. is an average crop per acre ; but in the best soils 300, 400, and 500 lbs. is often obtained. *It is a perennial in the southern part of the Peninsula, and can be picked several times in the year.*

" SUGAR.—Florida is called ' the Sugar State.' The cane matures to seed, produces well from the rattoon for 5, 8, or 10 years, which is one quarter of the expense saved in its production. The ordinary yield per acre is nearly twice as great as in Louisiana. The rich lands already described yield three and four hogsheads per acre as against one hogshead in Louisiana. Some counties average 3,200 lbs. to the acre, worth $480 ; 2,500 lbs. is a common average.

"The *peach* attains its highest perfections in Florida. The tree is long-lived, vigorous, and bears every year a sure crop. Profits, from $500 to $1,000 per acre.

"*Pomegranates, olives, bananas, pine-apples, not excelled in quality and quantity on the globe. Profits very large per acre.*

"*Quinces yield a profit of* $1,000 *per acre readily. Quality excellent.*

"*Apples, pears, plums, apricots, nectarines, cherries, do well.*

"*Strawberries, blackberries,* mulberries, huckleberries, gooseberries, currants, cranberries, *excel.* Quality superior; bear long. *Strawberries yield a profit of* $500 *to* $1,000 *per acre.*

"*Sapodillo, tamarind, paw-paw,* plaintain, cocoanut, date, almonds, pecan-nut, all flourish, and yield large profits."

As examples of the description and mode of cultivation of these fruits and vegetables, in the Reports referred to, two examples are copied from the United States' Agricultural Reports, as follows:—

UNITED STATES AGRICULTURAL REPORTS.

THE BANANA (MUSA PARADISIACA).

"Of the banana and plantain (*Musa sapientum*) there are several species. They are increased by suckers, and require a rich moist soil with warm exposure. These plants are successfully cultivated as far north as Fernandino, in 30° 345′ north latitude. The best variety for cultivation north of 28° north latitude is the one known as *Musa paradisiaca Cavendishii.* This is the most hardy, and seldom attains a height above 8 feet, while the more tender kinds often grow 20 feet high. When the plant is fruiting, and all the flowers are set, it is advisable to cut off the spadix an inch or two above the last tier of perfectly formed fruit, in order to hasten and perfect the remaining fruit.

There are few more excellent or delicious dessert fruits than the banana, and, as a food plant, its importance and value, as compared with other food plants, can hardly be over-estimated. *When it is realized that a plantation of bananas once established has never to be renewed, and that 1 acre of this fruit will produce as much food as 130 acres of wheat,* or 45 *acres of potatoes, its value and importance will be readily acknowledged.* The fruit matures early in South Florida, each bunch aggregating from fifty to one hundred bananas. The banana returns to the soil in the decay of its gigantic leaves almost as much nutriment as it takes from it. No plant known produces the same amount of nutriment from the same space of ground, a fact which finds recognition in the opinion entertained of it by Oriental Christians, who at one time thought it the tree of forbidden fruit, as the banana alone furnished everything sufficient for the necessities of the first man. Chemical analysis shows that the fruit contains in proper proportions all that is necessary to sustain the human system in warm climates.

As this plant is a great feeder, and when once planted lasts a lifetime, it is of the utmost importance that plantings should be made upon strong, rich soil, or that the plants be kept highly manured, to secure permanent supplies of the best fruit. In Brazil and other tropical countries plantations are formed by setting the plants 20 feet apart. Plants of the *Musa paradisiaca* variety should be set ten feet apart each way, and they will soon cover the ground, as they increase rapidly under favourable circumstances.

Each plant produces one, and one only, bunch of bananas, when the stem is cut down with a sharp spade or axe, to give place to succeeding plants.

"When the enormous yield of this fruit is considered, and it is taken into account that when once properly planted it needs no other attention than simply gathering the fruit, and that at reasonable prices the demand is almost unlimited, it is evident that its extensive cultivation will be made very profitable."

A thousand dollars profit per acre can be readily realized.

UNITED STATES AGRICULTURAL REPORTS.

THE DATE PALM.

"This excellent and valuable fruit is cultivated with entire success south of 28° north latitude, and the tree often perfects its fruit as far north as 30° north latitude. Numerous large and beautiful specimens of this tree may be seen in the gardens at St. Augustine. It is one of the most beautiful trees of the vegetable kingdom. Its long, graceful, ever-verdant, ever-waving, ever-changing branches make it the most picturesque of all others for landscape gardening, and should adorn the grounds of every homestead in Florida. The fruit is greatly and justly esteemed by the inhabitants of Egypt, Arabia, and Persia, on account of its concentrated and nutritious properties; large numbers subsist almost entirely upon it. It is generally the sole food of the Arabs and their camels on their long and tedious journeys over the Desert, the voyagers feeding upon the fruit, and the animals upon the stones. The inhabitants of these countries also boast of the medicinal qualities of the date fruit, and of the numerous uses to which the different productions of this tree may be applied. From the leaves they make couches, baskets, bags, mats and brushes; from the branches or stalks, cages for their poultry and fences for their gardens; from the fibres of the trunk, thread, ropes, and rigging; from the sap, a spirituous liquor; and the body of the tree furnishes fuel.

"The date-palm is propagated from the seeds and suckers, but more successfully from the former. The cultivation of this fruit should be greatly extended, as it may become an important and profitable resource of the inhabitants of Southern Florida. The bunches or clusters of this fruit often attain a weight of 15 pounds."

GRAPES.

"The grape is the glory and crowning fruit of Florida; grows luxuriantly. In quality, for table and wines, has no superior in any country. The forests abound everywhere with delicious wild grapes. 'In the southern portion of the State two crops of grapes are gathered in a year.' No enemy attacks the vine or fruit. The following varieties grow to perfection:—

Scuppernong	Brincle
Black Hamburg	Diana
White Muscat	Warren
Concord	Catawba
Golden Chessalas	Isabella, &c., &c.
Delaware	

"*The profits are* $1,000 *to* $2,000 *per acre.*

"Yield 1,500 gallons wine per acre.

"FRUITS AND VEGETABLES A PERPETUAL GOLDEN HARVEST FOR FLORIDA.

"It must not be forgotten that every vegetable and fruit raised or grown in Florida has a ready-cash market in New York, Boston, Philadelphia, Baltimore,

Washington, and other Northern cities and towns, which will purchase all that Florida can produce.

"Let the fact be remembered that winter and EARLY FRUITS AND EARLY VEGETABLES ALWAYS COMMAND THE HIGHEST, AND OFTEN EXORBITANT, PRICES, AND THAT FLORIDA CAN POUR HER RICH FRUITS AND VEGETABLES INTO THESE MARKETS OVER FOUR MONTHS EARLIER THAN ANY OTHER STATE IN THE UNION, AND IT MUST APPEAR SELF-EVIDENT THAT FLORIDA HAS A RICH HARVEST, AND MUST HAVE IMMENSE INCOMES FROM THESE CONTINUING RE-SOURCES FOR ALL TIME TO COME, IN WHICH SHE CAN HAVE NO COMPETITOR. She has the exclusive market for all these for full four months in each year, while one-half of the States are bound up in ice and snow, and she can supply her vegetables all the year round. Say nothing of her staple productions, and let her rely only on her forests, fruits, and vegetables, her future riches from her soil will exceed any other State in the Union.

"CATTLE, HORSES, HOGS, AND SHEEP.

"Cattle raising in the State is easy work. Green, rich pastures, growing all the year, abound through-out the State. The prairies and forests are in many places covered with immense herds of cattle. All that is required is to brand your cattle, and keep your herdsman.

"The fine Durham and other choice breeds flourish there.

"Many single owners have from 20,000 to 40,000 head of horned cattle.

"The export is over 200,000 head per annum.

"Horses and mules do well, are scarce, and very high in price. Great profit lies in raising them in this State.

"Sheep do well. The wool and meat are of good quality.

"Hogs can be raised ad libitum. The State is full of tame and wild hogs. Nuts, roots, and grass are their food, on which they grow fat. Pork is of fine quality. There is a large annual export of hogs.

"Compare stock-raising in Florida with the Northern States. In the North, food must be raised by the farmer to feed his flock full six months each year. In Florida, the required food grows spontaneous all the year. The profit in stock-raising in Florida is immense.

"OYSTERS AND TURTLES.

Indian River, Biscayne Bay, the Channel to Key West, and the whole sea-coast around Florida, contain an inexhaustible supply of oysters of excellent quality. There is no part of the world known where they propagate so rapidly.

"The oyster trade and consumption of the United States has become immense. $85,000,000 are annually expended there in the purchase of oysters in the shell at wholesale.

"In 1872 the coast of Virginia shipped to the Northern cities 30,000,000 bushels of oysters, for which $30,000,000 were paid. The supply is falling off fast and prices augmenting in proportion. Florida can supply the United States with good oysters and first-class turtle, which are now being shipped in con-siderable quantity to New York. These make the finest soups, stews, and fries. Large incomes will be realised by this Company and the people of Florida, who will engage in the shipment of these luxuries to the Northern cities.

"FISH.

All the creeks, rivers, lakes, bays, channels, and sea-coast of Florida seem to be alive and swarm with fish of the most noted and superior varieties, such as the mullet, bass, trout (of fresh and sea-water), perch, Spanish mackerel, shad, sheepshead, and many other kinds. Mr. Adams assert in his book, that 'fisheries are established all along on the Gulf coast. 'Probably no river on the globe of equal size affords an equal supply of good fish for food for man as the St. John's. This will also become another vast source of profit to Florida.

"WILD GAME.

"Florida is said to be ' the paradise of the hunter.'

"Deer, bear, turkeys, squirrels, rabbits, ducks, geese, brants, snipe, woodcock, pheasants, partridges, quail, and other birds and animals, exist in great numbers and quantity in the State.

"' Deer are abundant.' Indeed, the whole State used to be called 'a vast deer park.' The woods abound with wild honey. Domesticated bees are worth a dollar per hive, and are profitable. Honey is worth 60 cents per gallon.

"Thousands of Northern people go to Florida annually to enjoy the rich sport of fishing and hunting, and the history of their sports is often interesting and even thrilling.

"This meagre sketch must suffice. Consult the books for full details. They are worth a perusal to any one interested in that novel country.

"It must not be inferred that Florida is an Eden, and that all one need do is to go there, sit down, and receive God's natural blessing without efforts. It requires faithful toil, good judgment, and great perseverance there as elsewhere, to make a good living or to become rich."

The United States Agricultural Report for 1862, gives an interesting description of the climate, soil, forests, and productions of Florida.

EXTRACTS.

"The whole State is diversified with beautiful lakes and ponds, abounding in fish and fowl of various kinds, and of the most delicate flavor, and can support a population of 100 to the square mile, with one-half the labor required to live in the Eastern or Middle States."

"A large portion of the country is covered with Pine-forests, the trees standing at a considerable distance apart, without under-growth; grass and flowers spread luxuriantly over the surface of the earth during the whole year, and being unusually intersected with streams of pure water; cattle find excellent pasture all the year. The pine lands, though often termed "barrens," is in most instances not less pro-ductive than the numerous live-oak and other hard timbered hummocks of the richest soil, so finely adapted to the culture of sugar, cotton, tobacco, corn, rice, indigo, and fruits. Limestone and marl underlie pretty generally the whole Peninsula."

"It produces the long staple or Sea Island cotton of commerce, over any part of the Peninsula, with a pro-ductiveness surpassing the coasts of South Carolina and Georgia, to which this staple has been hitherto limited, and can supply any quantity of it required, to which the consumption will reach.

"It produces sugar with great advantage over Louisiana and Texas, having a superior climate for the cane, and has sugar lands enough to supply the con-sumption of the whole United States."

"Cuba tobacco is, next to sugar, most in favour with planters. The flavour is thought to be not inferior to the production of the famous district of Vuelt de Abajo, in the island of Cuba. The sandy soil near the sea-coast is well adapted for this production. Ordinary seasons give three good cuttings from the same stalks. 700 pounds is an average crop to the acre, which, when Virginia and Kentucky tobacco would not bring more than 6 cents, readily sold in the market at from 50 to 75 cents per pound."

"Rice is a valuable crop. Pine lands, upon which cattle have been herded for a few weeks, have often pro-duced 60 bushels of rice to the acre. With one month's labour, one hand, with a horse and plough, can cultivate ten acres of rice."

"Indigo was the principal staple of the Florida planter during the British occupation of the country. Except sugar, this is the most certain crop in Florida. It is indigenous to the country, abounding in the pine barrens, and even in the old fields cultivated by the British nearly a century ago, in spite of time and the constant cultivation of other crops."

"The climate is the best in the world for the pro-duction silk. Every species of mulberry grows there. The cochineal insect is a native of Florida. 'The uopal, on which the insect feeds,' is also a native plant."

"Corn is the most important article of food in a southern climate. To the negro it is indispensable. Although Florida lies south of the corn-growing belt, very good crops are, nevertheless, produced in the State. 40 bushels to the acre is often gathered on the best land, but from 10 to 15 bushels is the average crop."

"The sweet potato and the yam find in the Florida pine land their natural soils. 400 bushels are often produced to the acre. The common potato produces a good crop, if planted in the winter. Cabbages planted in November grow to a great size. Mellons, squashes, and pumpkins are produced with indifferent culture, and are of delicious flavour. Peas, beans, and indeed all the garden vegetables of the temperate or the torrid zone succeed perfectly well in Florida."

"Fruits are abundant and in great variety; figs are abundant and of the richest flavour; the quince, peaches, nectarines, and apricots succeed perfectly.

"The Florida Orange is larger and more aromatic than the Cuban. The pomegranite, the guava, citron, the shaddock, or " forbidden fruit," lemons, and limes are produced with ease, and everywhere abundantly.

"Wild plums and grapes are in great variety. Some of the cultivated species of the plum produces two crops annually.

"The pine-apple and banana are cultivated with great success. The olive and the tamarind are growing in many places. Arrowroot is a profitable crop. The pistache was greatly cultivated by the Seminoles. This vine produces a large crop on sandy land; it is a native of Spain, whence it was transferred to the gardens of Italy. Grasses are numerous and nutritious; there are few spots of uncultivated land not covered with grass. Deer as well as cattle, in vast herds, fatten on the wild grasses of the forests and prairies.

"As the opinion has been very widely disseminated that Florida is composed of swamps and overglades, or sandy plains and barrens, a brief description of her lands will be interesting to the agriculturists generally, and particularly to those who desire to produce in our own country almost everything which our comfort or our luxury draws from other countries."

(Here follows a description of the different soils,

similar to that already hereinbefore given in the body of this Report.)

"There is one general feature in the topography of Florida, which no other country in the United States possesses, and which affords great security to the health of its inhabitants.

"It is this: that the Pine lands, which form the basis of the country, and which is almost universally healthy, are nearly everywhere studded, at intervals of a few miles, with hummock lands of the richest quality. These hummocks are not, as is usually sup-posed, low, wet lands; on the contrary, they are high, dry, and undulating, and never require either ditching or draining. They vary in extent from 20 acres to 20,000 acres.

"Hence the inhabitants have it everywhere in their power to select RESIDENCES in the Pine lands, at such convenient distances from the hummocks, as will enable them to cultivate the latter without endangering their health, if it should so happen that any of the hummocks prove to be less healthy than the pine woods.

"Indeed, it is found that residences in the hum-mocks themselves are generally perfectly healthy a few years after they have been cleared.

"Newly cleared lands are generally attended with the development of more or less malaria. In Florida the diseases which result from such clearings are usually of the mildest type (simply intermittent fever), while in nearly all the other Southern States they are most frequently of a severe grade of bilious fever.

"A general interspersion of rich hummocks, sur-rounded by high, dry, rolling, healthy pine woods, is a topographical feature peculiar to Florida, and forms in this respect a striking contrast with Louisiana, Texas, or Mississippi, whose sugar and cotton lands are generally surrounded by vast alluvial re rions, subject to frequent inundations, so that it is impossible to obtain a healthy residence within many miles of them."

NOTE (B).

The following important private letter was called out by several English-lumber houses. Mr. Little is entirely reliable, a large dealer in American lumber, and his opinions are entitled to full respect and con-sideration :—

"THE TIMBER QUESTION.

"Sirs,—I find, in conversing with the timber mer-chants of Liverpool, Glasgow, and this city, on the subject of timber, that the question of the supply for any lengthened period is one to which they have given but little thought, and, indeed, this is not to be won-dered at when it is found that the people of the United States and Canada, who are more immediately con-cerned, have, I might say, only now begun to reflect on the question; and that mainly through the instrumen-tality of one of the oldest lumbermen in Canada, who brought the subject to the notice of the public in a communication presented to the National Board of Trade Convention, held at Chicago in October last, which was published, with other subsequent letters on the subject, in the American and Canadian press; and I now see that the President has just sent to the Senate and House of Representatives a memorial upon the cultivation of timber and preservation of forests, heartily approving thereof, and asking that a commission be appointed to ascertain what means can be adopted to provide against their waste—a course, I may remark, that should have been taken years ago.

"It appears you are now getting large supplies of your best timber from Canada and the United States, but from the rapidity with which we are stripping our forests for our own requirements, it is quite evident to my mind that ten years will not have elapsed before we will be forced to enter into competition with you as purchasers in the North of Europe, since the only extensive pine territory we can then have will be that on the Pacific side, and this source of supply is so far away from the points of consumption, that it would be cheaper to get it from this side of the Atlantic.

"The annual consumption of pine lumber alone in the United States is now over 16,000,000 loads. The amount of all kinds of sawed lumber, according to the Congressional returns for the year ending 30th June, 1870, was over 21,000,000 loads, to which, if we add the large increase which has taken place since that time, all descriptions of timber, round, flatted, and hewn, the timber used in the manufacture of shingles, the import of timber from Canada; the present annual consumption should not now be computed at less than 30,000,000 loads, or an amount more than double all the sailing tonnage of Europe and America combined.

"From the foregoing some idea may be formed of the position in which we will be placed in a very few years, for an article to us so indispensable, considering that the greater part of our country is prairie and treeless. Indeed, the vast country drained by the Mississippi and comprising more than one half the entire territory of the United States, has not been inaptly described by a writer on the subject as a huge farm with a very small grove in its north-east corner; and if you will turn to a map of the United States when investigating the matter, and compare the immense area of prairie lands included in the States in that section, as hereinafter mentioned, with the timber area in Michigan, Wisconsin, and Minnesota, you will readily see the correctness of this remark.

"The Eastern, or New England States, comprising Maine, New Hampshire, Vermont, Massachusetts, Connecticut, and Rhode Island, and the Middle States of New York, New Jersey, Delaware, Maryland, Pennsylvania, Ohio, and Indiana, were at one time dense forests, and within a few years most of them had large tracts of the finest pine timber. These States are to-day almost destitute of that wood, and, indeed, Maine alone excepted, have but little of any kind now left, and at the present time they are sawing up all kinds of timber, and are compelled to purchase largely from Michigan and Canada to supplement their almost exhausted stock.

"To the south of these are the States of Virginia, North Carolina, South Carolina, Georgia, Florida, Alabama, Mississippi, Louisiana, Arkansas, Tennessee, and Kentucky, having yellow and pitch pine and cypress, all valuable woods, and when it is considered that many of these States are among the oldest in the Union, having been lumbered on for very many years, and are steadily undergoing depletion both for home consumption and exportation of these timbers and hardwoods, there can be but little left to dispose of for any great length of time. The whole eleven produced less sawed lumber in 1870 than the production and consumption of the single State of Pennsylvania, or little more than one half the production of Michigan.

"West and north-west to the Rocky Mountains we have Texas, New Mexico, Arizona, Colorado, Kansas, Nebraska, Dakota, Eastern Montana, Illinois, Iowa, most of Missouri, that part of Minnesota west of the Mississippi, and the southern part of Wisconsin, all chiefly prairie, and an almost treeless territory. This whole Western World, as it might be called, together with the New England and Middle States above referred to, are now dependent mainly for lumber and timber on the small amount of white pine still remaining in the State of Michigan and the north-eastern portions of Wisconsin and Minnesota, the whole estimated under 170,000,000 loads.

"On the Pacific side there is Washington and Oregon, which alone have timber to spare, and which they are now distributing to the South along the whole western coast of North and South America, the remaining States of California and Nevada having only about one-fifth part timber, or an amount hardly sufficient for their own requirements.

"There is to the North of us the Dominion of Canada, which is supposed by some to be an endless or unbroken forest, when there is not one-tenth part of it forest of any kind. British Columbia on the Pacific side, which is entirely beyond our reach, may have timber to spare. Then there is the Sashkatchewan Valley, with an extent of country principally prairie, large enough, it is said, to make thirteen States the size of the State of New York. Next comes the Red River country and Manitoba, without timber to any extent. Then the rocky, barren district north of Lakes Huron and Superior. Here we reach the present province of Ontario, formerly Canada West or Upper Canada. This was truly a magnificent forest country, probably unsurpassed on the face of the globe, abounding in the finest pine, oak, elm, ash, walnut, and whitewood to be found anywhere, but the most of this timber was burnt off to clear the land for farms, or used for buildings and fences, and a large amount of that remaining has been otherwise used up or exported; so that to-day the oak, ash, elm, walnut, and whitewood are about gone; the oak which now leaves Quebec is principally from Michigan or Ohio; the walnut and whitewood you get are from Indiana, Ohio, or some other Western State; the pine would have been burnt off, too, in the same way, but for the difficulty of clearing the lands, owing to the number of trees and the greater amount of timber to be got rid of. The pine timber has of late years had a commercial value for our markets, but it is only within a few years that anything but that known to you as first quality white pine deals would bear the cost of transportation. To-day the culls or refuse are dealt in by us in New York as regularly as any other quality of the wood. This province of Ontario is at the present time using improvements, and excepting, perhaps, that part of her pine bordering on the Ottawa and its tributaries, she would be acting only prudently by retaining every remaining stick for her own use.

"Now we come to the Province of Quebec, which, fortunately for us, is so near at hand, that our State of New York is its natural market, and on the banks of the Ottawa and St. Maurice Rivers and their tributaries lies nearly the whole wealth of pine timber to spare in the Dominion of Canada east of the Rocky Mountains; and let us now consider how long these two streams can stand the constant drain on them for timber for your market, our market, the markets of South America, and the consumption of the Province itself. From these you get almost your whole stock of Quebec deals and white pine timber; we get a large amount of pine boards and timber; heavy shipments are constantly going to South America and elsewhere; and then there is the requirements of the Province itself, of no inconsiderate amount. The spruce district is confined chiefly to the Lower St. Lawrence, the St. Francis District or Eastern Townships, and the Provinces of New Brunswick and Nova Scotia; and when it is seen these pine and spruce sections have been worked upon for years, both for export and for home consumption, many of them the greater part of a century, we need not be surprised, when advised by those who prof se to be well informed on the subject, that the pine yet remaining in the Provinces of Ontario, Quebec, Nova Scotia, and New Brunswick, would not afford a full supply of timber to the United States alone for a period of three years.

"It is often remarked that timber will soon be getting scarce. It has now reached that point. It is to-day exceedingly scarce. As an evidence of this fact, I find from an editorial in the *Quebec Chronicle*, of March 5, the statement that, owing to a lack of snow, and difficulty in obtaining money for operations, Canada and the United States have got in but from one-third to one-half their usual stock of lumber the past winter, and, as a consequence, lumber is rapidly rising in price in the Western markets. There is no doubt that the above-mentioned causes have operated to some extent in curtailing the production; but can anyone fancy, with deals selling higher in this market and Canada than ever before, that only one-half a stock would be got out if timber was abundant? Attribute the circumstance to anything—a scarcity of snow, a scarcity of money; but why ignore the prime cause—a scarcity of timber?

"The State of Michigan, owing to its formation, being two narrow peninsulas, with extensive rivers running through them in all directions, and having a comparatively even surface to work on for lumbering, is enabled by the assistance of railroads, which penetrate the forests in all directions, to get out the enormous amount of about double the entire Canadian production; but were it not for the help of these roads, it would be simply impossible to do so—the water could not float the logs to market. This is truly burning the candle at both ends. A few years will end the matter. Imagine one section—Saginaw—increasing its production of sawed pine lumber from 222,500 loads in 1863, to over 1,000,000 loads in 1873, and this has been but little over the proportionate increase of the whole State, for the value of lumber sawed in 1870 was more than four times that sawed in 1860, and the production of this State (Michigan) in 1872 amounted to 5,000,000 loads, principally sawed white pine deals and boards.

"As the question is so frequently asked of lumbermen, why they ordinarily only mention pine or spruce, when speaking of the amount of timber on timber lands, I would state that these are with us the great commercial woods; also being light, and easily floated down the streams, they can be taken with little expense from the most remote sections of the country, wherever water-courses exist.

"To show how little thought is given to the subject of timber I am almost invariably asked by gentlemen on this side the Atlantic if the timber lands are generally good for agriculture—which of course most of them are—usually the better the timber the better the land; but fancy the question addressed to a proprietor of coal lands asking him the value of such lands for growing turnips. In our country, lands with good timber are now considered of more value than those cleared for agriculture, and the time is not far distant when a few acres of wood land will be worth entire farms, with all their improvements. Corn or turnips may be grown in a season, but it takes a century to grow a standard pine saw log.

"In conclusion, Sirs, in view of the question as above presented, it might be asked, what would be the state of the public mind of this country if assured the coal supply would be exhausted in some ten or twelve years? The timber supply in North America is a matter of almost as much consequence to us as that of the coal supply in Great Britain to the community here; and

yet, notwithstanding we are on the very eve of so terrible a calamity as its total exhaustion, a calamity in which both this country and Canada must also suffer, hardly a thought is given to the subject, except by a few, who, in view of the great advance which must take place in the immediate future, are now investing largely in timber lands.

"I am, Sirs,
"Your obedient servant,
"WILLIAM LITTLE,
(Canada).

"To Charles Heaven, Esq.,
"and Others, London, March 30th, 1874."

The fact has been established in America, that in the event of the rapid destruction of American forests and enormous consumption of timber and lumber being continued at the same ratio of increase for the next twenty years as during the last twenty years, that there will be no native forests left—perhaps even before the end of this period.

The Federal and most of the State Governments have taken active steps for the preservation of forests, to prevent their rapid destruction, and to promote the cultivation and growth of new forests.

The President of the United States addressed a special message to Congress on this subject, and the Congressional Committee on Public Lands made an elaborate and exhaustive Report, No. 259, in 1874, in answer, and reported a Bill to Congress for the passage of a law, headed with this preamble:—

"Whereas it is established that the supply of timber within the United States is rapidly diminishing, and that great public injury must result from its continued waste, unless adequate means are taken for its preservation and production; Therefore,

"Be it enacted by the Senate and House of Representatives of the United States of America, in Congress assembled," &c.

Extracts of testimony taken from this Congressional Report shows that:—

"The great forests of the Western States are fast disappearing; the most of those of the Middle and Eastern States went long ago. In the whole United States but one vast tract of timber is left untouched. That covers about one-half of Washington territory and one third of Oregon. Here the yellow pine thrives in great perfection, some trees reaching 300 feet in height.

"The demand for lumber increases in the United States at the rate of 25 per cent. per annum. *The decrease of forests is at the rate of 7,000,000 acres annually. Few people have any idea of the immense va ue of the wood which is used for purposes generally considered unimportant. The fences of the United States are now valued at $1,800,000,000, and its costs annually $98,000,000 to keep them in repair. By far the greatest proportion of these are wood. The railroads of the United States use over 150,000,000 of ties annually, costing from 50 to 80 cents each, and these have to be renewed once in every seven years. In 1871, 10,000 acres of forest were stripped of their timber to supply fuel for the single city of Chicago.*

"In twenty years scarcely anything will be left of the vast forests of Wisconsin, Michigan, and Minnesota, and too late our farmers will see how short-sighted they have been in not making provisions for supplying the*

great demand for lumber which this wide-spread destruction is certain to cause.

"The annual products drawn by the people of the
United States from the forest exceeds $1,000,000,000,
or eight times the interest on the National Debt. This
being the case, the preservation of . our forests is a
matter of general interest and of national importance.

"To save our timber, we must not only cut no more
than is necessary, but cut it in a proper and economical
manner. We must stop the merciless waste and
primitive method of chopping with axes, and use saws,
scientifically.* The forests of Europe are protected
by law, and the removal of their timber is carefully
and economically performed.

"Not to speak of the decrease of moisture and
other climatic changes superinduced by removing
trees, let us look at the matter of low aspect, and compute the profit and the loss.

---

* To cut 100,000,000 cords of wood with the axe requires as many
days' labour and as many dollars ; if the use of hand cross-cut saws be
substituted, and only one-half the labour saved, the 50,000,000 now
thrown away are gained, besides the immense waste of fuel, making in
the two items of annual saving an amount equal to the interest of the
National Debt.

"Probably not less than 30,000,000 of the people of
America are warmed by wood fuel, consuming more
than 100,000,000 cords per annum, anyone knowing
the prodigal use in our newer timbered districts will
certify. If mills, railroads, and steamboats consume
one-third as much, reckoning the cost at $3 per cord, we
have $400,000,000 annually for fuel alone. An equal
consumption of timber for fencing, and a vast amount
for wooden buildings of all kinds, give the enormous
aggregate of $1,200,000,000 annually produced by our
forests for consumption.

"When we consider the fencing and farm buildings
required by our more than four million farms, if
reckoned at $150 annually to each farm, making
$600,000,000, and when all the uses of wood are
considered, few men who have travelled will deny that
more than $1,000,000,000 in products is derived from
our forests annually—five times the production of our
pig-iron, and twelve times our production of gold and
silver. Indeed, few single interests exceed in value the
enormous productions of our forests." (See Full Report of the Congress of the United States.)

FREDC. C. MATHIESON, Printer, Bartholomew House, Bank, London, E.C.

PART SECOND.

"EAST DIVISION" OF THE SHIP-CANAL,

AND THE

GREAT TIDE-WATER-CANAL ROUTE

FROM THE

PORT OF FERNANDINA, THROUGH THE PENINSULA

TO THE

PORT OF KEY WEST AND TO CUBA.

THE PROPOSITION

Is, to first complete the construction and equipment of this branch of the enterprise, and thereby increase the incomes and earnings to an amount sufficient to make the first Mortgage Bonds and Capital Shares proposed to be issued desirable investment securities at par, and enable the Company to readily realise all the money required to fully complete and equip the whole enterprise.

SOURCES OF INCOMES AND EARNINGS.

1. From sales of the Company's domain of 2,300,000 acres of land (valued at $30,000,000) for agricultural and horticultural purposes, and town and village building lots, &c., &c.
2. From the sales of timber and lumber on the Company's lands, valued at $16,000,000 net.
3. From canal tolls on the works completed, and to be completed on this division.

All these resources will be fully shown after necessary preliminary considerations.

CONSOLIDATION.

The two canal enterprises, their property and rights, have been legally consolidated, in conformity to the provisions of the "Act" approved, February 19, 1874.

The objects and great advantages resulting from this consolidation are self-evident.

Both canals, from their junction in the St. John's River, run thence over the same *route* and improvements to the Port of Fernandina, and by this action are brought under the same ownership and management. The Company of the Great Tide-Water Canal Route was the legal owner and possessor of the 2,300,000 acres of land, and other property of great value, and they furnished a solid foundation for raising

the money to complete the construction works; and, finally, this Great Tide-Water Canal Route is of itself one of the most important commercial enterprises in America, and its financial results must prove satisfactory to the capital required for its construction.

THE CHIEF COMMERCIAL ADVANTAGES
ARE—

1. It will promote and facilitate international commerce and direct trade between the United States and the West Indies, Central America, and South America. It will open up a land-locked, short, safe steam route to Key West, and thence across the Channel to Cuba and Havana, and will avoid the long, circuitous, and dangerous navigation through the Straits of Florida. It will utilise this magnificent system of inland tidewaters and tributary lakes and rivers, and always afford the cheapest transportation facilities for the larger portion of the export, import, and internal commerce of the State.

2. The commerce of the United States with the West Indies, Central America, South America, and Mexico is over $272,000,000; Cuba already exceeds $172,000,000 per annum (see "United States Senate Reports, Transportation Routes to the Sea," p. 195); and this international commerce between the United States and the other nations named is rapidly increasing. So great is this commerce becoming, that a scheme for building the Great Southern Railway, through the Peninsula to Key West, is now projected, but if built it can never compete with this Water route.

KEY WEST is an important Ocean Port for International and State commerce. There can be no other possible water route through the Peninsula to Key West, and the importance of this route is seen to a great extent from the character of Key West, as shown from an English stand-point.

A 2

(The following is from the British Reports on Commerce and Trade of 1875, Part II., made by the British Vice-Consul at Key West :—

" AS A NAVAL STATION.

" Key West has long been one of the principal naval stations of the United States, and it is said to possess more advantages for the same than any other port in the union.

" 1st. For its susceptibility of fortifications.

" 2nd. For ease and number of approaches with all winds.

" 3rd. The difficulty of blockade.

" 4th. The ease in which supplies may be thrown in in spite of the presence of an enemy.

" 5th. Abundance of wood and water.

" 6th. *The facility of communication* with and deriving all the advantages *by water,* of supplies from the northern and southern sections of the Union, provisions from Louisiana, spars and live oak from Florida and Georgia, cordage, iron, canvas, powder, and shot, &c., from the north.

" 7th. *It commands the outlet of the trade from Jamaica, the Caribbean Sea, Bay of Honduras, and Gulf of Mexico.*

" 8th. It holds in subjection the trade of Cuba.

" 9th. It is a check to the naval forces of whatever nation may possess Cuba ; it is to Cuba what Gibraltar is to Ceuta ; to the Gulf of Mexico what Gibraltar is to the Mediterranean.")

3. On the full completion of this route the smaller ocean steam ships and coasting vessels carrying Gulf commerce can pass directly through this route to the North Atlantic, and avoid the heavy losses through the "Florida Pass."

4. In time of peace it will furnish the United States Government many facilities to provision her forts, carry her mails, naval supplies of ship-timber, lumber, stores, &c., at the cheapest freights ; and in time of war a land-locked channel, and secure passage.

5. This great tide-water Canal line, with the Ship Canal, will make nearly all the rivers and lakes of the State available for steam navigation. More than 1,500 miles of internal navigation, permeating every section of the State, will thereby become utilized to carry on a vast inland and export commerce. Much the heaviest commerce of Florida is on the Atlantic coast side. This coast south of St. Augustine is wholly impracticable to afford facilities to this commerce, which is bound, before many years, to increase to a great extent. The dangers from the coral reefs, rocks, sand banks, and currents of Gulf Stream will not permit shipping ports being established on this coast. Most of this commerce, both export and import, is now forced through the Gulf Stream and the Straits of Florida at an immense loss.

6. The surplus productions of the State are practically *all ocean commerce,* viz., timber, lumber, Sea Island and short cotton, sugar, tobacco, rice, Indian corn, live stock ; and to the North Atlantic cities will be furnished regularly the tropical fruits, winter and spring garden vegetables, melons, sweet and early Irish potatoes, fish, oysters, turtles, and numerous other valuable products, almost without limit, which can all be shipped direct on this route at the cheapest freights possible for all time to come, and without transhipments, and in the best condition for markets. The Northern Cities consume annually nearly $200,000,000 of vegetables and fruits, obtained from the temperate and tropical zones. Florida can supply all the winter and early vegetables, and the semi-tropical and tropical fruits, now so largely imported from the West

Indies, and Central and South America. (See United States Reports on this point, also *The Times*, and British Legation Report of Mr. Watson).

7. Italy is the charming climate and resort for the people of Europe. Florida is the Italy of North America, and when the severe winters set in, then the invalids and pleasure-seekers of the North flock to Florida, and an average of 50,000 to 60,000 visitors spend their winters in the valleys of the St. John's and Indian River, along the water line of this Company. On the opening of this line from Fernandina to Key West, this population will be constantly travelling on this most charming route of the world. This will bring immense and annually increasing revenues to this Company.

8. On the completion of these improvements the Consolidated Atlantic and Gulf Ship Canal Company will possess 630 miles of Canal and improved water-courses, on which the Company will collect tolls for the commerce and vessels that pass and repass over them ; besides, 870 miles of tributary rivers and lakes will pour their commerce through the Company's routes, as the only way to reach the ocean. This tributary commerce will pay tolls to the Company.

9. The area of Florida is about 60,000 square miles, or nearly equal to the area of the six New England States. She is capable of supporting a population of 10,000,000, and can then export surplus products of the soil annually of a greater amount in value than any other State in the Federal Union.

The ultimate amount of this State commerce may be properly measured by the annual commerce of the States of Ohio, Indiana, Illinois, Michigan, Iowa, or Missouri, which the official statistics show to be enormous.

LOCATION AND DESCRIPTION.

This Route commences in the harbour and bay of Fernandina, running thence southerly, and by the Company's canal, connecting with the St. John's River, near its mouth ; thence south-westerly up the St. John's River and Lakes to Lake Washington ; thence by short canal to Indian River, Musquito Lagoon, and Halifax River ; thence down Indian River, Jupiter Narrows, and connecting canal to Lake Worth ; thence down through Lake Worth and canal to New River ; thence southerly through New River and connecting canal to Biscayne Bay ; thence south-westerly on Biscayne Bay and Channel, Barns Sound, and Florida Bay to the harbour of Key West, on the Gulf of Mexico ; thence across the Channel to the City of Havana, in Cuba, 84 miles. Length of the route through the Peninsula, 450 miles.

The Company has extended its route from Indian River, by way of Halifax River, to the City of St. Augustine, and thence North into the St. John's River. This will make a straight route from Fernandina to Key West, nearly the whole distance of tide waters, by connecting canals. It possesses so many advantages that the additional costs become inconsiderate.

FERNANDINA HARBOUR.

The *Alabama Statistical Register* of 1871 publishes a description of this noble harbour, from the Report of Senator Yulee, of Florida.

" The port of Fernandina, next to Norfolk and Pensacola, is the best in the United States.

" The entrance to this port is easy with all winds ; the channels (of which there are three) are straight ; the harbour deep, varying from 20 to 50 feet, and almost completely land-locked ; the anchorage extension and the holding-ground of the best description. The deep-water line reaches close to the shore for a length of two miles, so that a continued wall, but little advanced from the line of shore, will give wharfage for two miles, with depth of 20 to 30 feet at low water, and warehouses can line the whole wharf-front. The entrance from the sea to the wharves is about two miles, and from the plateau of the town the approach can be observed seaward as far as the telescope can sight. The depth of water on the bar varies from 20 to 23 feet at low water, and high tide 30 feet."

The *Official Guide* of Florida of 1873, says:—

" This is the best harbour of the Atlantic south of Norfolk, and is spacious enough to shelter the fleets of the United States, and to admit over a good bar and through a straight channel, at ordinary high tide, all classes of ocean vessels. Its port, Fernandina, is a small city, and, though stunted by the check its young growth received during the war, is now surely advancing towards its natural destination—the outlet for the products of the whole of Florida; the centre for its lumber trade and naval stores; and the Atlantic shipping port for the largest share of the Gulf commerce.

"From its insular position, Fernandina, fanned by the constant sea breezes, cool in summer and mild in winter, is entirely exempt from the malignant and contagious fevers that visit annually nearly all the larger and many of the smaller towns of the South. Thus she offers to the far-seeing capitalists the chance of building up a wide-spread and lucrative trade ; to invalids in search of health, a mild and salubrious climate ; and the pleasure-seeker will find in the fishing and hunting, in the shell road, and in her *unrivalled beach*, with its invigorating surf-baths, and its 15 miles of smooth, unbroken race track, sufficient attraction for a lengthy stay. With a liberal policy pursued by those who control her destiny, the future of Fernandina must be great and bright."

THE ST. JOHN'S RIVER.

The following short description of this great river is found in the Official Land Office Report of the United States Government for 1870 :—

" The numerous rivers of Florida afford great facilities for internal navigation, giving free access by steamers far into the interior, and rendering available extensive tracts of rich country, which would otherwise remain unsettled for many years to come. The St. John's River, the principal river of the State, rises in Lake Washington, and flowing in a *northerly direction*, through an *exceedingly level country*, empties into the Atlantic near the north-east corner of the State. For 150 miles from its mouth it has an average width of nearly two miles (in some places over five miles), *and is navigable for large sea-going steamers as far as Pilatka*, and for smaller steamers to Lake Washington. Many of its tributaries are also navigable for considerable distances, and it is estimated that this river and its branches afford 1,000 miles of water navigation."

The broad part of the river, for the distance above mentioned, is called the Lower St. John's, and the upper part, passing through a series of beautiful connecting lakes, to Lake Washington, is called the Upper St. John's. The Atlantic tide is perceptible to Lake George, and from Lake Harney, 250 miles to its mouth, it has a fall of only 3½ feet, showing the country is almost a *dead level*.

This river, from the junction of the Canal to its *débouchement* into the ocean, a distance of nearly 90 miles, may be properly considered as a vast bay and harbour of quiet, land-locked water, with anchorage

extension and holding ground of the best description, and of sufficient capacity to accommodate the combined navies and merchant ships of the United States, England, and France.

Here ships can lie in safety at nominal harbour dues, receive unlimited supplies of first-class coal from the near coal fields of Alabama at the lowest rates, make repairs, and receive other supplies. These are great advantages.

The balance of these waters to Key West, are described in geographies.

HARBOUR AND CITY OF KEY WEST.

The " Official Guide " of Florida thus describes this harbour:—

" The Island of Key West is about six miles long, and one wide. The City of Key West is situated at the westerly extremity, where there is a LARGE AND COMMODIOUS HARBOUR OF GREAT DEPTH OF WATER (from 30 to 70 feet deep), and of incalculable importance in a commercial point of view. It is the principal coaling station for the Gulf trade, an army and naval depot. The markets of New York, and other Northern cities, and Havana, are supplied from its port with immense quantities of fish, oysters, turtle, sponge, and numerous other commodities. It has a large commercial trade with the West Indies, Central and South America. It exports from Florida large quantities of lumber, timber, cattle, hogs, and sheep to Cuba. Five steam-ship lines—three from the Atlantic and two from the Gulf—trade regularly with its port. It also receives large amounts of imports, chiefly from Cuba and San Domingo. Fort Taylor is located here, and commands the entrance to the harbour. This is a fine structure, with castellated walls, bastions, and towers, mounted with 140 guns ; 30 15-inch Rodman guns are mounted on its massive walls. Along the beach, at intervals of a mile, are several martello towers of great strength ; and these, with Fort Taylor, give the island prominent features. There is an excellent ship route of deep waters from the harbour of Key West across the channel to the City of Havana, in Cuba, entirely free from keys, coral reefs, or sandbanks.

CHARTERS.

THE ATLANTIC AND GULF SHIP CANAL is ~~located, and its~~ corporate rights are derived, under an Act of the State of Florida, approved February 19th, 1874. (See Act and Charter, also legal opinion of highly respectable British solicitors of London on the same, hereinafter contained).

On the 28th day of July, 1866, the State granted a special charter, incorporating "The Southern Inland Navigation and Improvement Company of Florida," with liberal franchises, rights, concessions, and powers, thereby authorising and empowering this Company to connect the waters of THE GREAT TIDE-WATER CANAL ROUTE by a series of canals, aggregating twenty-five miles, also to improve these waters by dredging or otherwise, and to complete and perfect these canals, and maintain this route, build wharves and docks, collect tolls, construct and navigate steamers and other water craft; purchase, own, and improve real estate, with other rights, powers, and privileges full and complete.

Under this charter the Company organised and carried on these improvements. Since the American financial crisis, no work has been done for want of means to go on.

LAND GRANT ENDOWMENTS AND PURCHASE OF 2,300,000 ACRES.

In aid of the completion of these improvements, the United States Government and the State of Florida made liberal and very valuable land grants of 2,300,000 acres, located in the celebrated St. John's and Indian River Valleys, which have more than trebled in value since the financial crisis of 1873 in America. A full description and valuation of these lands are hereafter given.

Under the charter (Section 8) the Company has *the right of way through all lands owned by the State, and has the title to lands for four hundred feet on each side, on any of the Canals cut, or streams improved, as well as all lands that may be given to the State of Florida by the Government of the United States, to aid in any of the improvements contemplated by the Act.*

This is a most valuable property right owned by the Company on its line of 450 miles long. In addition to the great value of these belts of land, it secures a monopoly of the water frontage to the Company for the erection of wharves, fishing grounds, "boomage," and many other uses.

ESTIMATED COST OF CONSTRUCTION AND FULL EQUIPMENT OF THIS ROUTE.

State Engineer and Company's Engineers' Estimates $5,000,000
Sterling £1,000,000

Of this amount there is a margin of 25 per cent. for contingencies. A large portion of this amount was intended for constructing wharves, buildings, steamers, and other improvements authorised by the Charter.

WORK DONE.

Prior to the autumn of 1873, a large amount of construction work was done on the Great Tide-Water Canal Route, which, together with purchases of real estate paid for, amounted to the sum of $1,250,000. There are no debts, claims, or liens against the Company or its property.

CONSTRUCTION WORK TO BE FIRST COMPLETED. LARGE FINANCIAL BENEFITS WHICH WILL RESULT THEREFROM TO THE COMPANY.

1. To deepen and widen the Canal, which connects the St. John's River with the inside Tide Waters to Nassau Inlet, and the Port of Fernandina, &c. Cost not exceeding £50,000. (An expenditure of £20,000 will open this Canal for Ocean Ships to pass through). This will complete the "EAST DIVISION" of the Ship Canal into the Atlantic Ocean.

This work can be accomplished within six months.

The amount of export and import commerce which will pass through this "EAST DIVISION" the first year, will be safe to estimate at 1,000,000 tons net, which will pay Canal tolls—a minimum rate of one shilling per ton net, and will realize to the Company a net annual income of $250,000 from the beginning—*reimbursing the proposed outlay the first year.* Of course, after the construction of the "WEST DIVISION," the net earnings of the entire Ship Canal will be enormous, for which see full Report (p. 55.)

2. To deepen the channel, in places in the Upper St. John's River, for a distance of five miles from the outlet of Lake Washington, at a cost not exceeding £10,000.

This section, together with the work already completed, will open up to steam navigation the whole length of the St. John's River to its source in Lake Washington, which will then, together with "its branches, afford 1,000 miles of water navigation."

3. To construct the Canal, of less than six miles in length, which will connect Lake Washington with Indian River, and to remove several oyster banks in Indian River—cost £50,000. This improvement made, will establish steam communication with the whole of the celebrated Indian River Valley.

All these improvements can be finished within twelve months from the resumption of work; and they will complete 350 miles of the Company's Great Tide-Water Canal Route, extending from the Port of Fernandina to the south end of Indian River, and passing through the centre and entire lengths of the rich valleys of the St. John's and Indian Rivers.

(The remaining section to Key West should be completed the second year. For exact estimates of work and costs to complete that section, see the Estimates of the Engineers herewith submitted.)

COMMERCE OF THE ST. JOHN'S AND INDIAN VALLEYS, AND TRIBUTARY COUNTRY, &c., SHIPPED OVER THIS ROUTE ANNUALLY FROM THE COMPLETION OF THE GREAT TIDE-WATER CANAL ROUTE THROUGH THESE VALLEYS.

CHIEF EXPORTS.

The Annual Lumber product in 1869 *was* $10,000,000, *and in* 1875, $25,000,000.

300,000,000 feet of lumber, manufactured now by the twenty large saw mills on the St. John's, and from other additional mills on the tributary rivers, are exported from this region. Immense additional quantities of timber are squared and shipped in the log, to European and other markets. Also large quantities of live-oak spars, &c., for ship and boat construction, are exported in the log. Large as this commerce now is, its increase must become simply vast; for the United States Government declares that Florida is the best timbered State in the Federal Union—that four-fifths of its 60,000 square miles is covered with magnificent timber, &c.

A pretty correct idea of the importance and extent of forest products, to be transported over this route of over 1,200 miles of inland tide water, lake, river, and canal navigation, may be found by reference to the forests of the States of Pennsylvania, Maine, Michigan, Wisconsin, and other States, where all the rivers and numerous railways running through the timbered regions are almost exclusively employed in transporting the forest products of these States. It appears that the products taken from the forests of the United States amount to about $1,000,000,000 per annum, which shows the magnitude of the business (see United States Congressional Report on Forestry, 1874).

SUGAR, COTTON, TOBACCO, AND RICE.

The Government also declares officially that Florida is the best sugar and cotton State of the Union. Large quantities of all these staples are annually produced, and nearly all of them must find an outlet through this route.

CATTLE, HOGS, AND SHEEP.

Many of the stock-raisers of Florida are reported to own from 30,000 to 40,000 head of cattle a piece. All the surplus of this live stock will be shipped over this route. Large amounts of them are being now shipped to Cuba, and to other countries by circuitous routes.

OYSTERS, FISH, AND TURTLE.

It is officially declared by Government Reports, confirmed by all the authorities, " that 1,400 miles of seacoast around the Peninsula, prolific of oysters, fish, and turtles of excellent quality, almost beyond parallel in quantity, with bays, sounds, inlets, and inland navigable waters of an equal extent, offer the richest inducements to enterprise and capital." Large quantities of those are now shipped to foreign markets.

Indian River, for 150 miles long, by two to five miles broad, is almost literally full of oysters and turtles of the best quality.

The *wholesale* commerce of the Northern Cities, in oysters alone, amounts to about $65,000,000 per annum, of which the coast off Norfolk, Virginia, furnishes about 30,000,000 bushels, at a dollar per bushel — and the cry of scarcity of oysters has gone forth. Indian River oysters are highly prized for their fine flavor. From 10,000,000 to 15,000,000 bushels of these oysters, together with immense quantities of fish and turtles, will be shipped annually to the North and other countries over this route.

A large list of other products are also exported.—But

THE TROPICAL FRUITS, BERRIES, WINTER, AND EARLY SPRING VEGETABLES FOR THE MARKETS OF THE NORTHERN CITIES AND STATES, FORM FLORIDA'S ANNUAL GOLDEN HARVEST FOR TIME TO COME, IN WHICH SHE CONTROLS A MONOPOLY.

Under this head the reader is referred to the subsequent official and other evidence.

The consumption of fruits and garden vegetables in the Northern cities amounts annually to the enormous sum of over $200,000,000.

Florida can supply all the tropical and semi-tropical fruits, early berries, and garden vegetables for the whole winter and early spring, now so extensively imported from foreign tropical countries, and part grown in hot houses.

The immense profits in the culture of these products and the healthy climate of Florida have caused a large influx of population and wealth, chiefly into these valleys, and the commerce of the St. John's and tributaries is developing with great rapidity. (See the authorities quoted herein).

IMPORT COMMERCE.

The permanent population of the State is about 210,000, and the annual visiting population about 60,000 more, floating about chiefly in these valleys. Nine-tenths are operating in, or tributary to these valleys. In a country rapidly developing with capital, the importations must be considerable to supply the wants.

Now all the export and import trade of these valleys passes through the mouth of the St. John's River. The United States Government appropriates money to keep this mouth open. The shifting *quicksands* soon close up the channel over the bar, unless constantly dredged.

Upon the completion of the connecting Ship Canal between the St. John's River and the inside tide waters, all export and import commerce and trade to and from the North Atlantic Ocean will pass through the Company's canals and improvements, by way of the Port of Fernandina and Nassau inlet; and the mouth of the St. John's will be abandoned and closed to navigation; and all this commerce will pay tolls to this Company.

INTERNAL COMMERCE.

IN America, which is a new developing country, it is demonstrated that internal commerce over transportation Routes, is many times the amount and value of the through commerce; and more than the exports and imports together. (See United States Senate Report " Transportation Routes to the Seaboard." Vol. 1, pp. 84, 216).

The amount of local traffic is vast in all the States. In Illinois the local earnings on the 5,000 miles of her Railways is over 85 per cent. of the total earnings.

The value of local traffic *created* is also strikingly illustrated in the following case of the Pacific Railroad from Omaha to San Francisco, whose earnings (see the Report of General William J. Palmer, one of the most practical railway engineers and thorough railway managers in America, published in 1874) were as follows :—

" Gross earnings, $24,187,192, or about £4,800,000.
Net   ,,   13,504,838,   ,,   2,700,000.

" Its construction," he says, " has reversed, to a great extent, the course of the world's trade with the Indies, so that teas and other Asiatic merchandise now come from the West instead of the East, and England sends her mails to Australia by way of New York and California, *yet the bulk of the revenue of this railway is derived from local transportation, originating between the two termini of Omaha and San Francisco.* Immediately prior to the construction of this highway (in 1866), a single coach line, an occasional emigrant train from California, and the supply of the interior Government military posts, constituted the entire movement. Nearly the whole of this enormous transportation represented by the above figures was simply *created* by the construction of this railroad. It did not *exist before* and could not have existed till the railway was built."

There is scarcely an exception in all that vast Railway and River system of the Great Mississippi Valley.

It is declared in the United States Senate Report above quoted (on page 8) that " *the commerce of the cities of the Ohio River alone (a branch of the Mississippi River), has been carefully estimated at over* $1,600,000,000 *per annum.*"

The local commerce of Florida, for over a quarter of a million of people, moving up and down this great Tide-Water Canal Route, with its tributary rivers, affording over 1,500 miles of steam navigation, and all paying tribute to the Company's Canals and improve-

(8)

ments, must, of itself, pay large earnings from the beginning, and its increase will be in a geometrical proportion.

A very large item can also be made available by the Company, from *passenger carriage* (see full Report, p. 58) ; carrying the United States mails, and from freight transportation, on the Company's fine steamers and barges, as contemplated by the Company's charter, yielding a net income of over $500,000 per annum, and which can be increased to almost any desired extent.

From these details it seems clear that, from the present resources of the Company's lands and timber, and from the existing commerce shown and indicated, the Company's incomes the first year will be ample to pay all costs and charges for operating this enterprise, and pay the interest on the capital employed, besides leaving a large net surplus ; and that after the first year these earnings will aggregate an amount sufficient to bring about the results proposed for floating the Company's securities to construct the West Division of the Ship Canal enterprise.

Another fact must be borne in mind, that the absolute success of the " East Division and the Great Tide-Water Canal Route " in no way or manner depends upon the completion of the West Division of the Ship Canal.

ESTIMATED NET ANNUAL EARNINGS AND INCOMES FROM THE GREAT TIDE-WATER CANAL ROUTE, &c.

The costs for operating and maintaining will be less than 15 per cent. on the gross earnings.

Through freights, net	$1,000,000
From exports, imports, and internal commerce, net	2,400,000
From east division of the "Ship Canal"	250,000
Total net	$3,650,000

(*Note.*—The Erie is a horse canal of 363 miles long, and closed nearly half the year by ice. Its average annual net earnings from the beginning, for 26 years, was $2,302,940 from tolls alone.)

Add incomes from the sale and rents of lands	$500,000
From sale of timber and lumber ...	200,000
Total net ...	$4,150,000

These results will not be obtained the first year, nor perhaps for several years. But the certainty of their realisation at an early period is unquestionable. The costs for operating will be reduced to less than 5 per cent. of the earnings. Many railways and canals show much arger annual earnings, neither having anything like the advantages of location and surrounding wealth of this enterprise.

The Suez Canal derived, in 1875, a revenue from its domain of £34,000, or $170,000. The relative agricultural character of the Suez Canal lands, compared with the Company's Florida Canal lands, is like that of barren sand to a rich garden.

The *last two items* deserve consideration. *The incomes therefrom are immediate*, and the evidence quoted shows that enough lands can be sold now to realise $1,000,000 cash, and also a ready sale for the lumber and timber. These lands have doubled in value several times since the Company owns them, and they will do so again ; and their *increasing value* will more than repay all the capital required to complete the works, with the interest thereon. It is, therefore, financial policy to sell both gradually at fair and full rates.

The wisdom of this course is demonstrated in canal and numerous railway companies possessing land grants. The Illinois Central and other railway companies are quoted as illustrations of the rule.

It will also be seen from the estimates in the large Report that the incomes from these two items will be greatly increased after the west end of the Ship Canal is constructed. (Report, p. 55.)

The Company therefore proposes to borrow the present required amount of money for a reasonable time, and secure this sum by pledging or hypothecating its first Mortgage Land Grant and Franchise Sterling Bonds, or will sell the same ; and for that purpose the Company has created its

FIRST MORTGAGE 7 PER CENT. LAND GRANT FRANCHISE AND CONVERTIBLE STERLING BONDS. AMOUNT $5,000,000 OR £1,000,000.

Each bond of the denomination of $1,000 or 200 pounds sterling. Interest payable in gold coin of the United States, at the Agency of the Company, in the City of New York, or in English sterling, in the City of London, at the option of the holder, on the first day of May and the first day of November in each year, free of Government tax. Principal payable in the same way, on the first day of May, 1904, unless sooner redeemed by the sinking-fund allotment, or conversion into lands.

The mortgage provides that each "*Bond may at any* "*time be* CONVERTED *or exchanged by the holder thereof* "*into the Land* of this Company at par, upon the sur- "render of the bond with all the unpaid coupons at- "tached, at the then regular schedule prices named in " the mortgage."

The bonds are also entitled to the benefit of a sinking fund of one per cent. annually ; and after three years there shall be an annual redemption of said bonds, by lot, equal to the accumulations in the sinking fund. (See Bond and Mortgage).

A full description and valuation of the lands mortgaged and forming an absolute security for the payment of these Bonds, with other important facts will now be given.

The Company owns a vast and most valuable real estate, which forms a DOUBLE SECURITY—AN ABSOLUTE SECURITY OF ITSELF, WITHOUT THE CANALS AND THEIR EARNINGS—to pay every pound of the capital shares and bonded debt, and from this source leave a large margin of profits, exclusive of the canals and their earnings.

The Company is not without authority and precedent for coming to this conclusion.

The United States Government granted land endowments to the St. Mary's Ship Canal Company of Michigan, and to twenty-five railway companies up to 1872.

The Reports and Exhibits of these Companies, and Summaries of some of them published by the United States Government, are of real financial interest.

The St. Mary's Ship Canal Company obtained a grant of 600,000 acres. From the proceeds of sale of a portion of these lands the Company constructed the required improvements, and then turned the Canal over to the Government ; whilst, from further sales, the Company has paid its shareholders an annual dividend of 12 per cent. for the fourteen years last past, and still owns the most valuable part of the grant—

the present value of which is estimated at $4,000,000 cash. (See Company's full report.)

The annexed table shows the names of four of the railway companies above referred to, the average price per acre of the sales, and the rate per mile realised on their grants:—

Names of Companies.	Average per acre.	Realising per mile.
	$ c.	$
Grand Rapids and Indiana............	13 98	50,967⁵⁰
Burlington and Missouri River	11 70	15,000
Illinois Central	11 35	41,854¹¹
Hannibal and St. Joseph	11 00	42,500

The average price per acre received is $12. Most of these roads run through the timberless prairies, and these lands as a rule had no forests.

The real cost for construction of portions of these roads through the level prairies was only $15,000 per mile. Taking all the twenty-five companies and their grants—some running thousands of miles through the great American desert, destitute of both trees and good soil—the surface being covered with sand, sage-bush, and alkali; and taking a fair average of these lands, they will not compare favourably at all with the poorest and most indifferent lands of the Company; and yet the fact is officially published to the world—

"That the average price of all the sales made of all the land grants, good and bad, was over $7 per acre up to 1872."

For a fuller exhibit, take the case of the Illinois Central Railroad Company, which has a large share of its stock held in England, and is well known.

The Official Report by the United States of the result from this Company's grant is given and published in the Land Office Report of 1870, p. 209.

The Report says:—

"The aggregate amount of land donated under the Act was 2,595,053 acres, which, at the minimum Government price, was $3,243,750. The double of this sum represented the aid to be given thereby to the railway, viz., $6,487,500. The total of the sales made have realised to the Company an average of $11·85 per acre, amounting to $23,968,736. The balance undisposed of now averages $12·55 per acre, at which rate they will swell the actual pecuniary aid derived from the land endowment to $30,000,000, which is equal to the entire cost of the road and the equipment, entirely reimbursing the stockholders for their investment, while the profits remain undiminished."

Now, be it known that these lands were chiefly prairie, and not an acre of timber lands on the whole route. The lands are not better in quality, and can never bring as much net profit per acre from cultivation as the Florida lands. They are also farther off from the Eastern markets.

It is a fact not to be lost sight of that, as a rule, Land Grant First Mortgage Bonds are safer securities than the same Company's Franchise Bonds, inasmuch as they have a double basis of security—1st, the land and its values; 2nd, the liability of the Company, its franchises and assets.

American Land Grant Bonds are held in high estimation in America and Europe, and are now more sought after by investors than Railway Bonds.

The Union Pacific Railway Company's Land Grant First Mortgage Bonds command 97 to 98 per cent. cash in sterling in the London Market. They are esteemed as perfectly safe, and yet the fact is well known that the grants of this line are the poorest lands of any grant in America, destitute of timber, the larger part poor and unproductive soil, and the most remote from the markets.

The Company owns by grants and by perfect fee simple titles, free of all incumbrances ... ... 2,300,000 acres
And controls, and will obtain complete title to, further grants and purchases 6,000,000

Total acres 8,300,000

These lands are largely covered with valuable forests for all kinds of timber and lumber uses. The lands will return larger net profits per acre from agricultural and horticultural productions than any other lands in the United States outside of Florida, and they are handy to home and foreign markets. The State of Florida is also filling up more rapidly, both in regard to population and capital, than did the regions in which the above "Railway grants" are located.

VALUATION OF THE LANDS ON THE ABOVE BASIS.

8,300,000 acres at $12 per acre (being the average that has been realized by the four Companies referred to) ... $99,600,000

But 8,300,000, even at $7 per acre (official average of all Land Grant lands sold) $58,100,000

The Company has created £1,000,000 sterling Land Grant Bonds, and has secured the same by 1st Mortgage, covering 2,300,000 acres of the above lands, to which the Company holds perfect grants and titles. These lands are valued and scheduled in the mortgage by the State at $23,000,000.

With this solid property, the franchises and improvements in hand, the Company proposes to commence its basis of financing, the money to be applied first in completing the "East Division," and the balance of proceeds on the "West Division."

The following Government Official Reports fully describe the Lands of Florida and of the Company, their soils, productions, climate, &c., &c.

TITLES.—Parties desirous to purchase or loan money on real estate, must have reliable business evidence, showing the character, resources, and value of the property, and good titles.

The United States Government has, in this case, itself furnished this evidence.

The title to all the lands in Florida, except private valid grants, vested in the United States Government. Under Acts of Congress, the United States Government, through her official land surveyors had the Florida lands surveyed into townships, ranges, sections, quarter-sections, and 40 acre lots.

At the same time these surveyors also made topographical reports, showing the character, quality, and productiveness of the soils, the timber forests, and all other valuable resources on every tract so surveyed.

The Official surveys, maps, and topographical reports were filed and recorded, according to law, in the General Land Office of the United States at Washington. These officers are great experts, and possess accurate education, and these surveys and reports are made conclusive evidence, by which the United States

Government, the States, and the people are governed. Lands are sold and bought only on these surveys and reports.

Their accuracy is unquestionable.

The law further requires the Land Commissioners of "The General Land Office" annually to compile those topographical reports, surveys, and maps; and the United States Government publishes these annual volumes, called

"Land Office Reports."

These reports for 1868, 1869, 1870, 1871, 1872, 1873, 1874, contain the topographical reports, surveys, and maps of the Company's Lands, and furnish all the evidence desired.

The United States Government also issue annually, from the National Bureau of Agriculture, official evidence in volumes, called

"Department of Agriculture Reports."

These Reports furnish the highest evidence attainable on all the subjects treated of therein; and foreign Governments make frequent quotations therefrom as containing the best evidence on these subjects. As examples, see the British Reports on Commerce and Trade made by the British Legation Office and British Consuls in the United States, for frequent quotations. The volume of 1862 has an exhaustive report on the "Soil, Climate, and Productions of Florida"—the volume of 1867 on "Horticulture and the Fruits of Florida"; and the Reports of 1871, 1872, and 1873, are explicit on the productions and profits of farming in Florida, rapid increase of population, and the great rise in the price of lands, &c.

Further, we have the official evidence published by the State of Florida, in annual reports, from her Land Office Department, from the years 1869 to 1876, fully covering and elaborating the whole subject. (All the above reports are in hand for inspection.)

These reports impart reliable information on the climate of Florida, the variety and productiveness of her soils (yielding the largest variety of agricultural and horticultural productions of any State in the Union), profits in farming, planting, fruit and vegetable culture, the immense forests of Florida, large timber and lumber industries, live stock raising, fish, oysters, naval stores, and other important resources of the State, rapid increase of population and wealth, internal improvements, &c.

All these reports describe the Company's property and lands, soils, timber, and all other resources, and for greater assurance they are made a part of this statement.

QUOTATIONS FROM THESE REPORTS.

(For fuller description see also Appendix of the Ship Canal Report.)

"By far the finest lands in Florida, denominated ' Rich Lands,' are: 1st. The ' Swamp Lands;' 2nd. The Low and High Hummocks; 3rd. The Prairies, or ' Savannas;' and 4th. The first-class Pine Lands.

"The ' Swamp Lands' are unquestionably the most durably rich lands in the State; they are intrinsically the most valuable. They are formed entirely of humus, or decayed vegetable matter, of extraordinary depth, and, from long use in portions of the State, show evidence of inexhaustible fertility. They occupy natural *depressions*, or basins, which have been gradually filled up by deposits of vegetable *débris*, &c. Drainage, which is practicable, is, however, necessary to *render the greater portion* available for purposes of agriculture. In the United States Survey Reports they are called ' Marsh Lands : *the richest of all*. Alluvial deposits, full of decayed vegetable matter; indeed, most of them are little less than beds of peat. They only require to be drained to become inexhaustible mines of agricultural wealth; they furnish never-failing stores of muck to enrich thin pine lands; they will produce abundantly anything that can be put into them. But the great crop, and that which is destined to be one of the main interests of the State, and a great source of wealth, is sugar-cane. On these lands it grows luxuriantly, tasseling out at the top, which it does not do in other States.'

"It has been demonstrated that these lands will yield four hogsheads of sugar to the acre, a most convincing proof of their value. Sugar cane is here instanced as a measure of the fertility of the soil, because it is one of the most exhaustive crops known, and is generally grown without rest or rotation. It is, however, not the only criterion by which to judge of the *relative fertility of lands situated in different climates ;* for we find in the richest lands in Louisiana (the great sugar-growing State) the crop of sugar per acre is not more than one hogshead, or about one half that of Florida.

"This great disparity in the product of those countries is accounted for, not by inferiority in the lands of Louisiana or Texas, but by the fact that the early incursions of frost in both these States render it necessary to cut the cane in October, which is long before it has reached maturity, while in Florida it is permitted to mature without fear of frost. It is well known that it ' tassels ' in Florida, and it never does so in either Louisiana or Texas. When cane ' tassels,' it is evidence of its having reached *full maturity*." The words " Swamp " Lands may seem objectionable to people not informed. As has already been observed, immense amounts of the richest and highest-priced farming lands in America were once called "Swamp Lands," which have been drained. Fully one quarter of the State of Illinois has been thus reclaimed, and the United States Land Office Report of 1869 says :—

"It will be observed that originally fully one-third of what is now the State of Louisiana was in the condition of swamp, or overflowed land. Much of it has long been reclaimed, and under a high state of cultivation. Being an alluvial deposit, the lands, when reclaimed, became the most fertile and productive farms and plantations in the State, and have for many years yielded immense crops of cotton and sugar, and before the war commanded from $100 to $150 per acre in gold." (And will do so again.)

"Low Hummocks rank next, and are not inferior to the swamp lands in fertility, and, like them, consist chiefly of decomposed vegetable matter deep down. They are always moist, and some of them require drainage. They are always covered with a heavy growth of live, water, and other oaks, cypress, ash, gum, bay, cedar, &c., and when cleared and brought under cultivation they are very productive, and practically inexhaustible."

"The growth of trees, shrubs, and vines upon these low hummocks is most surprising, and so dense as to present an almost impenetrable vegetable barrier to all ingress. They are immensely fertile, indeed, almost incredibly so, as is sufficiently shown by the fact that from one acre has been produced 4,000 *pounds of sugar*, and other crops in proportion."

"**High Hummocks** are in the highest repute in Florida for purposes of agriculture. These differ from low hummocks in occupying higher ground, and in general presenting a gently undulating surface, covered with a heavy growth of great variety of lumber, of hard woods, already described, and composed of deep and rich soil, underlaid with marl, clay, or limestone. The very richest variety of hummock is the 'cabbage hummock,' so called from the cabbage palmetto trees, with which it is covered. These trees grow sometimes to the height of 100 feet or more, this soil being composed of shell and vegetable matter mixed, is of rare fertility." "It will be readily understood by anyone acquainted with agriculture, that such a soil, in such a climate as Florida, must be extremely productive. This soil scarcely ever suffers from too much wet, nor does drought affect it in the same degree as in other lands. High hummock lands produce, with but little labour of cultivation, all the crops in the country in an eminent degree. Such lands do not break up in heavy masses, nor are they infested with pernicious weeds or grasses. These lands are very abundant, whilst their extraordinary fertility and productiveness may be estimated by the fact that three, often four, hogsheads of sugar are made per acre, on lands which have been many years in constant cultivation."

"All these varieties of hummock are frequently enhanced in value by the presence of *wild orange trees*, sometimes singly, or in small groups, and again in large groves."

"**Prairie and Savanna Lands.**—The rich alluvials bordering on the streams, and known as Savannas, are subject to inundations, and are highly valuable for the production of sugar and rice. The low savannas, like the prairies of the more valuable portions, are mostly rich vegetable mould, or loam, like the rich prairies of Illinois; others have the appearance of clay, but upon close inspection, it is muck, mixed with marl.

"These lands are destitute of trees, but covered with luxuriant growth of nutritious, tall, perennial grasses, and of green savannas, covered with flowers, on which vast herds of cattle and sheep graze, both summer and winter, and grow fat without other food. Some of these herds are very large, as many as 30,000 to 40,000 head of cattle being marked by the brand of a single owner. These stock growers are amongst the wealthiest men in the State, and acquire it easier than those engaged in any other industry."

"**The Pine Lands** are divided into first, second, and third class.

"**The First-rate Pine Lands** in Florida have nothing analogous to them in the other States. The top is a deep, vegetable mould, beneath which, to the depth of several feet, is a chocolate-coloured, sandy loam, mixed for the most part with limestone pebbles, and resting on a substratum of marl, clay, or limestone. This land is also extremely fertile, producing splendid yields of all the most exhaustive crops for many years. Large portions have been cultivated in short cotton for many years, yielding from 500 to 1,000 lbs. of seed cotton, and some have produced 400 lbs. of Sea-Island cotton for fourteen consecutive years, and are still as productive as ever, so that the limit of their durability is still unknown."

"**The Second-rate Pine Lands**, which form the largest proportion of Florida, are all productive. They rest on a basis similar to that of the first-class. These lands afford fine natural pasturage, like the first-class. They are heavily timbered with the best species of yellow and pitch pine; they are for the most part high, rolling, healthy, and well-watered; they will produce the finest crops of Cuba tobacco, oranges, lemons,

limes, bananas, and other tropical productions, also Sea-Island and short cotton, sugar-cane, and every variety of garden vegetable, which make them more valuable than the best bottom lands in the Northern and Western States.

"The prevalent forest growth of Florida is yellow pine, and of course the soil may be in general characterised as 'light,' and is either sandy or loamy; but owing to peculiar climatic or atmospheric influences they are of far more intrinsic value where 'light' than is usually attributable to the same character of light soil at the North and West, as is evinced by the fact that a bale of cotton, or 3,000 pounds of sugar, have not unfrequently been made [from an acre of these pine lands. Indeed, many of the pine lands are so underlaid with marl or clay as to give all the strength of clay soils, without their stiffness and difficulty of cultivation."

"**The Third-rate Pine Lands**, or most inferior class, are by no means worthless; the greater portion of them is covered with valuable timber, and with luxuriant vegetation and good pasturage. A small portion is high, rolling, sandy, and sparsely covered with a stunted growth of 'Black Jack,' and some good pine."

"Besides the everglades, there is but a very small proportion of worthless lands, compared with any other State. There are no mountain wastes, barren plains, nor deserts, and the land with this soil, whilst it is unfit for the culture of cotton, sugar-cane, corn, and tobacco, may always be made available for the culture of different kinds of cereals, fruits, or vegetables."

"In the poorest pine barrens, the peach is a vigorous grower, and an abundant bearer, and the grape succeeds equally well. From the great and continually increasing demand for grapes and pure wine, for peaches, and other fruits, either dried, canned, pickled, or preserved, no more promising undertaking can be entered upon than the orchard and vineyard business in the pine districts of Florida. These fruits grow to great perfection on these lands. The most inferior class of these pine lands is the best adapted for the culture of Sisal hemp, which is one of the most remunerative crops produced in the State. It will yield this product, worth $300 per acre, with less cost than any crop that can be grown, and therefore these poorest lands in Florida will yield larger profits per acre than the richest lands of the Mississippi Valley can possibly produce from their staple crops."

"Every district in the State abounds with fertilizers of muck, marl, and phosphates in quantities sufficient to fertilize the poorer lands, when necessary, for ages to come."

Again, 1868 Report—"The great fertility of the soil is everywhere evinced by luxuriant crops produced, including those of the temperate and torrid zones, the latter predominating. Sea-Island cotton succeeds well in all parts of the Peninsular, with a productiveness rivalling the best portions of the coast of Georgia and South Carolina, while the sugar-cane thrives even better than in Louisiana or Texas, owing to the absence of frosts. The ordinary yield of sugar per acre in Florida is nearly twice that of Louisiana, and the cultivation much easier. The area in Florida suitable for the culture of this staple is amply sufficient to supply the demands of the United States. The sandy soil is well adapted to the cultivation of Cuba tobacco, which yields an average of 700 pounds per acre, and, in South Florida, admits of two cuttings per annum. Silk culture must become a leading branch of industry in Florida, since every species of mulberry grows profusely in this latitude as far south as 27°, and experiments in the production of silk have proved highly satisfactory. Indigo was formerly the principal staple of Florida, and, with the exception of sugar, is one of the most certain and profitable crops, admitting two cuttings annually. It is found growing wild throughout the State, and around old fields where a century ago it had been cultivated. *In this genial climate all the tropical and semi-tropical fruits, such as the orange, lemon, lime, olive, fig, citron, pine-apple, banana, guava, the palm, with all the other tropical fruits, are produced in as great perfection as in the more tropical climate of the West Indies, Central America, and Brazil, and with far less attention and greater immunity from injury by insects or vicissitudes of climate, than the common fruits of Northern orchards. These fruits are celebrated for their great size and superior flavour. Grapes thrive luxuriantly, and the peach is at home here.* Sisal and New Zealand hemp, jute, and all the cereal crops of the Northern and Western States, are grown here."

"Every description of garden vegetables of the temperate and the torrid zones is raised here with great success. Owing to the fact that vegetation grows all the year round, the winter vegetables required in the markets of the Northern cities can be supplied from Florida for four months each year, when no other State in the Union can produce them during this period. Tomatoes, peas, beans, cucumbers, potatoes, melon, cabbage, beets, asparagus, and, indeed, the whole list of spring vegetables, can be shipped to Northern ports, from two to three months earlier than from any other State; and both in respect to tropical fruits and the earliest garden vegetables, Florida possesses a monopoly of the markets for the northern cities over any other State, which must build up an industry of gigantic extent, and immense profit to the people of the State.

"Experiments made on the soil along the Atlantic coast, from Indian River to Cape Sable, embracing several millions of acres, prove the soil well adapted to the culture of coffee."

What is called Middle Florida possesses all the conditions of soil and climate for the production of the best teas, and tea will grow over the whole peninsular.

The superior climate of the State has much to do with the growth of all vegetation.

"The maximum temperature in summer is near 85° Fahrenheit, and in winter ranging 45°, rivalling the favourite climate of Italy."

The "Official Guide of Florida," by the Hon. J. S. Adams, says:—"The wealth of Florida *at present* mainly consists in her timber, and, as a consequence, the leading industry will for some time be the manufacture of timber. But as the forests give way the agriculturalist will push forward, and increase the crops of cotton, sugar, tobacco, rice, Indian corn, sweet and Irish potatoes; the gardener will grow the early and winter vegetables for the Northern market to an enormous extent; while the *fruit grower* will become a main element of prosperity to the future. No other State or country can present such an extensive list of fruits capable of being grown as Florida. And no State can exhibit a fruit grown on its soil which cannot be cultivated with more or less success here. The following is only a partial list of the fruits of the State:—Oranges of all kinds, lemons of every variety, limes, citron, mango, sour-top, custard-apple, cocoanut, shaddock, paw-paw, date, fig, peaches, nectarines, apricots, plums, plantains, *pine-apples,* sweet almond, bitter almond, pomegranates, maumée apple, sapodilla, alligator pears, cherries, apples, pears, tamarinds, guavas, grapes of great variety (the forests abound with wild grapes), currants, mulberries, strawberries of every kind in the greatest perfection, blackberries, dewberries, huckleberries, &c. In this list it will be seen that not only are all the fruits of the

northern latitudes represented, but many others in which the State enjoys a monopoly; add to this the water-melon, and the musk-melon, of the whole citrous family."

"*In the growth of the tropical and semi-tropical fruits Florida enjoys a monopoly which, when fairly developed, will make her one of the richest and most important of the United States. Oranges, lemons, pine-apples, bananas, and various other tropical fruits will yield an average profit of at least one thousand dollars per acre yearly.*" "*It is the adaptability of the climate to grow these productions that makes even the inferior lands of Florida susceptible of producing crops more valuable than those of the best lands in other parts of the Union. It is the appreciation of this fact that is awakening such an interest in the business, and bringing to our shores large numbers from nearly every State.*"

When the fact is borne in mind that the Atlantic cities and their contiguous population consume annually $200,000,000 of vegetables and fruits, including the tropical fruits and early vegetables imported from the West Indies, the Bahamas, and other tropical countries, all of which Florida can supply to meet the demands of the whole nation, it must be seen that this great and most profitable industry will be pushed forward to meet this immense demand, and that the fruits and vegetables of Florida will be produced and shipped on a scale beyond even our present conception

(UNITED STATES LAND OFFICE REPORTS, 1868, 1869, 1870, —UNITED STATES AGRICULTURAL REPORT, 1862— FLORIDA LAND OFFICE REPORT, 1869, 1873).

FORESTS.—TIMBER AND LUMBER.

Florida Land Office Report, 1868, says :

"Florida is, beyond question, the best timbered State in the Union. Out of about 38,000,000 acres, only some 3,000,000 or 4,000,000 is now included in farms; of the rest nineteen-twentieths (exclusive of the area covered by rivers and lakes) is covered with heavy forests. On all the least moist, and more level portions, the pine is the prevalent forest tree, either the yellow or pitch pine. It grows with great beauty, and attains a large size, furnishing some of the handsomest pine lumber to be found in the markets of the world. The extent of the pine lands and the possible amount of lumber that could be manufactured, would be almost incredible to one who has never visited Florida. There are probably more than 30,000 square miles of heavy pine forests within the limits of the State.

"In the moister lands, along the rivers and creeks, and on the margin and swamps, an almost indefinite variety of trees are to be found, of which the most valuable for timber and lumber are live oak, white oak, the hickory, the ash, the birch, the cedar, the magnolia, the sweet bay, and the cypress. Of all these varieties a great abundance is to be found throughout the State. Of pine of the best quality, of cedar, and cypress in particular, the supply for any purposes of manufacture may be said to be inexhaustible. *The larger proportion of what has loosely been called swamp in Florida, is simply low hummock, with a soil of inexhaustible fertility, and covered with a dense growth of mainly cypress, magnolia, and sweet bay.* The timber of the cypress more nearly resembles that of the northern basswood than anything else; can be used for all purposes to which basswood is applied, and for railway ties and sleepers, for durability, has no equal in any other variety of wood. It is more easily split than bass-wood; can be warped and bent into desirable shapes. For clothes' pins, for fork and rake and broom handles, and for pails and tubs, cypress furnishes a superior material, while the red cedar yields the best known material for pails, tubs, and chests of a nicer and more costly description.

"The timber of the magnolia, also, is susceptible of a variety of uses, and is now being extensively used for the nicer and finer kinds of wheelwright and cabinet work. *Of this timber the supply is very large.* The wood of the red or sweet bay, in fineness of texture and in its other valuable qualities, stand equal to mahogany, and most persons cannot distinguish it from mahogany. It is coming into great demand for cabinet work." "It abounds in the State."

"The resources of Florida in the direction of the manufacture of the wooden ware, tools of all descriptions made from wood, and fine cabinet work, are very great." "An inexhaustible abundance of material, at the cheapest possible rates, and very great accessibility by water communication, offer inducements for the manufacture of lumber, wooden ware, and all kinds of tools made of wood."

Also United States Land Office Report, 1868, p. 19 : "The principal forest trees of this State, some of which are eminently adapted for ship-building, are live oak, mahogany, magnolia, pine, cedar, and cypress. Mangrove, boxwood, mastic, satinwood, crabwood, and lignumvitæ, abound on the keys, and generally in the southern part of the State."

United States Land Office Report, 1869, p. 103, speaks of the timber of Southern Florida; also the timber of the Middle and North Florida :—

"The flora of this region embraces a great number of species, including many found in the tropics, as well as those indigenous to the temperate zone. Among the most important forest trees are the live, red, white, and water oaks, cedar, cherry, cypress, hickory, elm, pine, ash, gum, magnolia, birch, walnut, mahogany, and dogwood. The other varieties, found principally in the southern portion of the State, and on the keys, are lignumvitæ, boxwood, mastic, satinwood, palmetto, and crabwood. Large quantities of live oak are annually sent to various foreign and domestic ports for ship-building, and other purposes. THE LUMBER PRODUCT IS ESTIMATED AT TEN MILLION DOLLARS ANNUALLY, (IN 1869), and this interest is rapidly increasing. Florida is nearly all timbered; yellow and pitch pine form the basis. The undergrowth embraces an extensive variety of plants and vines, while flowers exist in the greatest profusion."

Present product is over $25,000,000 per annum.

FROM "FLORIDA SETTLER" AND "OFFICIAL GUIDE," 1873.

"LUMBER.

"First on the list of State productions we place lumber, as it holds at present the first rank among the industries of Florida, whether we consider the amount of capital involved, the value of the material produced, or the extent of the resources from which it is drawn. It can be asserted with confidence, that over no other State in the Union is valuable timber so extensively and uniformly distributed, and ere long the lumber business of this State will rival in extent that of any other. Within the last few years the manufacture of lumber has received here an enormous impetus, consequent upon a knowledge and recognition of the vast timber resources of the State, and *now the trade begins to assume gigantic proportions, with an almost unlimited power of expansion.* When any one contemplates, in the light of knowledge, the astonishing wealth of the State in timber, the question at once arises, Why has it remained so long almost untouched, and less favoured portions of the country sought after for the supply of lumber? Hitherto, nearly all the yellow-pine flooring consumed in the great cities of the North has been obtained from South and North Carolina. But at no time in their history have these States contained a tithe of the pine timber of superior quality to be found in Florida. It is by no means an exaggerated estimate when we put the heavy pine forests in the State as covering an area of 30,000 square miles.

VALUES.—The quality of the lumber is attested by the fact that it commands in market 10 per cent. more than that of any other section. The *New York Mercantile Journal,* in an article on the lumber market, states as to values :—

"Yellow-pine flooring and step-plank from Florida are in fair demand at $30 per 1,000 feet, while the inferior lumber made in North and South Carolina moves slowly at $23 to $25. The yellow pine, so called, growing in the Carolinas, is objectionable for many reasons. In the first place the tree is of a different and less enduring species, has a greater proportion of sap-wood and black knots; and in the second place it is from these trees that the manufacturers of pitch and turpentine procure their material, depriving them of the elements which give the durability and peculiar excellence of this kind of wood for building purposes. *Architects and owners should always require in their specifications that the yellow pine to be used in first-class buildings should be of the growth of Florida.*"

"The highly deserved reputation of the pine lumber furnished by the forest of the State, is attracting the attention of capitalists in all parts of the country; and besides those mills already established, some most gigantic enterprises are constructing to take advantage of the resources of the State."

Florida Land Office Report, 1873, says :—

"In 1871, Mr. Judah, the well-known and highly competent railway engineer, was employed by the Jacksonville, Pensacola, and Mobile Railroad Company to survey their route from Appalachicola River to Pensacola city. This company had a land grant of 600,000 acres, and Mr. Judah and his associates made a full Report on the value of these lands and the forests and timber thereon.—*Extracts from Judah's Report.*

"Nearly the entire body of these lands (600,000 acres) is covered with a dense growth of yellow pine of a quality unsurpassed by that of any other State in the Union. Some of the largest and finest lumber-mills anywhere to be found in the United States are located upon the Blackwater River, in the vicinity of the town of Milton, in Santa Rosa county. The amount of lumber annually shipped from this district is about 50,000,000 feet, yielding upwards of $500,000 to the manufacturers, and costing the millowners, delivered in the log, upwards of $40,000. . . .

"QUANTITY OF LUMBER ON THESE LANDS.

"Allowing twenty trees per acre fit for cutting into saw-logs, averaging 500 feet Board Measure per tree, and the quantity amounts to 6,000 million feet of lumber, which is worth, manufactured, at only $12, $72,000,000. At only five trees per acre, the quantity is 1,250,000,000 feet of lumber, worth $18,000,000. Allow it worth $2.50 per thousand feet standing (a fair estimate), and it will pay the whole cost of the road."

"It is a fact that timber makes anew again in twenty-five to thirty years; so that after going over a body of timber, cutting off that large enough for saw-logs, *leaving* the smaller timber, this smaller timber will have grown sufficiently in from twenty-five to thirty years to yield another supply equal to the first."

"Spar-timber exists nowhere in greater abundance or of better quality than upon these lands. Heavy European contracts have been filled from this locality, and contracts can be obtained to any extent that can be filled. Good spars bring from $100 to $300 each. Reliable associates have traversed these lands and report that they have seen lands where twelve spars could be cut from an acre. Allowing that *one spar* can be cut from each five acres, and it gives 125,000 spars, which at only $100 each are worth $12,000,000 at tide-water."

"It is not unlikely that the land may yield an average of one spar per acre, which would give us the value of spar-timber alone, standing, of $62,500,000. The spars of Florida are well known in Europe, and are believed to be equal to any in the United States."

"The value of such a domain as this can scarcely be estimated. The value of the lumber alone on these lands will exceed the total aggregate cost of the Illinois Central Railroad."

Mr. Judah's Report has been adopted as correct by the United States. See "Agricultural Reports," 1871.

"These railroad lands are nothing more than a fair sample of the lands throughout the State in respect to their capacity for lumber. But besides the pine, great varieties of the most valuable timber are to be found distributed all over the State, and capable of being worked up and put upon the market with highly remunerative results. The live and the water oaks of the State have a world-wide reputation, and though the demands of ship-building throughout the entire country, and in some parts of Europe, have for many years been supplied from the forests of the State, its resources in this are apparently untouched. The cedar swamps of Florida are at the present time supplying most of the pencil manufactories on this continent, while the immense quantities of cypress to be found scattered all over the Peninsula promise to furnish the most desirable railroad ties that can be found. Then for the manufacture of furniture, sashes, blinds, waggons, and wooden ware of every description, there is an unlimited supply of red bay, cherry, white oak, ash, birch, hickory, gum, elm, and a number of other equally valuable species of timber."

The Florida pine differs materially from the Northern. It is the tropical *long-leafed* variety, only grows in an exceedingly mild or warm climate—admits of a very fine finish and polish, much of it being well adapted for fine cabinet furniture. It has also a preservative quality, not found in any but the long-leafed kind. The yellow pine of Florida is probably not excelled anywhere. It justly commands a premium of 10 per cent. over other pine lumber.

SHIP-TIMBER.

Florida has more first-class ship-timber and lumber for naval construction, and of better quality, than *all* the balance of the United States put together. This fact is established by the Congressional Report on Forrestry of 1874. The Report says, p. 38 :—

"The amount of public lands reserved by authority of law is now very nearly as follows :—

				Acres.
" In Mississippi	...	...	...	26,218
„ Florida...	...	...	...	208,824
„ Louisiana	...	...	...	9,170
„ Alabama	...	...	...	240 "

Live and water oaks only grow in the Southern States. The Government having the power to select her lands for naval construction, made her chief and almost exclusive selection of her Florida lands for this purpose. If she could have selected any better else-where, *she would have done so.*

The "Florida Official Report," 1873, says :—

"Within the last year or two some fine saw-mills have been erected in Appalachicola, and immense quantities of lumber are manufactured and shipped to various quarters of the globe, and the city is again reviving."

The Pennsylvania Tie Company have erected a large mill, nearly completed, for the purpose of manufacturing the cypress railroad tie and sleeper. It is one of the most extensive establishments of the kind on the continent.

This cypress timber has proved to be the most durable railroad timber known. Ties and sleepers will last on and in the ground for 15 years, or equal to two or three sets of good oak ties. This timber abounds on the Company's " hummock " lands. It is used for many purposes, and will yield the Company large profits.

ESTIMATE.

Estimating the Company's forests and their values on the 8,300,000 acres at a minimum in quantity and in price, it is safe to say—

			Acres.
The pine forests cover at least		...	3,000,000
And other timber	...	...	1,000,000
Total timber lands	...	...	4,000,000

The common selling price of lumber is $15 per 1,000 feet Board Measure (B.M.), equal to 83½ cubic feet of hewn or squared timber.

But put this price at the present low, depressed rate, $12.

				Feet B.M.
Minimum yield per acre of pine lands at		...	4,000
„ „ „ cypress „		...	10,000
„ „ „ other lumber		...	4,000

Then

			Feet B.M.
3,000,000 acres pine lands at 4,000 feet yield...	...	...	12,000,000,000
500,000 acres cypress at 10,000 feet yield	...	...	5,000,000,000
500,000 acres cedar, mahogany, &c., at 4,000 feet yield...	...	...	2,000,000,000
Total	...	...	19,000,000,000

At $12 per 1,000 feet yield	...	...	$228,000,000
Deduct one-half for cost of manufacturing and marketing (high estimate)	...	...	114,000,000
Net profit	...	...	$114,000,000
Estimating at half these results net			57,000,000
On 2,300,000 acres	...		$14,000,000

This amount is independent of the timber cut and shipped in the log, such as ship-spars, live oak, water oak, and all timber for mines, of which this property can furnish many millions of dollars' value in the aggregate, and *all this variety* is needed, and has a ready gold market in England and elsewhere.

By examination of the Timber and Lumber Reports of Florida, Michigan, Wisconsin, Maine, and Pennsylvania, it will be seen the above estimate is below the minimum there reported.

Estimating the value of the trees "standing" at only 4,000 feet B.M. per acre, and $2¼ per 1,000 feet (a low average price, as shown from the Timber Reports of the Great Timber States), and we have a profit of $10 per acre,

or 4,000,000 acres at $10	...	...	$40,000,000
or 2,300,000 „ „ „	...	...	12,000,000

It will be seen by comparison that the estimates are far below those of Mr. Judah reported above. He gives a maximum value on 600,000 acres of $72,000,000, and a minimum of $18,000,000, besides spar timber alone at $62,500,000.

It is proper to remark here, that the rapid exhaustion of timber in America, and in all countries accessible by water-way, is fully shown by the Government Reports of Great Britain and the United States, briefly noticed in the Appendix. (Note B. in full Report.)

It is proper to remark further, that a large quantity of Florida timber is now being shipped to the English and other European ports. Much of it is worked up into cabinet furniture, and for such use is highly appreciated in the markets. London timber merchants now offer to this Company to purchase heavily of its Florida timber. Large quantities of it are supplied to the West Indies and South America.

THE LOCATION OF THE COMPANY'S 2,300,000 ACRES, AND FUTURE PROFITS THEREFROM.

To obtain an intelligent idea of the importance of the ready market and value of these lands, it should be borne in mind that they are located in East Florida, mostly in a solid body on each side, directly along and contiguous to the Company's "Great Tide-Water Canal Route," in the most desirable portion of the State, and handiest to water-navigation and markets.

They are shown on the official maps of surveys. The N. boundary commences a few miles above the city of Pilatka, on the Lower St. John's; thence S. on both sides of the Lower and Upper St. John's River and series of connecting lakes; thence again S. on both sides of Indian River, Lake Worth, and New River, terminating north of Biscayne Bay; thus extending N. and S. on each side of this magnificent chain of navigable waters and connecting canals, for a distance of 234 miles, extending E. to the Atlantic coast, and commanding that coast for this great distance; embracing a large portion of the rich St. John's and Indian River Valleys. The largest part of the immigration into the State is rapidly populating these valleys, and, as a consequence, the lands are rising greatly in value.

The present Executive Governor Stearns, who was formerly Surveyor-General of the United States for the District of Florida, Ex-Gov. Reed, and the Hon. M. A. Williams, one of the United States Surveyors, engaged for over twenty years in surveying Florida lands for the Government, have all made a written appraisal of the first-named 2,300,000 acres, and they put the valuation at $8, $20, and $25 per acre. Now it so happens that there are private plantations and large farms

held and owned by sundry individuals at intervals through this grant; and large portions of these private plantations and farms have been sold for cash during the last three years, and during the year last past, land has been sold on the St. John's for $50, and as high as $150 per acre; and much has been sold on the Indian River and Halifax River, the lowest at $10 per acre. Population is pouring into this part of the State very rapidly. United States Senators and other wealthy men of the Northern States are buying locations on these waters, and are building magnificent residences, and laying out beautiful tropical gardens, to spend their winters in this charming and salubrious climate, and thereby avoid the rigors of Northern winters.

Accurate admeasurements shew that Lake Washington is 13 feet higher than Indian River. It is proposed to cut the Company's 6 mile canal deep enough to drop the surface of the lake about 4 feet. This would leave a fall, still, of 9 feet from the lake, which will afford magnificent and most valuable water powers, sufficient to drive a large number of mills and manufactories all the year; and a large industrial city will accordingly grow up on this favoured site, bound to result in great profits to the Company.

Here the new and beautiful City of Eau Gallie is located, with its broadly laid-out streets, and beautiful natural parks of tropical groves and perpetual blooming flowers, having Salt-water Rivers and Ocean on one side of it, and Lake Washington—15 miles length of fresh water—on the other side. Above this latitude the frost line ceases. The fresh ocean breezes and trade winds continually fan and cool this charming spot.

The State Agricultural College, an Institution founded by the State and endowed by the United States, has been located on this new city site, with 5,000 acres of fine land as endowment.

South of Lake Harney, along the St. John's River, the Company owns 450,000 acres of land, which require special notice. There are no richer lands on the earth, —they are covered with perpetual green pastures, on which tens of thousands of heads of cattle feed winter and summer, and grow fat. These lands will abundantly raise any vegetable or fruit sown or planted on them. They will raise 4,000 pounds of sugar to the acre, and for Sea Island Cotton no better lands exist in America.

On the completion of the Company's Canal, these lands will be all thoroughly drained, and will then readily rent for $10 per acre, which will ultimately bring in a rental revenue to owners of $4,500,000 per annum. The whole tract is richly worth $100 per acre. (See official reports, &c.) The Mississippi River cotton and sugar lands sold readily for $100 to $150 per acre, in cash, before the late war. They will do so again.

But the Company's lands here located have the advantage in climate and soil, and will raise crops of greater value per acre.

A large body of her land granted will front on the great Ship Canal, and for a full description and location of the other grants, see official surveys, maps, and inventory.

CITY, TOWNS, AND VILLAGE SITES ALONG THE SHIP CANAL, &c.

At the Terminal Harbours of the Ship Canal, in the Atlantic and Gulf, and at Key West, large commercial cities must grow up under the control of the Ship Canal Company, and on the 680 miles of canals and improved water courses, the Company will establish depôts and wharves every 8 or 10 miles, and also lay out town and village sites. Railway and Canal Companies in America and other countries have done so, and have realised immense revenues and profits therefrom. The population settle upon and improve those points, and the Company should realise profits enough from this source to pay the whole construction cost of the works.

A highly respectable firm of English solicitors has fully examined and reported upon the legal status of this Company, upon all its papers, documents, titles of real estate, bonds, mortgage, &c., &c., and upon the value of the 2,300,000 acres mortgaged, and have delivered a statement of facts and legal conclusions therein to the following effect :—

1. That the charters and the organization of the Company thereunder are in due legal form.

2. That the bonds and mortgages securing the same, together with all the necessary intermediate steps, are all in due form of law, and that the Company is now in legal shape either to sell Bonds or borrow money on its property and securities.

3. That the titles to real estate are perfect. On this point they say, "It seems clear that the three grants mentioned (2,300,000 acres) are valid, and vest the title thereto in this Company, and that neither the United States nor the State of Florida can annul or withdraw either of them, and that by the deed of conveyance a free, clear, perfect, and absolute legal title is evidenced and vested in the Company in fee simple, without conditions whatsoever."

4. They lastly find the following official evidence relating to the value of these lands, and come to the conclusion that these lands are worth now in the market from $5 to $100 per acre, and are ample security for a loan of £1,000,000.

The following is their full report on this point:

"VALUE OF THE COMPANY'S LANDS.

These lands are located, in what is called "East Florida," in the Counties of Marion, Putnam, St. John's, Orange, Volusia, Brevard, and Dade, along and on each side of the Company's Tide-Water Canal line, for a continuous distance of over 230 miles (see Official Map, Grants, and Deed), including a large portion of the rich valleys of the St. John's and Indian Rivers. It appears also that interspersed through this body of land are occasional plantations, which, since the late Civil War in the United States, have been subdivided into smaller tracts, and sold, and now occupied ; while several of these counties, possessing lands outside of the Company's grants, have each a considerable population, which is rapidly increasing yearly.

POPULATION OF THESE COUNTIES.

Marion	...	...	...	16,000
Dade	...	...	...	10,000
Putnam and St. John's		... each	6,000
Volutia and Brevard	...	... about	5,000

A full description of the lands of the State and of this Company—variety of soils—agricultural and horticultural productions—extensive heavy forests, &c., &c., is contained in Official Reports, issued by the United States Government and by the State of Florida, named as follows :—

United States " Land Office Report," 1870, pp. 44 to 53.
   "   "   "   "   " 1868, pp. 17 to 23.
   "   "   "   "   " 1869, pp. 100 to 105.
United States " Department of Agriculture."
                Report, 1862, pp. 59 to 65.
   "   "   "   " 1868, pp. 140 to 147.
   "   "   "   " 1872, pp. 160 to 171.
   "   "   "   " 1873, pp. 510 to 511.
United States " Special Report on
   Immigration," Statistics, &c.   1872, pp. 138 to 147.
Annual Messages of the Governor of Florida,
   with accompanying Documents from the
   State Land Office Department, &c., from
   1869 to 1875.

In full corroboration of these Official Reports, it appears there are numerous Geographies, Histories, British and American books, periodicals, and papers, also showing the value of the Florida Lands.

It will also be found that, since the late American war, Florida has been rapidly increasing in population and wealth. The chief immigration and settlements appear to be into the St. John's and Indian River Valleys ; besides, this portion of Florida has become a great national resort for pleasure-seekers and invalids, who leave the Northern States during the severe winter months, and spend their winters in the salubrious climate of Florida. It is reported that from 40,000 to 60,000 visitors spend their winters annually in East Florida.

In the Annual Survey Report to the United States Government, by M. L. Stearns, United States Surveyor-General in Florida, dated August 31, 1870 (see U.S. Land Office Report, pp. 331 to 333), this officer reports that " The Eastern portion from the St. John's River to the Coast, and including Indian River, is settling up very rapidly, perhaps more so than any other part of the State, and consequently that section presents a greater variety of interests than any other. The lumber trade is very important. There are on the St. John's River some twenty steam saw-mills, three-fourths of them at or near Jacksonville. The richest sugar lands in the State lie in various localities along the Indian river, and offer an inexhaustible mine of wealth to the industrious and enterprising farmer. The natural advantages of the State are ample."

The Official Agricultural Report of the United States for 1871, page 164, says:—" One great advantage which these (Florida) Lands possess over Western lands lies in their ability to produce six great staple productions, the most valuable known, and of which the supply cannot equal the demand, while the western lands produce but two great staples, viz., wheat and corn. These staples are yellow pine lumber, the best timber for naval construction, house-building and cabinet work. Cotton (both Sea Island and short staple), tobacco, sugar and rice, in addition to which may be enumerated, among other products, hay, corn, oats, potatoes (sweet and Irish), all kinds of vegetables, oranges, bananas, figs, peaches, quinces, and many other tropical fruits, which can be grown nowhere else in the United States as well as here."

From the foregoing official Government authorities it appears quite clear that the Florida lands, including those belonging to the Company, contain a very large amount of valuable forests for a great variety of timber and lumber, of yellow and pitch pine, live oak, water-red and white oaks, cedar, cherry, cypress, hickory, elm, ash, gum, magnolia, birch, walnut, mahogany, satinwood, and in some portions, lignum vitæ, box-wood, mastic, palmetto, crabwood, &c.

That the soil and climate are specially adapted to the culture and growth of all tropical and semi-tropical fruits, viz., the orange, lemon, lime, citron, fig, banana, plantain, mango, soursop, custard-apple, cocoa-nut, shaddock, paw-paw, date, nectarine, apricots, pine-apples, plums, peaches, cherries, apples, pears, tamarinds, almonds, grapes of great variety, strawberries, blackberries, currants, mulberries, &c., &c.

In addition to this list add all the garden and field vegetables of the Temperate and Torrid zones, which grow there summer and winter. In the culture of these fruits and winter and early vegetables, Florida claims a monopoly over any other part of North America. The Northern cities and States import vast quantities of these fruits and vegetables annually from foreign countries, which Florida can supply.

Very many cases are mentioned of the large profits realized per acre in the cultivation of the *staples*, as compared with other States, and extraordinary profits are shown in the raising of the orange, banana, fig, grape, strawberries, and other fruits, and in the winter and early vegetables. These features are attracting a large immigration to Florida from the Northern States since the war, and it is claimed that the Florida Lands possess a special value over other rich lands in other States, because of their adaptation to the growth of the tropical fruits and winter vegetables, for the Northern States and cities will afford a continual market for these products.

VALUE PER ACRE OF COMPANY'S LANDS.

The following letter and valuation is entitled to consideration, viz. :—

"OFFICE OF SURVEYOR GENERAL,
"Tallahassee, Fla. *Aug. 25th*, 1870.
"Sirs,
"From our knowledge and information, which we have of the land ceded and granted to your Company by the Trustees of the Internal Improvement Fund of the State of Florida, we would appraise their value at from $8 to $10 per acre, upon the completion of the Canals and Improvements contemplated by the Charter of the said 'Southern Inland Navigation and Improvement Company.'

"HARRISON REED, Governor, and President of the Board Internal Improvement Fund."
"M. S. STEARNS, United States Surveyor General.
"J. S. ADAMS, Commissioner of Lands and Immigration.
"T. H. OSBORN, and others."

In appraisements and letters, dated January 28th and March 29th, 1871, by Mr. M. A. Williams, one of the United States Land Surveyors of Florida for twenty-five years, he says :—

"I have, within the last twenty (20) years, either surveyed for the United States' Government, or examined for the State of Florida most of the lands granted to 'The Southern Inland Navigation and Improvement Company.' I have no doubt that a very large portion of these lands would be worth and would sell for from $10 to $25 per acre upon the completion of the Company's Canals," &c.

He says he has spent more than twenty-five years in surveying public lands in Florida for the United States Government, that the Company's Lands extend from Palatka on the St. John's to Biscayne Bay, that he is "well acquainted with the character of these lands on the entire route," that he "selected a very large portion of these lands" for the State from the United States Lands, that they are among "the richest and most valuable in the State." Part require draining (see Judge Fry's Synoptical Report, p. 15, and Engineers' Reports, "cutting the canal from Lake Washington to Indian River, so as to drop the surface of the Lake 4 feet, will drain the Company's Lands "). Williams further says :—" Your line of improvements will open the only available tropical portion of Florida, and will unquestionably be the most *attractive portion of the State*, and the most desirable for the thousands of visitors who annually seek this climate for health and pleasure, and it will also be the most desirable for the production of all the tropical fruits," &c.

The United States Agricultural Report for 1871, and the United States Special Report on Statistics and immigration, show the value of the lands of the Southern Slave States in 1860, and the large decline of price during the late American war, as the result of that war. Of Florida they say—"In some sections of the State lands declined during this period from 20 to 50 per cent., but on the St. John's River and Indian River they have advanced *one-third in value* since the date named," and on page 165 of the first-named report the Government says: "The price of wild land in Dade County is about $50 per acre. Cultivated lands at Key West and Boca Chico can be sold at prices varying from $500 to $1,000 per acre, according to the stock of fruit growing."

The large amount of construction work performed, and the rapid increase of population in the last few years, have fully demonstrated the above valuation of the Governor, Land Commissioners, and the United States Surveyors.

"The message of Governor Harrison Reed to the Legislature, delivered January 4, 1872, claims that the *increase of population during the last three years* has been 40,000, mainly as a result of the labours of the Immigration Bureau in exhibiting systematically the peculiar resources of the State. He especially calls attention to the fact that 1,200 miles of sea-coast, prolific of oysters, fish, and turtle, almost beyond parallel, with bays and inlets, and inland navigable waters of an equal extent, offer the richest inducements to enterprise and capital."

In the "Annual Message" of Governor Stearns to the Florida Legislature, with "Accompanying Documents" of his Cabinet officers, for the year 1875. Land Office Department, p. 5, it is officially declared that:

"The past year has marked the commencement of a new era in the history of our State, in the unexampled influx of population which has taken place. We are in possession of sufficient data to be able to state that the accessions of wealth and population have been greater during the past twelve months than in any three previous years; and the consequence is a very perceptible effect on the material property of the State.

"This influx of immigration has been more apparent in the Eastern portion of the State, and is seen in the extraordinary advance in the price of lands; in the extensive purchases that have been made for the purpose of tropical fruit culture; in the springing up of new and enterprising settlements, and the spirit of life and activity which is observable throughout regions where solitude hitherto reigned supreme.

"There is, perhaps, no State in the Union about which there is so much enquiry at present as Florida." This last-named Report shows, that in *Marion County* "very good unimproved farming land can be bought for $50 per acre."

In *Putnam County* the "price of land varies from a Government Homestead to $100 or more per acre," and "First rate orange land on the East side of the St. John's River is held as high as $100 per acre.

St. John's County varies about the same.

c

Volusia County (where the Company owns a very large body of land). *" Private lands in small lots can be purchased at from $5 to $100 per acre.* (The lands of this County are very superior in quality).

Brevard County " is fast showing the effects of energy and capital," and lands sell outside of the Company's grant at from $10 upwards per acre.

The United States Agricultural Reports of 1873 shows:

"*That Orange County* is making rapid progress in population and wealth. It unites the advantages of diversified and beautiful scenery, a remarkably healthy climate, a productive and well-watered soil, and easy access to market. The climate and soil have proved by trial to be well adapted to the growth of oranges, lemons, and almost every other variety of semi-tropical fruits, as well as the principal vegetables. These attractions having become known are drawing immigrants from almost every State in the Union.

Lands which five years ago could be bought at 25 cents to $1 per acre now bring $50 to $150 per acre."

The Trustees of the Internal Improvement Fund, who made these grants, appraised and fixed a schedule price $10 per acre (see Deed of Trust, p. 10, sec. 2). The law required the Board to " fix the price of the public lands granted in the Trust" (see Act 1855, sec. 22, " Bush's Digest" 375).

From the foregoing Official authorities, both of the United States Government and of the State, we have a full exhibit of the character, value, and market price of the lands granted to the Company.

Large portions of these grants are worth from $5 to $100 per acre, and in our opinion the evidence shows, that the average price of $10 per acre, as estimated by the Board of Trustees, is a fair valuation.

Another mode of valuation is given by the United States Government, in the numerous grants of lands, donated by the Government in aid of Railway and Canal construction. An Official Report is published by the Government, showing that all land grant lands, sold by the Companies to the year 1870, realized an average price of $7 per acre. In some instances the grants averaged from $8 to $12 per acre. The Hannibal and St. Joseph Railway Company sold their lands at an average of $11 per acre. The Grand Rapids and Indiana Railway Company realized an average of $13.98. The Burlington and Missouri River Railroad Company, averaged $11.70 and the Illinois Central (well-known in London) averaged $11.35 per acre. This Company's grant contained 2,595,000 acres. The sales made to 1870 amounted $24,000,000 cash, and the residue is selling since at an average $12.50 per acre. The whole grant will net to the Company $30,000,000 cash. (See United States Land Office Report, Sept. 1870.)

The LOAN of £1,000,000 *secured by the Company's First Mortgage Bonds,* under the Trust Deed, covering two million three-hundred thousand (2,300,000) acres of lands, with other property, improvements, franchises, and rights, is and must be sufficient, safe, and most ample security for this Loan.

The *value* of these *lands alone* at the appraisement and scheduled rate in the Trust Deed is *four times the amount of the required Loan.*

At the *average rate of $7 per acre* for all land grants sold to 1870, they will be nearly *three times* the Loan.

Mr. Bennock, of London, after examining the evidence of their value, states they are worth " over 50 times the amount of the Loan required."

An important consideration to the Lender is found in the ability of the Company to pay the interest and principal of this Loan as they mature.

1st. From Tolls.

2nd. From the sale of Timber and Lumber.

3rd. From the sale of Lands.

The Company is in position now to collect tolls on the vessels and Commerce passing over its improvements.

It seems the Commerce on the St. John's River, Indian River, and Lakes, is quite large, and increasing rapidly.

It is reported in the United States Land Office Reports that the annual export of timber and lumber from Florida in 1869 was $10,000,000, besides home consumption. This timber it is reported commands a premium of 10 per cent. in the City of New York over lumber from other States. Liverpool, London, and other British ports receive and furnish a ready market for this timber and lumber. Letters have been shewn from lumber merchants in London to this Company, offering to purchase from the Company amounts up to nearly £200,000. The Company's forests are readily accessible, and most favourably situated for shipment of timber and lumber. It has already been shewn that there is a large immigration into the St. John's and Indiana River Valleys, where the Company's land is situated, and that these lands have risen rapidly in value. Taking into consideration these facts, together with Reports of the large annual sales of land grant lands made by the Illinois Central, Grand Rapids, and Indiana, Burlington, and Missouri River, and numerous other Railway Companies, it would seem clear that the Company can from this source commence to receive large returns immediately."

"SHIP CANAL.

" It appears that The Atlantic and Gulf Ship Canal is incorporated and located under the Act of the State of Florida, entitled ' An Act to provide a General Law for the Incorporation of Railroads and Canals,' approved February 19th, 1874.

This Act is the Charter right of the Company—the franchises, rights, and powers it confers are complete and very liberal, and it would seem that the franchise is perpetual, and the Company has power to fix the rate of tolls and compensation for the use of the Canal, and to collect the same, to purchase, hold, use, and sell and convey real, personal, and mixed property, take and hold voluntary grants of land to aid in construction, powers to borrow money and execute Trust Deeds or Mortgages on the Company's property to secure such loan, &c., &c.

The provisions are comprehensive, and seem to guard the rights and privileges of the Company well.

To anyone wishing to become interested in this enterprise (financially or otherwise) it will be interesting and well worth the while to read and study the provisions of this Charter. Legislation so favourable to a Company is seldom obtained in England.

The commercial and international character of this Ship Canal, its importance, necessity, benefits, &c., are fully exhibited in the full and Synoptical Reports compiled by Judge John H. Fry, principally from Government authorities. We recommend that these Reports and the authorities quoted from be well read and studied.

In conclusion, it is our opinion that the propositions and terms offered for the loans are an inducement to capitalists, and that the security for the loan seems safe and ample in amount."

Important Leader in the *Times* and the Official British Report on Commerce and Trade—On the Thrift of Florida—Increase of Population—Immense Profits in Tropical Fruit-culture, and rapid rise in the price of Lands in the St. John's Valley, right in the heart of the Company's Grants of 2,800,000 acres.

*Leader in the "*TIMES,*" London, June 28, 1876.*

"The latest volume of the Reports of the Secretary of Legations, which has been recently presented to Parliament, includes a contribution of more than ordinary interest. This is a careful analysis of the 'trade and some resources of the United States for the year 1875," and, apart from its general value, it embraces the first impartial review of the economical condition in the South that has been published in this country since the re-election of President Grant to the Presidency. The period of four years, which is now drawing to a close, was marked by a few startling events; but it is all the more likely that it was fruitful in steady, if silent, progress among those communities which, after the desolating convulsions of the war, could only hope to repair their strength by rest. The writer of the Report, Mr. Grant Watson, was First Secretary of Legation at Washington, until, on the nomination of Lord Lytton to the Indian Viceroyalty, he was promoted to the Lisbon Legation. His conclusions are sober and inobtrusive; his survey of facts is wide and searching, and, upon the whole, his Report is a most praiseworthy addition to our knowledge of the United States.

In Mr. Watson's judgment the South had, at the close of last year, reached a turn in its fortunes at which the abiding consequences of the war were being overcome by the strong permanent elements of industrial prosperity. The worst days clearly were past. The riches of the soil, the generosity of the climate, and the abundance of labour had begun to tell, and wealth was being recreated with amazing rapidity. The Civil War had rent the old fabric of society from top to bottom, but some of the fragments fell into new relations, and others obtained scope for free growth by the ruin of the rest. The slave-owning aristocracy of former days was wholly disappeared. But there were other slaveholders who were no aristocrats, who worked with their own hands—the 'mean whites,' as their betters used to call them—and these, recovering from the shock of the conflict, are now becoming steadily prosperous, while, in spite of some political disturbances and consequent suffering, there is 'a general diffusion of means for ease and comfort unknown before.' By the side of this class the Negro freedmen cultivate for the most part their own holdings. 'Cotton culture has been democratized by emancipation.' No single estates now yield 1,000 or 2,000 bales for individual owners; but the small farmers, white and black, "raise cotton for their own profit individually, and the aggregate of their little crops nearly reaches, and will soon exceed that which was produced before the war.' Mr. Watson reckons the production of 1875 at 3,800,000 bales, and the value of this quantity is 'diffused among many thousands, or perhaps, millions of persons or families." Wealth begets wants, and the elevation of living among the "mean whites" and the freedmen has developed an immense increase in the consumption by the South of Northern manufactures. Of this development there are no precise statistics, but Mr. Watson calculates that the Southern consumption of Northern commodities is now at least quadruple, and may possibly be tenfold that of the period before the war, while it is known to be constantly augmenting. The condition of the freedmen, who are now politically

enfranchised as well as emancipated, is, of course, not wholly bright; but some have amassed "wealth," many thousands, "own houses and pay taxes," and Mr. Watson does not hesitate to say that they will ultimately become "a Conservative element" in the State. "Their labour is adding largely to the wealth of the South, and is essential to its further development."

Energetic efforts are being made in various directions to hasten and to guide this process of renovating growth.

As an example, Mr. Grant Watson points to *the case of Florida, which the war and the consequent ruin of the planters may be said to have first brought to the knowledge of the North, and opened to the influx of Northern enterprise and capital. The "Land of Flowers," where Ponce de Leon placed his fabled "fountain of youth," has in late years attracted, by the charm of its climate, crowds of invalids from the Northern States, and this communication has at length disclosed to the shrewd Northern mind the capacities of this fertile peninsula. Especially since the crisis of 1873 paralysed trade and industry in the North, setting capital seeking after investment and labour for employment, the development of the resources of Florida, which, as a fruit-producing country, has not a rival in the world, have received a great share of attention, and whenever the crisis at the North comes to an end, reviving speculation, as Mr. Watson predicts, "will turn thither, and give a still greater impetus to this already rapid movement." The orange groves of Florida are in themselves sources of wealth as rich as the most famous lodes of Nevada. The fruit is "cultivated as easily, and produces as quickly as the apple, and yields in full bearing from 1,000 to 2,500 per cent. per acre to the owner on the ground, at present prices, and with but trifling labour." The Florida orange ripens deliciously, and will certainly supplant, in the markets of the Northern Cities, the half-matured foreign fruit of which at present New York alone consumes 500 millions annually. The land fitted for this profitable and pleasant occupation has, of course, gone up rapidly in price. A large tract was purchased on the St. John's River eight years ago at about one dollar an acre, and has lately been re-sold for orange planting at prices varying from 50 to 120 dollars; while other estates, bought some four or five years ago at 25 dollars an acre, and planted with orange trees, brought a couple of years since not less than 1,000 dollars an acre. In this neighbourhood, a Swedish colony has been established, it is stated, with the most encouraging results. The most severe frosts do not touch the fruit trees, though on the glowing shores of the Lago di Garda, as travellers in Lombardy and Venetia will remember, the tender lemon has to be carefully covered during the winter. It is plain* that a new industry of great value has been opened, and that it possesses attractions to win the Scandinavian settlers from Ohio and Wisconsin. This, however, is only a typical instance of a movement which, according to Mr. Watson, is progressing in many parts of the Southern States—wherever, indeed, the natural advantages of climate and soil, set free by the break-up of the old social system, invite Northern capital and enterprise. Unless this progress should be unexpectedly checked, the calamities of the Civil War will quickly be obliterated by the rising tide of a prosperity almost without parallel, even in American experience.

*British Commercial Trade Reports, No. 6 (1876), Part
II., by Her Majesty's Secretaries of Embassy and
Legation, &c., &c. Presented to both Houses of
Parliament, by command of Her Majesty, May,
1876.*

"REPORT BY MR. WATSON ON THE TRADE AND SOME
RESOURCES OF THE UNITED STATES, FOR 1875; WITH
A PREFACE ON THE MATERIAL CONDITION OF THE
SOUTHERN STATES.

"WHILE the Northern States of the Union, especially
in their commercial and manufacturing interests, are
greatly suffering at the present moment, a turn would
appear, finally, to have been reached at the South,
whose soil, climate, and abundant labour are now telling
upon it in rapidly augmenting prosperity.

The class of former slave-owners have been, for the
most part, ruined and permanently impoverished; but
the lower strata—those who themselves work—have
recovered from the devastation of the war, and a general
diffusion of means for ease and comfort, unknown
before, may be observed, although certain localities are
still agitated, and are suffering by reason of political
disturbances.

Cotton culture has been democratized by emancipation. While no longer crops yielding from 1,000 to
2,000 bales are raised to enrich single families and
develop luxurious and extravagant tastes in these, the
negroes whom they formerly owned, and who as slaves
were scantily and coarsely clothed, having few wants,
now raise cotton for their own profit individually, and
the aggregate of their little crops nearly reaches, and
will soon exceed, that which was produced before the
war; and its result—for last year, about 3,800,000
bales—is diffused amongst many thousands, or perhaps
millions of persons or families, and goes to supply the
increasing wants of this numerous class of new consumers; and, while no statistics are published, the
consumption by the South of articles manufactured at
the North has probably more than quadrupled (it may
be tenfold) that of before the war, and it is constantly
augmenting.

The former slave, now a freeman (voter), as well as
freedman, has become very generally an owner of the
soil which he cultivates; in many instances he has
amassed wealth; many thousands own houses and pay
taxes, and will eventually become a conservative
element thereby of society, though now greatly under
the lead of political adventurers. Many are naturally
lazy, thriftless, and, in some towns where they swarm,
a pest of society; but it cannot be doubted that their
labour is adding largely to the wealth of the South,
and that it is essential to its further development.

*Florida would, like Texas, appear especially to have
been favoured in rapid development of its resources and
increase of wealth. Its remarkably fine climate has
attracted invalids in crowds, and these have brought
more particularly to the attention of the North the
advantages of its soil and peninsular position for semi-
tropical fruit-culture, especially the orange, which is
now taken hold of there with northern energy and a great
deal of northern capital. The almost fabulous returns
from it are attracting crowds who are thrown out of
employment by the crisis at the North, and their money
as well, no longer to be profitably employed there; and,
while the present movement is owing mainly to the
necessities of the people which make Florida's harvest,
it is probable that when the reaction comes at the North,
with the passage of the present crisis, speculation will
turn thither and give a still greater impetus to this
already rapid development. Amongst other things that
might be cited as instances of the latent wealth of this
favoured region may be especially mentioned—*

*Oranges, which are cultivated as easily, and produce
as quickly as the apple, and yield in full bearing from
1,000 to 2,500 per cent. per acre to the owner, on the
ground, at present prices, and with but trifling labour.
This superior ripe fruit must ere long in supplanting
the half-ripe foreign fruit, of which now (oranges and
lemons) there are nearly 1,000,000,000 imported into
the United States annually (to New York alone
500,000,000, or half of the entire amount).*

*To give an illustration of this increase of prosperity
in the State of Florida, in this one direction, some facts,
the correctness of which may be relied on, may prove of
interest, relating to one property on the St. John's River,
the "Sanford Grant," of twenty-five square miles, which
was purchased in 1868 at about one dollar per acre.
Lands for orange culture upon it have been sold in the
past year at an average of 50 dollars, and up to 150
dollars per acre. Land there purchased four years ago
at 25 dollars an acre and planted in orange trees, has
been sold three years later at 1,000 dollars per acre, and
its neighbourhood in Orange County abounds in similar
instances.*

SANFORD'S GRANT, ORANGE COUNTY.

"The undersigned," says a widely circulated advertisement, "offers for sale to actual settlers, or improvers only, and in lots to suit buyers, the lands
embraced in the above property, consisting of about
twenty-five square miles.

"A portion of this tract—about 6,000 acres—is
believed to be the choicest orange land in Florida. A
Swedish Colony, established for four years on the
centre of the grant, and rapidly increasing, furnishes
reliable, intelligent labour, and an incontestible proof
of its unsurpassing healthfulness.

"A settlement from Wisconsin, and another from
Ohio, with a post office ('Twin Lakes'), at either extremity of the grant, demonstrates in the most striking
manner the large profits derived from orange-culture
when well directed. Full bearing groves in the neighbourhood abundantly testify to the large and certain
income resulting from such labour on a small outlay.
It is beyond the line of injurious frosts. The unusual
severe cold on the 15th instant, which blighted the
banana tops even so far south as Enterprise, left no
trace on the grant opposite, protected by the warmer
waters of Lake Monroe on the north; and at General
Sanford's large grove (Belair)—sixty-five acres—with
many hundreds of tropical and thousands of semi-
tropical and imported plants, not a leaf was touched.
Green peas, strawberries, tomatoes, &c., can be grown
the winter through in the open air, in profitable union
with the orange-culture.

"The Swedish Colony will undertake to clear fence,
plant, and cultivate (on guarantee) lands for orange
groves, of which eighty are already in different stages
of development.

"Besides the Sanford House, which will open on
the 1st January, be open for 150 guests, and which,
when completed next year, will be the largest hotel in
the State, boarding-houses, churches, schools, post and
express offices, saw-mills, stores, &c., present the usual
conveniences to settlers on and near the grant.

"Steamers, ten times weekly to Jacksonville, offer
the indispensable facilities of direct water communication with market to fruit and vegetable-growers.

"The prices of land are from 5 dols. to 100 dols. per
acre, according to quality and location. Special rates
for villa sites upon high banks of lakes.

On the lower pine lands, unfit for orange-culture, five acres will be given to each of the first twenty families who settle upon them.

"L. M. MOORE,
"*Land Agent for the Grant (and Postmaster), Sandford, Florida.*"

Amongst the produce of Florida may be mentioned many varieties of fruit, such as the banana, the guava, the bread-fruit, &c., the sugar-cane, starches, medicinal roots and herbs, cotton, tobacco, paper, grapes, endless variety of fishes, and lime-sand."

A most interesting book, of 806 pages, and illustrated, has been published in Glasgow in 1875, entitled, "The Southern States of North America," by Mr. Edward King, and sold by W. G. Blackie and Co., in which a valuable chapter of 65 pages is devoted to Florida: its Climate, Fruits, Culture, &c., &c.

[*Extracts.*]

"The wealth of Northern cities is erecting fine pleasure houses in St. Augustine, surrounded with noble orchards and gardens. A brilliant society gathers there every winter, and depart reluctantly when spring comes on. Hundreds of families have determined to make it honceforth their winter homes."

"In December, the days are ordinarily bright and sunny, a salt, sea wind blowing across the peninsula; from ten uutil four o'clock one can sit out doors, bathed in floods of delicious light."

"The number of persons whom I saw during my journey, who had migrated to the Eastern or Southern sections of the State, 'more than half-dead with consumption,' and who are now robust and vigorous, was sufficient to convince me of the great benefits derived from a residence there."

"Physicians all agree that the conditions necessary to insure life to the consumptive are admirably provided in the climatic resources of the peninsula. The European medical men are beginning to send many patients to Florida."

"For the healthy, and those seeking pleasure, it will become a winter paradiso; for the ailing it is a refuge and strength."

"The mornings of December, January, February, and March, the four *absolutely perfect months of East Florida,* are wonderfully soft and balmy; the sun shines generously, but there is no suspicion of annoying heat. The breeze gently rustles the enormous leaves of the banana, or playfully tumbles a golden orange to the ground."

"The *Indian River Valley* is difficult of access, *but swarms of travellers are now finding their way there.* Hardly 1,000 miles from New York, one may find the most delicate and delightful tropical scenery, and may dwell in a climate which neither Hawaii, nor Southern Italy, can excel."

"Among the cocoanuts and the mangroves here, invalids may certainly count on laying a new hold upon life; and the invalid who comes here pale and racked with a harrowing cough is, after a few weeks, seen tramping about in the cool of morning with gun and fishing-rod, a very Nimrod and Walton combined. It can be made one of the richest garden spots in America."

"When the necessary dredging and building of canals has been accomplished, so that the INDIAN RIVER ORANGE may have an outlet, viâ St. John's River, the North will be SUPPLIED with oranges of MORE DELICATE TEXTURE THAN IT HAS YET SEEN; THE NUMBER OF GROVES ALONG THE RIVER WILL BE LEGION."

"The fitness of Florida for the growth of tropical and semi-tropical fruits is astonishing. Not only do the orange, the lemon, the lime, and the citron flourish there, but the peach, the grape, the fig, the pomegranate, the plum, all varieties of berries, the olive, the banana, and the pine-apple grow luxuriantly. Black Hamburg and white Muscat grapes fruit finely in the open air; the Concord and the Scuppernong are grown in vast quantities. The guava, the tamarind, the wonderful alligator pear, the plaintain, the cocoanut, and the date, the almond and the pecan, luxuriate in southern Florida, and the Indian River country. Within these boundaries a tropic land, rich and stranger, will one day be inhabited by thousands of fruit-growers, and where beautiful towns and perhaps cities will spring up."
—"A good tree will bear from 1,000 to 3,000 oranges yearly. Some trees at Mandarine have produced 5,500, many of the oranges weighing nearly a pound."
—"One young grove on Indian River, with 1,350 trees, produced in a season 700,000 oranges. They were sold for $25 to $68 per 1,000 case, and netted to its owner over $20,000."—"Col. Heart's grove nets him from $12,000 to $15,000 yearly."—"Dr. Moragne has a grove that nets him over $20,000 per annum."—"Only one man is required to attend one of these groves, who requires one or two negro men to help pick and market them."—"The culture of oranges will certainly become one of the prime industries of Florida."

Such millionaires as Mr. Astor, A. T. Stewart, Col. John P. Howard, General Sanford, Hon Mr. Anthony, U.S. Senator of Rhode Island, and many others, have embarked capital in these valleys for tropical fruit culture, and winter residences.

Another Report says:—

"The celebrated Dummitt and Burnham plantations on Indian River are yielding annual fortunes to their owners."

"At a very low estimate ten acres will yield a revenue of $15,000 to $20,000 per annum, which is *life long.* These estimates can everywhere be substantiated. The products of a single grove of *five acres* on the St. John's River were sold last year for $15,000."

"*Bananas pay even more.* An acre will yield 1,500 bunches, which will bring upwards of $3 per bunch, or over $4,500 per acre."

Mr. King, page 403, shows the class of men who are engaging in this interesting industry:—

"Property is becoming exceedingly good, yearly rising in value."—"In a few years those of Mr. Stockwell, of Maine, with 400 bearing trees; Mr. Burr, of Morristown, N.J.; the Estate of Mosten (200 each); Mr. Brown, of New York, 2,000 young trees; Dr. Parsons, the Long Island Nurseryman, and others, will yield fortunes to their owners. Col. Dancey has a lemon grove of over 200 trees. Among noticeable groves are those of Mr. Cowgill, the State Comptroller; Dr. Mays, at Orange Mill; a number of New York gentlemen at Federal Point; Captain J. W. Stark, and the fine estate of Captain Rossignol. There are also many successful orange groves scattered from Rawlestown to San Mattco, Murphy's Island, Buffalo Bluff, Welaka, and Beecher. There are many groves on the Ochlawaka River, and more than 1,000,000 *trees* are already budded there."

Besides such leading men of wealth, thousands of men, who have not over £100 cash, are engaged in these industries. They purchase a few acres, plant them in orange and other fruit trees, and between the rows of trees they cultivate enough vegetables to pay all their expenses for living and for making further improvements, and in a few years their fruit will yield them larger returns than their capital and labour can bring them in other industries.

The Land Office Reports of Florida, for 1875, p. 18, in speaking of the character of immigrants settling in Florida, says:—

"They are men of the same type as those who have made that belt of country, extending from the Atlantic to the Pacific, and from the Ohio River to the Lakes, the grandest theatre of industrial activity on the continent. They are men possessed of cunning hands, resolute hearts, and clear heads; and to such no finer field than Florida was ever presented for occupancy. It is a field overflowing with the elements of wealth and substantial enjoyment. It has an abundance of raw material and rich soil, upon which all the fruits, all the crops, and all the animals necessary to man's subsistence, comfort and convenience, can be cultivated and propagated, and a climate so congenial to his physical nature that the very exuberance of his spirits doubles his pleasures and robs adversity of half its woes."

Harper's New Monthly Magazine, No. 308, January, 1876, in an article on "Florida," p. 290, says:—

"*Orange County, without railroad help, or metal, or minerals, has by its orange groves alone increased in wealth from twenty to a hundredfold in six years.*"

In a new work just published (1876), entitled, "Camp Life in Florida," by Hallock (whose books on American subjects are considered high and reliable authority), says:—

"Now, more than ever, is attention being directed to the Land of Flowers. Winter visitors in vast numbers migrate thither as regularly as birds of passage. Twenty thousand people visited St. Augustine last winter, and will be multiplied in the next. The hotel accommodations there have been trebled within five years, and are still increasing, not only at Jacksonville, Green Grove Springs, and other favourite resorts on the St. John's River, but also on the *Eastern Seaboard* and the South West Coast hotels are being erected for use in the approaching season. New steamers have been added to the St. John's River Lines, and increased facilities opened for communication with the North.

"Agricultural resources have been developed beyond expectation, lands have been opened that are richly adapted to the cultivation of the orange, banana, guava, and pine-apple, while the monthly markets for green peas, cucumber, strawberries, tomatoes, and melons, offer pecuniary temptation to gardeners that cannot be overlooked. Agricultural and Emigration Societies have been established, and newspapers devoted to the economic interests of the State.

"Lands for well located farms have appreciated *five times* their value *in three years*, and real estates has advanced to fancy prices at the principal wateringplaces. Northern merchants have built princely residences there; settlements have been made at numerous points on the coast and in the interior; old familiar places are no longer recognised. Such changes have a few years brought.

"There is no place on this continent like Florida for both *game and fish*.

"Frost seldom, if ever, injures the sugar-cane, it tassels, and *grows from 15 to 20 feet high*.

"The settlers find much profit in the culture and sale of fruits and vegetables for the Northern markets. Even in the interior of the State, notably at Lake City, many of the citizens are speaking of giving up the cultivation of cotton, and turning their attention to English peas and other vegetables for shipment to Northern States.

"A few years ago, with the exception of Welaka, scarcely anything was to be seen but the *interminable forests along the St. John's River*. There was scarcely a settlement or clearing to mark the advance of civilization. What a change now appears! Landings, clearings, houses, and orange groves map out to the eye of the traveller the rapid improvement now going on.

"There seems no doubt that the population and developed resources of Florida are destined to double in ten years. Those who have some prescience will do well now to take time by the forelock, that they may reap coming advantages.

Mr. Ledyard Bill's late published history of "Florida, and the St. John's Valley," after describing the young city of Jacksonville, with its ocean commerce equal to some cities in the north of three times its population, with the steamers, brigs, and schooners in its harbour, and towns and noted mineral springs, hotels, and social life on the St. John's, concludes, " that the banks of St. John's will in time be as famous for their vineyards and wine as are those of the Rhine in Europe," and the almost endless productions of the tropical fruits of every variety that grow in the tropics, and the early vegetables required in the Northern cities, now mostly imported from the West Indies, Central America, and the Bahamas to an enormous extent, will make the St. John's River, with its lakes and lagoons, a tropical orchard, vineyard, and garden from end to end."

He further says:—

"*Even the pine lands of the poorest quality suit the grape, and more wine can be made from an acre of this land than from any two acres of the ordinary winegrowing in Europe. The highest yield in Europe is not over five hundred gallons to the acre, whereas, in Florida, over fifteen hundred gallons is a common yield. When these facts become known fully, it must excite the grape-growing population of worn-out France and Italy to try their fortunes in our most favoured land.*

"There is no sort of necessity for America importing the miserable adulterations that she is now doing, and sending her gold across the ocean by the millions in exchange, when within her own boundaries she is favoured beyond all lands in soil and climate adapted to the production of superior wine, and in such quantities as not only to supply the home demand, but have a surplus for exportation.

The orange of Florida excels the fruit of any other country, both in size and sweetness. This the general testimony of competent judges, and we unqualifiedly concur, *especially when we remember those grown in what is known as the Indian River country. These seldom reach any of the northern markets, the home consumption being sufficient to require them all.*

"The orange is the longest lived fruit-tree known to us; it will flourish and bear fruit for more than 100 years.

"*The present groves will run an average yield of* 2,000 *per tree; they can be marketed at* 25 *dollars per* 1,000. *This would give a return of* 50 *dollars per tree, or to an acre of about* 500 *trees* 5,000 *dollars.* The labour of one man is quite sufficient to tend the largest grove in Florida, except the time of gathering, when two are required.

"Mr. Howard, from New York, has within a year past (1869) invested nearly 50,000 dollars in St. Augustine in real estate, which is feeling the effect of the healthy influx, property having already risen to fourfold its value five years ago, and still not high. The residence of Senator Gilbert was bought by him at the close of the war for $8,000, and we judge it worth $40,000 now."

M. Lanier, a Frenchman, has just published (1876) a Book on Florida, somewhat after the style of Murray's Guide Books. On page 132 he furnishes a list of towns and stations on the St. John's River. There are 42 towns and stations from Jacksonville to Salt Lake on the St. John's. Five years ago there were less than ten. He describes the St. John's and Indian River Valleys fully. He says :—

"Green-Cove-Springs is one of the most popular winter resorts on the St. John's. The Springs, with the Clarendon Hotel adjoining, are but a short distance from the river. Connected with this hotel are hot and cold baths, and swimming baths of spring water.

"*These waters contain sulphates of magnesia and lime, chlorides of sodium and iron, and sulphurated hydrogen, and have a temperature of 76° Fahrenheit.*

"*They are used for the cure of rheumatism, gout, Bright's disease of the kidneys, and such affections. Beside the Clarendon, the Union House, a charmingly erected hotel offers accommodation to visitors; and there are good private boarding houses.*" * * *

"Melonville is on the right hand side of Lake Monroe, and is in a neighbourhood which is beginning to exhibit much activity in settlements and improvements. Hereabouts are many orange-growers, the flourishing Swedish Colony brought over by General Sanford in 1871. Eureka, Eau-Clair, Wekiva, Lake Jennie, Lake Maitland, Lake Conway, Fort Reid, and other settlements. Extensive interests have been established here in orange groves. Adjoining General Sanford's lands are those of Mr. William Astor, consisting of 8,000 acres of timber and orange lands. Not far off is the Fort Butler Grant, in which Mr. Astor is said to be interested, on which are numerous groves of wild oranges, and the charming little Lake of Schermerhorn." At Enterprise he says :—

"Consumptives are said to flourish in this climate, and there are many stories told of *cadaverous persons* coming here, and turning out successful huntsmen and fishermen, of ruddy face and portentous appetites after a few weeks spent."

Of the Indian River Country he says :

"The general character of the lands in the Indian River Country appears to be a strip of high rich soil, lying immediately on the Western shore, from a half-mile to a mile in width, then coming Westward a belt containing "hummocks and savanas" of great fertility from one to two miles in width, then ridges of light hummock, then still Westward rich grazing lands."

"Upon these lands, oranges, sugar cane, bananas, pine-apples, lemons, limes, guavas, strawberries, blackberries, grapes, figs, nectarines, apricots, corn, indigo, sweet-potatoes, melons, and all manner of garden vegetable grown and yield profusely.

"Along this Indian River country is a marvellously bland air, and I have been told of many over-worked men and incipient consumptives who have here found new life. The waters are full of fish, oysters, and turtles of the best varieties for table use; the woods abound in deer, wild turkeys, and other games, and the whole land amounts to a perpetual invitation to the over-worked, the invalid, the air-poisoned, the nervously-prostrate people to come down with yacht and tent, with rod and gun, and re-build brain, and muscle, and nerve. *The price of lands ranges from 5 to 50 dollars per acre.*"

"*The largest sized and finest flavoured oranges grow in this charming Valley. Many persons hold the Indian River Orange to be typic fruit.*"

"Judge Du Pont informs me that he has raised from Pine Land 69 barrels of syrup per acre, bringing the handsome sum of $400 per acre."

"As to the profits, you can make $300 an acre sure." "Figs are yielding a profit of from $1,000 to $1,200 per acre, and instances are reported of Banana yield of $5,000 per acre."

The Indian River valley lies south of the frost-line, and all the official and private Reports on Florida speak of this locality as possessing the finest climate, and altogether the best fruit and vegetable-producing region of the whole State.

The Company owns about 1,000,000 acres in this interesting valley.

Without elaborating further, it must appear self-evident to any thinking mind that to appraise the Company's Lands at ten dollars per acre is to set a low price, and that the Company may confidently expect to realise an average of, at least, ten dollars.

This will make the mortgage security in lands over $23,000,000 cash basis. Mr. Conover, one of the United States Senators from Florida, telegraphed to London, in answer to inquiries from London parties, that the lands belonging to the Company "will sell, now, in cash at from $3 to $30 per acre, making an average of $16.50 per acre, cash now.

SUMMARY CONCLUSIONS UPON THE COMPANY'S REAL ESTATE—ITS GREAT VALUE—WITH AN ESTIMATE OF ANNUAL INCOMES THEREFROM.

The official Reports of the Governments of the United States, Florida, and Great Britain, together with the Reports and Statements from other unquestionable high character, quoted and referred to, established the following facts :—

1. That four-fifths of the area of the lands in Florida are covered with magnificent forests, furnishing timber and lumber, of the most superior quality, for ship and house construction, cabinet and ornamental work, &c., of which many millions of dollars' worth are annually shipped to the Northern Cities, to Europe, the West Indies, South America, and to other markets. These timber resources alone are bound to make the State rich, as the timber in the States of Maine, Michigan, and Wisconsin, made them rich.

2. That the soil of Florida is varied, rich, and very productive, successfully growing all the variety of staple crops of the United States; that all the tropical fruits grow there to perfection; that the garden vegetables grow all the year round, winter and summer; that the markets of the Northern and North-Western Cities, and States, and Canada, which are bound up in ice and winter four or five months each year, can be fully supplied with these tropical fruits, and winter and early spring vegetables, and that in these respects Florida can control and monopolize the Northern markets, which now consume over $200,000,000 annually in fruit and vegetables.

3. That the State is rapidly increasing in population and wealth; that great progress is making in developing and utilising her timber, agricultural, and horticultural resources; and as a consequence and fact, her lands are rising rapidly in price.

4. That the population is chiefly settling in the St. John's and Indian River Valleys along the lines of the

Company's Canals and Routes, and the principle development is taking place in these Valleys.

5. That that Company owns and has perfect grants and titles to 2,300,000 acres of rich lands located in the St. John's and Indian River valleys, along the Company's Canals and Water Routes, and in and about all the settlements, which are now making the remarkable demonstrations in tropical fruit and vegetable culture, *showing larger profits per acre than any other lands in North America can produce.* It is in the central region of the Company's lands in Orange County, where the wonderful development in tropical fruit culture is reported upon by the British Legation Office at Washington in 1876, and so aptly treated in an able leader in the *Times* of June 23rd, 1876, showing that lands were purchased there, eight years ago, at about one dollar per acre, and the same are now selling for fifty dollars to hundred-fifty dollars per acre, and that the profits from Orange culture is from 1,000 to 2,500 per cent. per acre yearly, and that Northern capital is flowing into that region, &c.

6. The evidence and common history of that country show, that the INDIAN RIVER VALLEY, on account of its being south of the terminal frost line, its unsurpassed favourable climate, and its great adaptability of soil, IS FAR SUPERIOR FOR THE SUCCESSFUL CULTIVATION OF THE ORANGE AND ALL THE TROPICAL FRUITS, than the St. John's Valley is, or any more northerly portion of the country, for in the latter Valley and more northerly regions, not ALL the *tropical fruits can be successfully raised,* and the quality of the fruit is not so good, as is shown by the fact that Indian River Oranges and fruits command a premium price in the markets, and 1,000,000 acres of the Company's lands are located in the Indian River Valley.

7. Tens of thousands of people from the Northern States annually spend their winter season in Florida for pleasure or health, and to avoid four to five months of the severe rigors of winter, ice, and chilling atmosphere of the North ; and on account of the superior climate of the St. John's and Indian River Valleys, the conveniences, improvements, and attractions of those Valleys, nearly the whole of this visiting population go to the different cities, towns, villages, mineral springs, and settlements in these Valleys, and spend their visiting seasons there.

8. *That the market value of the Company's lands is from $5 to $100 per acre, cash. The value of the Company's lands in hand, 2,300,000 acres, exceeds $30,000,000. The 6,000,000 acres will run a much less price per acre.*

9. THE ESTIMATED ANNUAL INCOMES FROM THE COMPANY'S LANDS.

Taking into consideration the annual sales and incomes heretofore realized by Railway and other companies from their Government land grants in aid of their enterprises, &c., and the demand for the Company's timber and lands, it would seem safe to estimate, from the sale of timber, from sale of lands for agricultural and horticultural purposes, from the sale of town and village lots, from ground rents and other issues, and profits from the realty and buildings, an aggregate of $3,000,000
On the east division, before the completion of the west division 1,000,000
On the east division, by its completion from Fernandina to Lake Worth ... 500,000

From this must be deducted 15 per cent. to cover all expenses.

The United States Agricultural Report for 1862, gives an interesting description of the climate, soil, forests, and productions of Florida.

EXTRACTS.

" The whole State is diversified with beautiful lakes and ponds, abounding in fish and fowl of various kinds, and of the most delicate flavour, and can support a population of 100 to the square mile, with one-half the labour required to live in the Eastern or Middle States."

" A large portion of the country is covered with *Pine-forests,* the trees standing at a considerable distance apart, without under-growth ; grass and flowers spread luxuriantly over the surface of the earth during the whole year, and, being unusually intersected with streams of pure water, cattle find excellent pasture all the year. The pine lands, though often termed "barrens," is in most instances not less productive than the numerous live-oak and other hard timbered hummocks of the richest soil, so finely adapted to the culture of sugar, cotton, tobacco, corn, rice, indigo, and fruits. Limestone and marl underlie pretty generally the whole Peninsula."

" *It produces the long staple or Sea Island cotton of commerce, over any part of the Peninsula, with a productiveness surpassing the coasts of South Carolina and Georgia, to which this staple has been hitherto limited, and can supply any quantity of it required, to which the consumption will reach.*

" *It produces sugar with great advantage over Louisiana and Texas, having a superior climate for the cane, and has sugar lands enough to supply the consumption of the whole United States.*"

" Cuba tobacco is, next to sugar, most in favour with planters. The flavour is thought to be not inferior to the production of the famous district of Vueltade Abajo, in the island of Cuba. The sandy soil near the sea-coast is well adapted for this production. Ordinary seasons give three good cuttings from the same stalks. 700 pounds is an average crop to the acre, which, when Virginia and Kentucky tobacco would not bring more than 6 cents, readily sold in the market at from 50 to 75 cents per pound."

" Rice is a valuable crop. Pine lands, upon which cattle have been herded for a few weeks, have often produced 60 bushels of rice to the acre. With one month's labour, one hand, with a horse and plough, can cultivate ten acres of rice."

" Indigo was the principal staple of the Florida planter during the British occupation of the country. Except sugar, this is the most certain crop in Florida. It is indigenous to the country, abounding in the pine barrens, and even in the old fields cultivated by the British nearly a century ago, in spite of time and the constant cultivation of other crops."

" The climate is the best in the world for the production of silk. Every species of mulberry grows there. The cochineal insect is a native of Florida. 'The nopal, on which the insect feeds,' is also a native plant."

" Corn is the most important article of food in a southern climate. To the negro it is indispensable. Although Florida lies south of the corn-growing belt, very good crops are nevertheless produced in the State. 40 bushels to the acre is often gathered on the best land, but from 10 to 15 bushels is the average crop."

" The sweet potato and the yam find in the Florida pine land their natural soils. 400 bushels are often produced to the acre. The common potato produces a good crop, if planted in the winter. Cabbages planted

(25)

in November grow to a great size. Mellons, squashes, and pumpkins are produced with indifferent culture, and are of delicious flavour. Peas, beans, and indeed *all* the garden vegetables of the temperate or the torrid zone succeed perfectly well in Florida."

" Fruits are abundant and in great variety; figs are abundant and of the richest flavour; the quince, peaches, nectarines, and apricots succeed perfectly.

" The Florida Orange is larger and more aromatic than the Cuban. The pomegranite, the guava, citron, the shaddock, or "forbidden fruit," lemons, and limes are produced with ease, and everywhere abundantly.

" Wild plums and grapes are in great variety. Some of the cultivated species of the plum produces two crops annually.

" The pine-apple and banana are cultivated with great success. The olive and the tamarind are growing in many places. Arrowroot is a profitable crop. The pistache was greatly cultivated by the Seminoles. This vine produces a large crop on sandy land; it is a native of Spain, whence it was transferred to the gardens of Italy. Grasses are numerous and nutritious; there are few spots of uncultivated land not covered with grass. Deer, as well as cattle, in vast herds, fatten on the wild grasses of the forests and prairies.

" As the opinion has been very widely disseminated that Florida is composed of swamps and everglades, or sandy plains and barrens, a brief description of her lands will be interesting to the agriculturists generally, and particularly to those who desire to produce in our own country almost everything which our comfort or our luxury draws from other countries."

(Here follows a description of the different soils, similar to that already hereinbefore given in the body of this Report.)

" There is one general feature in the topography of Florida, which no other country in the United States possesses, and which affords great security to the health of its inhabitants.

" It is this: that the Pine lands, which form the basis of the country, and which is almost universally healthy, are nearly everywhere studded, at intervals of a few miles, with hummock lands of the richest quality. These hummocks are not, as is usually supposed, low, wet lands; on the contrary, they are high, dry, and undulating, and never require either ditching or draining. They vary in extent from 20 acres to 20,000 acres.

" Hence the inhabitants have it everywhere in their power to select RESIDENCES in the Pine lands, at such convenient distances from the hummocks as will enable them to cultivate the latter without endangering their health, if it should so happen that any of the hummocks prove to be less healthy than the pine woods.

" Indeed, it is found that residences in the hummocks themselves are generally perfectly healthy a few years after they have been cleared.

" Newly cleared lands are generally attended with the development of more or less malaria. In Florida the diseases which result from such clearings are usually of the mildest type (simply intermittent fever), while in nearly all the other Southern States they are most frequently of a severe grade of bilious fever.

" A general interspersion of rich hummocks, surrounded by high, dry, rolling, healthy pine woods, is a topographical feature peculiar to Florida, and forms in this respect a striking contrast with Louisiana, Texas, or Mississippi, whose sugar and cotton lands are generally surrounded by vast alluvial regions, subject to frequent inundations, so that it is impossible to obtain a healthy residence within many miles of them."

(*Editorial* from the *Evening Standard*, London, November 10, 1876.)

" A new warning of approaching danger—this time of an agricultural, not a political nature—reaches us from India. The soil is becoming ungrateful. That the results of cultivation are less bountiful than formerly, there is, unfortunately, no disputing. In old times the rulers of Hindostan, the Emperor Akbar amongst them, were in the habit of chronicling, for purposes of State policy, the yield of the land at certain periods. In the public record, known as the *Ayeen Akbary*, it is stated that two centuries ago the harvest of picked cotton was 223 lbs. per acre; by 1823 it was only 128 lbs.; in the last decade 67 lbs.; and it has now declined to an average of 52 lbs. per acre. Rice which, according to the same ancient report, yielded 1,338 lbs. per acre, has since fallen to 800 lbs. and 900 lbs., and wheat from 1,155 lbs. to 660 lbs. The reason of this decrease is not far to seek. The climate of the East is as exhausting to the soil as to the human system; the earth must be ploughed more deeply, and re-invigorated by fertilising elements. The duty of providing a remedy for this state of things is incumbent upon the Government, which is placed in the position of landlord, from the fact of its receiving a tithe of the grain crops. Lord Mayo dealt with the difficulty in a statesmanlike manner, and acknowledged the obligations of the governing power. ' The duties,' said the late Viceroy, ' which in England are performed by a good landlord, fall, in India, in a great measure, upon the Government. The only Indian landlord who can command the requisite knowledge and capital for the improvement of the land is the State,' and nowhere, it may be added, has the State so immediate and direct an interest in such questions."

This is another evidence showing the great value of the Florida Cotton Lands.

America has the best cotton lands, and produces the best cotton in the world. Tens of millions of acres will produce from 400 pounds and upwards per acre of picked cotton, and the whole State of Florida successfully produces the LONG or SEA ISLAND COTTON, the most valuable fabric the soil can grow, and ranking next to silk in value.

G. S. Norris, Esq., of Baltimore, now in Europe, on business to sell Florida lands and induce emigration to Florida, has published an important Report on the Florida lands, resources, climate, &c., which contains important " Letters of the Bishop of Florida, Rev. Edward Meaney, B.A. (Oxon.); Rev. Owen B. Thackara, Archdeacon; Rev. O. Q. S. Waldron, Ex. Gov. Harrison Reed; M. A. Williams, United States Land Surveyor; and Samuel A. Swan," all men of the highest integrity, fully confirming the statements and Reports herein quoted on this subject, which will well repay a perusal.

Please turn to the " Appendix " of the Ship Canal Report for a short history of Florida, its climate, health, soils, timber productions, large profits in agriculture and horticulture, &c.

Also turn to the same Report, page 52, title "CANAL PROPERTIES CONSIDERED," and read the short history of the Suez and numerous other canals, and grand financial successes and results exhibited; and chapters 1st and 5th of the same Report show that the *Florida Ship Canal* is the grandest commercial and financial enterprise of the present or any other age.

D

Finally a word on

THE NORTH SEA CANAL—JUST OPENED.

On the 1st of November, 1876, the King of Holland opened that Canal.

An interesting fact, growing out of the *swamp* lands reclaimed by that enterprise, is worthy of note here.

The correspondence published in the *Daily News*, London, October 30th, 1876, says :—

"That the land on each side of the Canal has been reclaimed, and has fetched enormously high prices, amounting, in some cases, to £120 an acre. There are 12,000 acres of reclaimed lands, and by the concession they become the property of the Company."

The special correspondence published in the *Times*, London, November 2nd, 1876, says :—

"The gross cost of that Canal is more than £2,000,000. But the *net cost in cash* will be probably not much more than £1,000,000. The polders (reclaimed lands) have realised at Dutch auction an average of £80 per acre, and are not all sold. Some parts near Amsterdam, and valuable for building purposes, have brought £340 per acre. For agricultural purposes £120 an acre has been paid. The total amount reclaimed and to be reclaimed is 12,450 acres. Some 8,500 have been disposed of, &c."

The Leader published in the *Times*, London, November 18th, 1876, in exhibiting the merits of that enterprise, says :—

"The cost was estimated at £2,000,000, but the net expenses will, it is believed, be brought down to little more than half that sum, by causes peculiar to Holland.

Large tracts of land have, as we have said, been snatched from the waters of the adjoining Lake, and they afford admirable fertile soil. More than 12,000 acres have thus been added to the territory of Holland, and the land is so valuable as to have fetched an average of £80 an acre.

"Some of it, indeed, has been sold for agricultural purposes at £120 an acre, a sum that may well excite the envy of those among our own proprietors who can measure their unreclaimed lands by thousands of acres."

The average price per acre of that not yet sold will not be less, perhaps, than that which is sold.

The result is, that the realization from this small body of re-claimed swamp land nearly pays the entire net amount of the construction cost of the North Sea Canal.

This is a striking example of the aid derived from lands in constructing internal improvements.

The Illinois Central Railway Company practically realized $30,000,000 from its land grants, of a little over 2,500,000 acres, and to-day could realize more than twice this amount for the same lands.

The Company's 2,300,000 acres are amongst the richest lands in the State, and 1,000,000 at least are of the very best orange-producing quality in Florida. Indeed, the Indian River lands for orange culture are the best in the State.

It is hardly improbable to suppose that a number of Companies will be organized both in the United States and Europe to utilize portions of the Company's vast domain of 8,300,000 acres of land, for the cultivation of *Sea Island cotton*, sugar, Cuban tobacco, rice, and especially tropical fruits and garden vegetables ; also to manufacture timber, and export oysters and fish, and that a large emigration is bound to go to Florida from Europe to enjoy its fine climate and great advantages offered.

CONCLUSIONS.

From the foregoing elaborate Report and cumulative evidence in support, the facts are submitted, in confidence and assurance, that the capital required to complete this branch of the enterprise is absolutely secure.

1st. From the certain earnings of the enterprise.

2nd. It is secured by the timber and lumber alone on the Company's lands.

3rd. The 2,300,000 acres of the richest and most valuable lands in the State are good security for this capital.

4th. The franchises, rights, improvements, real, personal, and mixed property, form an aggregate security for the Bonds and Stock proposed to be issued, which are most ample and first-class for the investment of Capital.

JOHN H. FRY,

Attorney for the Company.

www.ingramcontent.com/pod-product-compliance
Lightning Source LLC
Chambersburg PA
CBHW031443270326
41930CB00007B/840

9 7 8 3 3 3 7 1 4 6 7 3 3